INFLATION ACCOUNTING

INFLATION ACCOUNTING
Reporting of
General and Specific
Price Changes

Robert Bloom, Ph.D.
and
Araya Debessay, Ph.D., C.M.A.

PRAEGER

PRAEGER SPECIAL STUDIES • PRAEGER SCIENTIFIC

New York • Philadelphia • Eastbourne, UK
Toronto • Hong Kong • Tokyo • Sydney

Library of Congress Cataloging in Publication Data

Bloom, Robert.

Inflation accounting.

Bibliography: p.
Includes index.
1. Accounting—Effect of inflation on. I. Debessay,
Araya. II. Title.
HF5658.5.B56 1984   657′.48   83–26973
ISBN 0–03–062367–7 (alk. paper)

Published in 1984 by Praeger Publishers
CBS Educational and Professional Publishing,
a Division of CBS Inc.
521 Fifth Avenue, New York, NY 10175 USA

456789 052 987654321

Printed in the United States of America
on acid-free paper

To Our Families

PREFACE

This book is designed to provide a comprehensive analysis of the concepts, issues, and techniques in accounting for changing prices. The main title of the book—Inflation Accounting—is used in the broad sense to encompass the financial reporting problems stemming from general and specific price-level changes. There are no comprehensive up-to-date supplementary books on this subject. Accordingly, this book has been prepared to fill a void in the market.

Intended for undergraduate and graduate accounting students, the book can be used effectively in a variety of accounting courses. Moreover, this book should appeal to individuals seeking an analysis of the methods and techniques of accounting for changing prices, assuming they are familiar with accounting fundamentals. The subject concerns prospective and practicing accountants as well as financial statement users. The specific objectives of the book are as follows:

1. To trace the evolution of thought on accounting for changing prices primarily in the United States
2. To examine the concepts of capital maintenance, and in so doing relate them to the problem of income measurement in a period of changing prices
3. To analyze and compare the alternative inflation-accounting models
4. To analyze and evaluate the disclosure requirements of FASB Statement No. 33, "Financial Reporting and Changing Prices" (1979)
5. To discuss and compare the objectives vis-a-vis the specific provisions of pronouncements on accounting for price changes in the United States and abroad
6. To analyze and compare the treatment of monetary items in selected inflation-accounting pronouncements, including general purchasing-power gains and losses, monetary working-capital adjustments, and gearing (financial-leverage) adjustments
7. To examine the empirical research findings on the informational content of inflation-accounting disclosures

Because of the importance attached to the measurement of income, consideration is given to the nature of income and its computation in accounting. Models of accounting for price changes are viewed as alternatives or companions to conventional historical-cost accounting. This book deals with the following alternative models: (1) historical-cost/constant-dollar; (2) current cost; and (3) exit price. The mechanics of preparing financial statements adjusted for price changes are specified, using the foregoing models. Additionally, an analysis of working capital and gearing adjustments is provided.

Thus, this book furnishes a conceptual and pragmatic framework to examine the current and perennial debate on accounting for price changes in external financial reporting. Along with a descriptive analysis of proposed accounting methods, the arguments for and against each alternative are extensively discussed. We evaluate each model, relating it to the conceptual framework of financial reporting. This book also emphasizes a comparative, international view of issues in accounting for general and specific price changes by focusing attention on the recent British, Canadian, and Australian pronouncements on the subject. These highly industrialized, English-speaking countries were selected to illustrate significant similarities and differences with the United States in the development of inflation-accounting standards. This book also provides an assessment of the alternative accounting models based on the objectives and qualitative characteristics of financial reporting.

In sum, we intend to furnish a lucid analysis of the conceptual issues underlying accounting for price changes besides the practical issues involved in utilizing a supplementary accounting framework within annual financial reports. This book is not intended to be encyclopedic. On the contrary, our primary purpose is to identify and examine the significant issues governing the subject of accounting for general and specific price changes, which should provide insights on a broader scale to the process of introducing major changes in the nature of financial reporting.

ACKNOWLEDGMENTS

Although we did not always follow their advice, a number of prominent accounting researchers provided helpful comments to us on the prospectus, outline, and/or chapters of this book:

Dale Buckmaster, University of Delaware
Lawrence A. Friedman, University of Kansas
Reg S. Gynther, Coopers & Lybrand, Australia
Eugene A. Imhoff, Jr., University of Michigan
Richard V. Mattessich, University of British Columbia
Maurice Moonitz, University of California at Berkeley
Carl L. Nelson, Columbia University
Richard A. Scott, University of Virginia
George H. Sorter, New York University
Robert T. Sprouse, Financial Accounting Standards Board
Geoffrey Whittington, University of Bristol

Additionally, we wish to acknowledge the dependable research assistance provided by Thomas N. Kuenzi at the University of Wisconsin-Whitewater; May Tam at Illinois Institute of Technology; and Robert Scott, Jeffrey Russell, Robert Bernosky, and Bruce Campbell at the University of Delaware. Also appreciated is the diligent typing and administrative assistance furnished by Julianna Cheung, Cheryl Feller, Astrid Peterson, Hazel Wilson, and especially Fern Rasmussen at the University of Wisconsin-Whitewater; and Nancy Benson, Thelma Flewelling, Gail Hall, and Judy Lahocki at the University of Delaware.

CONTENTS

LIST OF EXHIBITS

INFLATION ACCOUNTING

1

THE CONVENTIONAL ACCOUNTING MODEL: ITS ORIGIN, DEVELOPMENT, STRENGTHS, AND WEAKNESSES

INTRODUCTION

The conventional accounting model, also referred to as the historical-cost model, has come increasingly under attack in recent years. Although arguments against the conventional model have intensified during periods of inflation, the model has been criticized for serious deficiencies even in the absence of inflation. It should be emphasized, however, that the conventional model has strong proponents who contend that it has played a significant role in the past and will continue to be important in financial reporting in the future.[1]

The challenge of devising a satisfactory accounting model to accommodate the financial-reporting problems stemming from changing prices has compelled the accounting profession in most countries of the world to go back to the drawing boards. Several alternative models have been proposed, tested, and evaluated. We will analyze the alternative models later in this book. Our concern in this chapter is with the conventional accounting model. Although its continued existence does not seem to be seriously threatened at this stage, the alternative models represent significant departures from the conventional model.

To evaluate the strengths and weaknesses of the conventional model and to appreciate the need for alternative accounting models, it is important to establish, as a starting point, a clear understanding of the objectives of financial reporting. Then it will be a matter of assessing the ability of the given model to satisfy the prescribed objectives, both under stable and unstable price levels.

In dealing with the objectives of financial reporting as a basis for evaluating the conventional model (and also the alternative models

analyzed later in this book), we have found it necessary to restrict
the scope of our analysis to publicly held corporations, as opposed to
proprietorships, partnerships, and closely held corporations. Thus,
we focus on the financial-reporting environment dominated by publicly
held corporations in which investors and creditors are assumed to be
the primary users of financial reports.

It is important to note that the conventional accounting model
has been in existence much longer than any of the competing models.
This model has developed as the reporting environment has undergone
extensive changes. A study of the historical evolution of accounting
should provide a useful background for evaluating the conventional
accounting model. Accordingly, this chapter presents a historical
overview of the origin and development of the conventional accounting
model. This overview is followed by a discussion of the contemporary
financial-reporting environment, providing a framework for our analysis of the strengths and weaknesses of the conventional model.

EVOLUTION OF ACCOUNTING PRACTICE

Accounting historians trace the roots of accounting back to
4500 B.C. [2] The early civilization in the Mesopotamian Valley, with
the active trading that then prevailed, required some form of record-
keeping system. Traces of such ancient commercial records in the
form of clay tablets have been discovered by archaeologists. [3] Similarly, evidence can be found of papyri records during the Egyptian
civilization and parchment documents from the Middle Ages. [4] Although little is written about such ancient accounting systems, it is
evident that trading operations could not have been executed in such
times without some form of accounting.

Credit for developing the modern double-entry bookkeeping system is given to the Italian monk Luca Pacioli, who is referred to as
the "father of modern accounting." His book De Computis et Scripturis,
published in 1494, was the first text on bookkeeping. [5] A. C. Littleton,
who studied the evolution of accounting, observes that: "The careful
reader of Pacioli's text is likely to be amazed to note how little basic
change there has been in bookkeeping." [6] It should be emphasized that
the fundamentals of bookkeeping have not changed despite the changes
that have occurred in the form and operations of business organizations. Even though the mechanics of bookkeeping have not changed
significantly, accounting and financial reporting have developed pro-
gressively with changes in the business environment. [7] This development should not be surprising, however, since accounting reports
respond to the changing information needs of users.

The history of accounting can be divided into three periods

according to the relative importance of three forms of business organizations:[8] (1) the single venture or partnership; (2) the closely held corporation; and (3) the large corporation, having many stockholders, management separate from its ownership, and securities that are traded in major capital markets.

In the early days of maritime trade, "trading was more a matter of single ventures, the conclusion of which defined the accounting period; careful assessment of profit as distinct from capital was hardly necessary."[9] For such business ventures, emphasis is placed on proper record keeping from the beginning to the end of the venture in order to provide an accounting to the venture partners. To elaborate on the single venture model, assume the purchase of a ship by a group of investors for the purpose of undertaking a <u>single cargo voyage during a particular time frame</u>. Once an investment is made in this venture, it cannot be sold. There is no secondary market for such an investment. At the end of the trip, the ship is sold and the profit determined. Upon distribution of the profit to the investors, the venture terminates. The role of the accoutant in such a venture is essentially limited to generating accounting data for use by the venture partners, which entails the preparation of a cash-flow income statement and the provision of accounting data to facilitate the liquidation of the venture. The accounting model for such a venture differs from the conventional model in several respects.

1. There would be no interim financial statements because such statements would serve no useful purpose in a single-period venture model.
2. The process of cost allocation to reflect depreciation and amortization is unnecessary since there is only one period in the life of the venture.
3. There is no need for accrual accounting. Cash-flow reports would be sufficient to provide information regarding results of venture operations. The actual income is determined with certainty at the end of the venture.
4. There is no need for preparing an end-of-period balance sheet because the venture does not represent a going concern. At the end of the venture, a liquidation statement is prepared to reflect the liquidation value of the net assets of the venture.

As business enterprises evolved from single-period ventures into more permanent individual proprietorships and partnerships, accounting also had to change accordingly—e.g., moving toward the accrual basis and cost-allocation. However, in such early business organizations, the role of accounting was primarily to satisfy the information need of the owners.

The introduction of the corporation, with its limited-liability attribute, emphasized the need to ensure that financial statements did not contain anything "that might be fraudulent against creditors."[10] Moreover, since the legal capital of the business served to protect the creditors, it was important to establish accounting procedures to measure the income for the period in order to ensure that no distribution from permanent capital was made without the knowledge and, in certain cases, the consent of creditors. Here again the role of accounting in closely held corporations was primarily confined to satisfying the information needs of owners, subject to the constraint that the creditors' rights be protected. Commenting on the nature of accounting for limited-ownership corporations, George O. May observes:[11]

> [I]t was still permissible for stockholders to adopt such accounting methods for the determination of profits and the amounts available for dividends as they might see fit, so long as these did not impair the just rights of creditors.

In view of the emphasis on protecting creditors' interests, the balance sheet emerged as the most prominent financial statement, informing creditors about the solvency and liquidity of the business organization. At this stage of accounting development—that is, the nineteenth century—apart from the concern for creditors' informational needs, there was little interest in disclosure of accounting information. In the majority of cases, financial secrecy was the order of the day. Firms were not willing to disclose even their sales revenue figures lest they disclose information to competitors. Accounting information was considered to be proprietary. Since most of the corporations were then closely held and owned and managed by the same people, there was no compelling public desire for external disclosure. In general, there was little concern for the information needs of external users, and thus those who relied on financial statements had to do so at their own risk. This attitude reflected the doctrine of caveat emptor ("let the buyer beware").[12] Additionally, weak state laws existed regarding public disclosure; and the accounting profession was still in its infancy.

The growth of modern corporations during the early part of the twentieth century played a significant role in the development of accounting. Because such corporations were generally owned by individuals and institutions who were not associated with the day-to-day operations, they required more informative and reliable financial statements. In particular, the stewardship role of accounting broadened during this period. In a narrow sense, stewardship refers to management's custody and safekeeping of resources furnished by owners and creditors of the firm. This view of stewardship is clearly inadequate to the extent that owners and investors expect profitable operations from the corporation. Accordingly, the role of accounting as a source of information useful for judging management's stewardship performance assumed prominence, marking a shift in emphasis from the balance sheet to the income statement. The importance of income generated progress in both income measurement and in asset valuation. Viewed from this perspective, there is no doubt that the emergence of major corporations played an important role in the development of accounting. As Littleton observes from his study of accounting evolution:[13]

> Because of limited liability there was a legal obligation to retain in the business the amount of the capital contribution. It became important, therefore, to be able to make an accurate calculation of the amount of assets which could safely be distributed. . . . The necessity for such calculations gave added importance to knowledge enabling one properly to distinguish assets and expenses.
>
> Because the incorporation of an enterprise resulted in a definite continuity of economic existence . . . , there was an economic obligation to maintain the productive power of the enterprise . . . [which required] sound theory to guide the management in making periodic calculations of the profits.
>
> And finally, because corporations were aggregates of capital under delegated management it was necessary to substitute "figure knowledge" for direct knowledge of investors. Financial statements became the medium of stockholders' knowledge of their affairs and thus gave added importance to well chosen account classifications which would make the statements clear and comprehensible.

Other factors also influenced the evolution of accounting. Among such factors is the 1913 constitutional amendment which authorized the federal government to impose an income tax on businesses and individuals. These tax laws necessitated the maintenance of accounting records, enhanced the importance of income measurement, and required accounting procedures and practices to separate income from capital. As a result, special attention was given to depreciation accounting and inventory valuation techniques.

In the aftermath of the stock market crash of 1929 and the Great Depression, there was a concerted effort on the part of the federal government, the major stock exchanges, and the accounting profession to improve financial reporting.[14] Although there is insufficient evidence, it is alleged that the various accounting practices of the 1920s were partly responsible for the stock market crash of 1929. Among the accounting and financing practices that have been attributed to the stock market collapse are the following:[15]

1. The preparation of false and misleading financial statements so that corporate officials could profit at the expense of duped investors. It was not unusual during this period to find assets written up to appraised values on the balance sheets of firms that possessed no real earning power.
2. The manipulation of security prices by giving false impressions of capital market activity—by artificially driving up security prices and allowing profiteers to reap significant gains before security prices fell to their actual levels.
3. The use of extensive credit margins, which many investors were unable to cover.
4. The existence of information-inefficient capital markets, which enabled corporate officials and other "insiders" to benefit from the withholding or the release of information until they could capitalize upon it.

The collapse of the stock market and the Depression were instrumental in effectuating improvements in financial reporting. The enactment of the Securities Acts of 1933 and 1934 marked an important milestone in the history of financial reporting and in the efficiency of capital markets. The 1933 act is concerned primarily with full and fair disclosure of all material facts connected with securities offered in interstate commerce. The 1934 act is essentially concerned with the regulation of security trading on the secondary markets. [16] Thus, with the active participation of the government and the accounting profession, financial reporting was subjected to new regulations that contributed significantly toward enhancing the credibility of corporate financial statements.

To sum up, accounting has evolved as the business environment has changed. With the expansion of business activities and the growth of business organizations from single ventures to proprietorships and partnerships, and then to limited liability corporations and the contemporary publicly held corporations, the role of accounting has expanded to meet the information needs of the participating parties. In those instances where financial reporting was abused, the intervention of the government and the profession was instrumental in restoring credibility.

CONTEMPORARY FINANCIAL-REPORTING ENVIRONMENT

Although a great deal of business activity is performed by single proprietorships, partnerships, and privately owned corporations in the United States today, it is the financial-reporting issues of publicly owned corporations that have become the major concern to the accounting standard-setting bodies. The primary emphasis of the Financial Accounting Standards Board (FASB) is on the information needs of investors, as reflected in its Statement of Financial Accounting Concepts No. 1, "Objectives of Financial Reporting," (1978). The Securities Acts of 1933 and 1934 also stress the welfare of investors and the "fairness" of the markets in which investors buy and sell securities.[17]

The modern corporation engages in complex, large-scale production processes and distribution networks requiring extensive physical capital. In turn, the corporation has to attract substantial financial capital from the public by issuing equity and debt securities that are traded in the capital markets. From the corporations' point of view, financial reporting can be considered a means of marketing the corporation's securities to potential investors and encouraging investors to maintain their holdings in the corporation. From the investor's viewpoint, the investment process involves the sacrifice of current consumption for securities that are claims to future cash flows.

The purpose of investing in securities is to maximize wealth. A rational investor would, therefore, select from among a set of investment opportunities the portfolio of investments that would maximize the return for a given risk or minimize the risk for a given expected return. It is expected that investors could reduce the risk involved in their security investments by holding a diversified portfolio. This means that the risk of a given investment is evaluated in relation to the investor's portfolio.[18] Return-on-investment in securities is defined as the change in the market value of the securities plus any dividends received during a given period. The investment risk is the expected variance of the expected return.

The objective of financial reporting from the investor's point of view, therefore, should be to provide information to enable the investor to assess the future returns and associated risks of available alternative investment opportunities. Stated differently, corporate financial reports should provide information to aid investors in predicting the amounts, timing, and related uncertainties of net cash flows from investments.

In its Statement of Financial Accounting Concepts No. 1 (1978), the FASB has set forth the following objectives:

> Financial reporting should provide information that is useful to present and potential investors, and creditors and other users in making rational investment, credit and similar decisions. The information should be comprehensible to those who have a reasonable understanding of business and economic activities and are willing to study the information with reasonable diligence.

Financial reporting should provide information to help present and potential investors and creditors and other users in assessing the amounts, timing and uncertainty of prospective cash receipts from dividends or interest and the proceeds from the sale, redemption, or maturity of securities or loans. Since investors and creditors' cash flows are related to enterprise cash flows, financial reporting should provide information to help investors, creditors, and others assess the amounts, timing, and uncertainty of prospective net cash inflows to the related enterprise.

Financial reporting should provide information about the economic resources of an enterprise, the claims to those resources (obligations of the enterprise to transfer resources to other entities and owners' equity), and the effects of transactions, events, and circumstances that change its resources and claims to those resources.

From a broader societal concern, financial reporting should foster proper allocation of societal resources. Given efficient capital markets, successful firms, that is, firms that promise higher expected returns for a given level of risk, would be able to attract investors and thereby serve to channel resources to be best utilized. This presupposes that investors have information to distinguish the successful from the unsuccessful firms. Thus, an overall objective of financial reporting should be to foster an efficient allocation of social resources. To achieve this aim, accounting information ought to be useful in assessing the firm's future cash flows and the risks associated with the flows.

Our next aim is to evaluate the extent to which the conventional accounting model meets the challenges of financial reporting in the contemporary business environment. Accordingly, a discussion of the strengths and weaknesses of the conventional model is presented below.

Strengths of the Conventional Accounting Model

The most fundamental strength of the conventional accounting model is that, unlike the alternative accounting models, it reflects historical prices that are generally the result of arm's-length transactions. Therefore, the data are generally considered reliable, i.e., faithfully representative, unbiased, and independently verifiable by external parties. In fact, the verifiability feature makes the conventional model the preference of the public accounting profession.

Because the conventional model is essentially based on actual transactions, it is perceived to provide data that are less disputable than are conveyed by alternative accounting models. An interesting defense of the conventional, historical-cost model is expressed by Solomon Barkin, a labor union economist.[19] Barkin advocates this model in view of its ability to present actual events without arbitrary adjustments by management. He argues that "the determination of income is a <u>political question</u> that cannot be resolved by accountants, economists, or lawyers who are truly technicians for implementing agreements."[20] In his view, "accountants should simply provide a record of past transactions, leaving any interpretations to the user." Accordingly, Barkin recommends strict adherence to historical cost in order to facilitate equity in the bargaining process, asserting that "if corporate income was arbitrarily adjusted to show the impact of inflation, labor would be in an untenable bargaining position."[21]

The conventional model also appeals to creditors, particularly during periods of increasing prices when the conventional model tends to understate the value of the resources of a firm. Such understatement should provide a margin of safety to creditors.

Another important reason for the continued use of the conventional model is that it is the only legally recognized model that serves as the basis for taxation. This model provides the basis for defining legal capital and, therefore, furnishes the benchmark for the dividend declaration. Moreover, trust deeds, contracts, and many other statutory and common law instruments are enacted or negotiated on the basis of historical costs.

The conventional model is defended on the following additional grounds:

1. "Users' understanding of the effect of changing prices may be enhanced if they are able to compare the measurements in the primary financial statements with measurements that reflect changing prices."[22]
2. "Users are accustomed to the present financial statements."[23]
3. "Historical cost valuation is among all valuation methods currently proposed, the method that is least costly to society considering the social costs of recording, reporting, auditing, settling disputes."[24]

The foregoing discussion has provided several arguments in defense of the conventional accounting model. There are also strong arguments against this model, which are presented below.

Weaknesses of the Conventional Accounting Model

At the present time, there appears to be a general consensus that the conventional financial statements are deficient in conveying economic data that could help investors in their investment decision making. Furthermore, the conventional accounting statements are not helpful in promoting an efficient allocation of societal resources.[25] Even Y. Ijiri, who is a staunch defender of the historical-cost model, admits that his defense of the model "is not addressed to those who evaluate highly the contribution by historical cost accounting but nonetheless advocate the need for improving it and supplementing it by other procedures."[26]

The weaknesses of the conventional model are essentially related to the underlying principles of the model. As Kenneth MacNeal pointed out 44 years ago, "the conventional financial statements must necessarily be untrue and misleading due to the unsound principles upon which the conventional accounting methods are based."[27] MacNeal adds that: "For more than four hundred years, since the publication of Pacioli's book on double entry bookkeeping in 1494, the accounting methods, and hence accounting reports, have been based on expediency rather than on truth."[28] Indeed, there is a great deal of truth in MacNeal's assertions. It is interesting to note, however, that the deficiencies of the conventional model tend to be more pronounced during inflationary periods. The recent inflationary conditions experienced in the United States and other countries have renewed strong interest in finding a better, alternative accounting model. However, although the deficiencies of the conventional model tend to be highlighted during inflationary periods, the model has fundamental weaknesses that could undermine financial reporting even in the absence of inflation. A discussion of some of the major problems underlying the model follows.

Generally Accepted Accounting Principles

The conventional financial statements are prepared in conformity with "generally accepted accounting principles." Such principles allow for the presentation of transactions using more than one method—e.g., inventory valuation. Accordingly, one can prepare different sets of financial statements for the same firm by choosing alternative, generally accepted methods for computing depreciation, inventory and valuation to cite two examples. As a result, there is a serious credibility gap in financial reporting. Furthermore, as R. J. Chambers alleges, there is no definitive source of generally accepted accounting principles. After listing several sources of the accepted principles— which include FASB statements and interpretations, Accounting Prin-

ciples Board (APB) Statements and Opinions, American Institute of
Certified Public Accountants (AICPA) accounting research bulletins,
AICPA accounting interpretations and statements of position, AICPA
industry audit guides and accounting guides, industry accounting practices, pronouncements of other professional associations, statements
of regulatory agencies such as the Security Exchange Commission
(SEC), accounting textbooks and articles, and common business us-
age—Chambers observes: "This whole array of sources is so open-
minded that it is no exaggeration to say that almost anything can be
a 'generally accepted principle'."[29] He contends that "the availability
of alternative rules makes it possible for companies to select sets of
rules which 'on the whole' grossly misrepresent income."[30]

Historical-Cost/Realized-Revenue Principle

The conventional accounting model may be described as the
"historical-cost/realized-revenue" approach to income measurement
and asset valuation.[31] The historical-cost principle requires that
accounting records be maintained at original transaction prices and
that these values be retained throughout the accounting process to
serve as the basis for values in the financial statements.

While it is true that historical cost generally represents "fair
market value" at the time of transaction, given that we have informed,
rational buyers and sellers in a competitive market structure, as time
passes, however, the economic value of an asset may conceivably
change substantially, especially during a period of inflation. This
phenomenon renders the historical-cost balance sheet of limited significance to interested external parties such as investors and creditors, who may well be more concerned about the current value of the
economic resources owned by an enterprise than about the original
cost of these resources. In "The Fable of the Two Factories," which
assumes inefficient capital markets and no financial intermediaries
or sophisticated financial analysts, MacNeal demonstrates the misleading aspects of the historical-cost principle.[32] In "The Fable of
the Two Flour Mills," MacNeal shows how two identical assets—purchased at different prices and hence reflected on the balance sheet
at different acquisition costs—serve to mislead investors, who rely
on the auditor's opinion, which states that the financial statements
fairly present the financial position of the firm in conformity with
generally accepted accounting principles. When confronted with the
misleading nature of this opinion, the auditor maintains that he relies
on the historical-cost principle. A synopsis of MacNeal's fables is
provided at the end of this chapter.

Conventional accounting income is measured by matching historical costs at which the transactions were originally recorded with

realized revenues. Aside from certain cost items, such as wages, and other current operating expenses, which tend to reflect current costs, the historical cost of units sold and the reported historical-cost depreciation may not represent the current cost of these items. In general, whenever there is a time lag between acquisition and utilization, historical cost may well differ significantly from current cost. The longer the time lag, the more substantial the difference between the reported amounts and the current values is likely to be. Accordingly, the conventional accounting model tends to report "inflated" profits during a period of increasing prices. Revenues tend to increase, but that part of the cost of goods sold representing earlier purchases of plant and inventories will generally be based on lower costs, producing inflated profits. The conventional reported income contains realized holding gains, but without making any distinction between normal operating income and holding gains. As a result, from the investor's point of view, the relevance of the conventionally reported income, which commingles regular operating income and holding gains, may conceivably be limited.

As noted earlier, the conventional model is based on the realization principle, which calls for the recognition of revenue when it has been realized. Realization requires the conversion of a resource into cash or near-cash through a market transaction. The realization principle has an important implication affecting both the balance sheet and the income statement. In the balance sheet, the realization principle dictates adherence to the historical cost of the assets until the resource is sold, despite any changes in the value of the resources held by the firm. The realization principle requires that only realized revenues be included in the income statement. Accordingly, objections have been leveled against the realization principle, asserting that it is "an unnecessary principle which leads not only to a misleading and confusing computation of income, but also to an equally misleading and confusing portrayal of resource values in the balance sheet."[33] MacNeal has presented "The Fable of the Two Flour Mills" and "The Fable of the Two Investment Trusts,"[34] both of which clearly demonstrate how misleading financial statements can be due to adherence to the realization principle.

One exception is made in the conventional model when the value of the inventories falls below original historical cost. The "lower of cost or market" rule recognizes a loss due to a decline in the market value of inventories even though no market transaction has occurred. This departure from the realization principle is justified by the "conservatism" principle. Another exception arises in the valuation of inventories of certain minerals, such as gold and agricultural products. Such inventories are recorded at their net realizable value (i.e., the selling price less estimated costs to complete and sell). The latter exception is justified on the grounds that (1) such inventories have a controlled market with a fixed price applicable to all quantities, and (2) there are no significant costs of disposal involved.

The revenue realization principle produces an income measure that is consistent with the maintenance of the original money capital of the firm. In a period of rising prices, however, maintaining the original money capital is insufficient to sustain the firm's operating capability due to the increased replacement costs of inventory and the plant and equipment consumed in normal operations. As discussed earlier, the conventional approach of matching historical costs with realized revenue generates inflated profits during periods of rising prices. Such inflated profits cannot be regarded as a measure of "distributable income" simply because the total distribution of such income, in the form of dividends to owners, would impair the operating capacity of the firms, unless external financing could be secured to replace inventory sold and operating assets consumed at the current higher prices.

Stable Monetary Unit Principle

Another key problem of the conventional accounting model stems from the use of the dollar as the measurement unit under the assumption that it is a stable unit of measurement. Recent experience, however, has shown that the dollar has serious limitations as a means of communicating financial information. Unlike other units of measurement, such as the ounce or the meter, the dollar is an unstable unit. Because the value of money, as a medium of exchange, is based on its ability to command goods and services (i.e., its purchasing power), during inflation, as the general price level of the goods and services rises, the purchasing power of the dollar declines. The opposite is true with deflation. Thus, the value of the dollar fluctuates with changes in the general price-level movement. The stable monetary principle assumes that (1) there is no inflation, or (2) the rate of inflation can be ignored.

Experience has shown that the rate of inflation has not been constant from year to year. The significant inflationary conditions during the past several years have created serious measurement problems in financial reporting. The measurement-unit problem has long been recognized in the accounting literature. W. A. Paton noted in 1922:

> The value of the dollar—its general purchasing power—is subject to serious change over a period of years. . . . Accountants . . . deal with an unstable, variable unit and comparisons of unadjusted accounting statements prepared at intervals are accordingly always more or less unsatisfactory and are often positively misleading. [35]

Paton considered "the instability of the accountant's yardstick as one of the fundamental limitations of accounting."[36]

The historical-cost principle underlying the conventional model together with the stable monetary-unit principle results in a balance sheet with assets acquired at different times with dollars of varying purchasing power. In the income statement, the conventional accounting model also reports costs and expenses in monetary units that differ from one another and from the units used to measure revenue items. If we assume that the difference in purchasing power of the monetary unit between two points in time is significant, then one cannot achieve meaningful results by adding or subtracting "different" dollars. Although the amounts are denominated in the same currency, their economic significance is tantamount to dealing with different currencies.

Elementary rules of arithmetic would require that one use a homogeneous unit of measurement to add, subtract, or compare amounts. In discussing the measurement-unit problem, Chambers asserts:

> In the whole process of conventional accounting there is a basic illogicality in that we add, subtract, and compute relationships between things that are not the same in economic reality although they are denominated in the same term, "dollar."[37]

Henry Sweeney contends that the use of the nominal dollars is a key deficiency of conventional accounting:

> The success of the whole system of business depends upon the truthfulness of reports. The truthfulness of reports depends mainly upon the truthfulness of accounting. The truthfulness of accounting depends largely upon the truthfulness of the dollar—and the dollar is a liar! For it says one thing and means another.[38]

In view of the measurement-unit problem, investors cannot make meaningful interperiod comparisons of accounting data or analysis of past trends (such as growth in assets, earnings, and dividends).

To sum up, the conventional model has several serious deficiencies, which stem from two of its underlying principles: revenue realization and stable money unit. Additionally, there are problems that arise because of several acceptable, alternative accounting methods, resulting in a multitude of possibilities for presenting the same transactions. As an outspoken critic of conventional accounting puts it:

It is futile to expect a "financial position" to be "fairly presented" if the asset components are represented variously by actual money amounts (e.g., cash, receivables and payables), by historical costs, (e.g., for investments in land and marketable securities), by depreciated historical costs (e.g., for plant and machinery, vehicles and buildings), and by such other odd amounts as LIFO, the lower of cost and market prices, and so on (e.g., for inventories). Aggregates of such amounts have no meaning whatever; they fairly present nothing in the nature of a dated financial position. [39]

SUMMARY AND CONCLUSION

This chapter examined the conventional accounting model. To appreciate the strengths and weaknesses of this model, we traced its origin and development. The conventional model has its roots as far back as 4500 B.C. The fundamentals of contemporary accounting, however, are credited to Pacioli (1494).

Our review of the evolution of accounting reveals that accounting has developed parallel to developments in the business environment. In the early days of venture enterprises, accounting, by necessity, was rudimentary, relying on the cash basis, with no consideration of valuation and cost-allocation issues. When more permanent types of business organizations came into existence, the need for accrual accounting and cost allocation arose. In those early business organizations, which were essentially owner-managed, accounting was primarily for the owners' and creditors' use. Because the most important external users of financial statements were creditors, mostly bankers, the balance sheet emerged as the principal financial statement, conveying information about the solvency and liquidity of the business entity. In order to protect the creditors, the principle of "conservatism" became an important standard in the preparation of the financial statement.

The establishment of publicly owned corporations had a strong influence on the development of accounting and financial reporting. With the dominant role played by the corporation in today's business environment, and the existence of many investors who are divorced from the day-to-day operations of the corporation, the need for reliable information has assumed special importance. To this end, the accounting profession and the government, through the Securities and Exchange Commission, have endeavored to improve the scope and quality of financial reporting.

Our evaluation of the conventional accounting model has focused on its adequacy as a means of financial reporting for publicly held corporations, with particular emphasis on investors and creditors as the primary users of financial statements. The major strength of the conventional accounting model is that it is based on arm's-length transactions. Therefore, conventional accounting data are generally reliable. Moreover, the model is acceptable for legal matters. On the other hand, the model has major shortcomings. That there are several alternative accounting methods permitted as "generally accepted accounting principles" serves to promote a credibility gap in financial reporting. Alternative accounting procedures allow transactions to be reported in different ways. Additionally, the revenue realization principle tends to generate financial statements that do not reflect cash flows, particularly in periods of changing prices. Under inflationary conditions, the balance sheet tends to understate the values of the resources of a firm since these resources are reported at their historical costs. By contrast, the income statement tends to report "inflated" profits, by matching historical costs with realized revenues. Finally, because the conventional model is based on the "stable monetary unit" principles, or assumption, the instability of the dollar has created serious measurement problems in financial reporting.

Given that financial reports constitute a key source of information on which investment, credit, and other economic decisions are made, it is important that these reports provide relevant and reliable information. Confidence in financial reporting is important to facilitate an equitable allocation of capital.

In view of the deficiencies of the conventional model, several alternative accounting models have been proposed. These models will be examined later in this book. The next chapter traces the historical evolution of inflation accounting in the United States.

APPENDIX: MacNEAL'S FABLES

In his classic book, MacNeal presents three fables to illustrate how faulty conventional accounting principles—in particular, realization and conservatism—are. The moral of these fables is that " . . . the sophistry, illogic, and the untruth of accounting principles . . . produce figures deceiving accountants, businessmen, and the public alike." A summary of each fable follows:

The Fable of the Two Factories

A builder sold two identical factories to two different men. One building was sold for $5,000, the other for $20,000. Only the builder himself knew the cost to the factories. Each man who bought a factory subsequently had an accountant prepare a balance sheet. Thus, one balance sheet showed assets of $5,000, while the other (for the identical factory) showed assets worth $20,000; the stock equities were $5,000 and $20,000, respectively. Each man then sold additional stock for $5,000. A banker who invested in the $5,000 factory received a one-half interest, while the farmer, the only person in the area who did not know that both factories were identical and worth the same, received only a one-fifth interest.

The man in whose factory the farmer had invested was later arrested for defrauding the farmer. This man blamed the accountant, who was soon arrested and tried in court. The accountant admitted that he had had no idea what value either factory had, although he had thought the price difference for the two identical factories was absurd. According to the accountant, he had done the best he could by using the original cost prices as the values for the factories. When the jurors met to decide on a verdict, some wondered why the accountant had not made additional inquiries or had not obtained estimates of the factory prices. Others felt that the accountant had been correct, for an accountant cannot know the current price of a factory. After three days, no consensus was reached, and the accountant was freed.

The Fable of the Two Flour Mills

Two men who owned corporations each began leasing a different flour mill on January 1. Each corporation had $150,000 cash. Since the annual rent was $1,000, each treasury had $149,000 remaining.

On January 1, Henry invested in wheat, buying 100,000 bushels at $1.00 a bushel, while Bill invested $100,000 at 6 percent interest. At the end of the year, wheat was selling at $2 a bushel, so Bill called in both his principal and interest and purchased 50,000 bushels at $2 a bushel for wheat, apprehensive that wheat prices would rise. On

December 31, Henry made an unrealized profit of $100,000 (100%), while Bill earned $6,000 interest. An accountant prepared statements for each man. Henry's assets were valued at $149,000, and his loss was $1,000, the annual rent. Bill's balance sheet showed assets of $155,000 (149,000 + $6,000 cash interest), while his income was $5,000 ($6,000 interest − $1,000 rent).

A farmer wanted to invest in one of the flour mills but could not understand financial statements. Therefore, he asked his banker to explain them. The banker asserted that Bill's mill had more assets and made money, while Henry's mill had fewer assets and incurred a loss for the year. Accordingly, the farmer invested in Bill's mill, and subsequently regretted that action. Henry's mill was really worth $249,000 as compared to Bill's $155,000. Thus, Henry earned $99,000 during the year, while Bill earned only $5,000. Henry then converted his wheat into flour during January and sold it for $100,000 profit. Bill did the same, earning no profit at all.

The accountant was later questioned. He argued that he was correct in not anticipating unrealized profits and in valuing inventories at the lower of cost or market, in accordance with generally accepted principles governing the conventional accounting model.

The Fable of the Two Investment Trusts

Financiers formed two investment trusts and purchased securities for both trusts in exactly the same amounts, prices, and kinds. After the first year, the financiers really went to work. Both trusts had earned profits, but in order to realize those profits, the securities of one trust were sold. The securities in the other trust were left intact.

Accountants were called in to prepare financial statements for each trust. Of course, the trusts were actually equal in value. However, realized profits (not unrealized profits) and the lower of cost or market values were reflected on the financial statements, so one trust appeared to be better than the other.

After the financial statements were published, one trust's stock price rose, while the other's fell. The financiers, knowing full well that each trust had actually earned the same profits, then sold holdings of the higher-priced trust and acquired additional stock of the lower-priced trust.

The following year, each trust also earned profits, and the same accountants prepared the financial statements. The trust, which had lower profits the year before, now showed higher profits, for its securities were sold during the year. The other trust showed lower profits, for its securities remained unsold.

NOTES

1. Y. Ijiri, for example, has presented a strong argument in defense of historical-cost accounting in his article, "In Defense of Historical Cost Accounting," in Asset Valuation and Income Determination, ed. R. R. Sterling, (Lawrence, Kans.: Scholars Book, 1971), pp. 1-14. We present arguments in defense of the historical-cost model later in the chapter.

2. O. R. Keister, "The Mechanics of Mesopotamian Record-Keeping," in Contemporary Studies in the Evolution of Accounting Thought, ed. M. Chatfield, (Belmont, Calif.: Dickenson, 1968), pp. 12-20.

3. Ibid., p. 13.

4. A. C. Littleton, Accounting Evolution to 1900 (New York: Russel and Russel, 1933, reprinted 1966.) Littleton's book provides an account of the historical evolution of accounting from antiquity to the beginning of the twentieth century.

5. H. R. Hatfield, "An Historical Defense of Bookkeeping," in Contemporary Studies in the Evolution of Accounting Thought, ed. M. Chatfield, (Belmont, Calif.: Dickenson, 1968), p. 3.

6. Littleton, Accounting Evolution to 1900, p. 77.

7. Ibid., p. 368.

8. G. O. May, Financial Accounting: A Distillation of Experience (New York: Macmillan, 1943), p. 51.

9. R. A. Irish, "The Evolution of Corporate Accounting," in Contemporary Studies in the Evolution of Accounting Thought, ed. M. Chatfield, (Belmont, Calif.: Dickenson, 1968), p. 58.

10. May, Financial Accounting, p. 51.

11. Ibid.

12. See D. F. Hawkins, "The Development of Modern Financial Reporting Practices Among American Manufacturing Corporations," The Business History Review (Autumn 1963): 135-68.

13. Littleton, Accounting Evolution to 1900, p. 366.

14. As a result of a series of meetings between representatives of the New York Stock Exchange and the American Institute of Accountants (later to become the American Institute of Certified Public Accountants) soon after the 1929 stock market crash, the concepts of fairness and consistency in the application of accounting principles were introduced into the auditor's report.

15. See K. F. Skousen, An Introduction to the SEC, 2nd ed. (Cincinnati, Ohio: Southwestern, 1980), pp. 4-5.

16. Ibid., pp. 19-26.

17. W. H. Beaver, Financial Reporting: An Accounting Revolution (Englewood Cliffs, N.J.: Prentice-Hall, 1981), p. 13.

18. For a rigorous definition of risk and return, see E. F. Fama, "Efficient Capital Markets: A Review of Theory and Empirical Work," Journal of Finance, May 1970, pp. 382-417; and W. Sharpe, Portfolio Theory and Capital Markets (New York: McGraw-Hill, 1970).

19. Quoted in B. Merino, ed., Business Income and Price Levels (New York: Arno Press, 1980), p. iv.

20. Ibid.

21. Ibid.

22. See FAS 33, par. 7, p. 3.

23. Ibid.

24. Ibid., p. 14.

25. See J. Ronen and G. H. Sorter, "Relevant Accounting," Journal of Business (April 1972): 259.

26. Ijiri, "In Defense of Historical Cost Accounting," p. 1.

27. K. MacNeal, Truth in Accounting (Philadelphia, Pa.: University of Pennsyvalnia Press, 1939; new ed., Houston, Tex.: Scholars Book, 1970), p. vii.

28. Ibid.

29. R. J. Chambers, "Fair Financial Reporting—In Law and Practice," in the Emanuel Saxe Distinguished Lecturers in Accounting 1976-1977 (New York: Bernard M. Baruch College), p. 12.

30. Ibid.

31. E. Stamp, "Income and Value Determination and Changing Price Levels: An Essay Towards a Theory," Accountants Journal (August 1972), p. 17.

32. MacNeal, Truth in Accounting, pp. 2-6.

33. T. A. Lee, Income and Value Measurement: Theory and Practice (Baltimore, Md.: University Park Press, 1975), p. 50. See also J. H. Myers, "The Critical Event and Recognition of New Profit," The Accounting Review, (October 1959): 528-32; American Accounting Association Committee, "The Realization Concept," The Accounting Review, (April 1965): 312-22; C. Horngren, "How Should We Interpret the Realization Concept?" The Accounting Review, (April 1965): 323-33.

34. MacNeal, Truth in Accounting, pp. 6-15.

35. W. A. Paton, Accounting Theory (1922, original ed.; reprinted, Houston, Tex.: Scholars Book, 1973), p. 427.

36. W. A. Paton, "Depreciation, Appreciation and Productive Capacity," The Journal of Accountancy, (July 1920): 1.

37. R. J. Chambers, Accounting, Finance and Management (Sydney, Australia: Arthur Anderson and Company, 1969), p. 310.

38. H. W. Sweeney, Stabilized Accounting (1936, original ed.; reprinted, Chicago: Holt, Rinehart and Winston, 1964), p. xliii.

39. Chambers, "Fair Financial Reporting," p. 10.

2

THE EVOLUTION OF FASB *STATEMENT NO. 33,* "FINANCIAL REPORTING AND CHANGING PRICES"

INTRODUCTION

The purpose of this chapter is to trace the historical evolution of FASB Statement No. 33 (FAS 33), the present inflation-accounting standard in the United States, which was issued in 1979. Selected antecedent literature on the subject of accounting for general and specific price changes is examined. While emphasis is placed on the evolution of inflation accounting in the United States, a comprehensive study of the roots of inflation accounting should also include an examination of European literature on the subject.

This analysis is intended to show that FAS 33 has substantial foundations in U.S. literature. While the ideas underlying FAS 33 have been previously proposed, earlier literature on this subject has been neglected. The current debate on inflation accounting represents a repetition of ideas that have long been conceptualized and articulated.

Disclosure Requirements of FAS 33

FAS 33 has been labeled "an experiment" to deal with the problem of changing prices in financial reporting. Toward this end, it mandates the disclosure of three types of supplementary financial data, reflecting: (a) general price-level adjusted historical cost data, (referred to in Statement No. 33 as "historical cost/constant dollar" [HC/CD] data), (b) "current cost" data, and (c) "current-cost/constant-dollar" data. More specifically, FAS 33 requires the following annual disclosures by firms having inventories and gross property, plant, and equipment exceeding $125 million or total assets of more than $1 billion net of accumulated depreciation:

1. Income from continuing operations taken from the conventional statements with general price-level adjustments made for cost of goods sold, depreciation, depletion, and amortization
2. Income from continuing operations taken from the conventional statements with current-cost adjustments for cost of goods sold, depreciation, depletion, and amortization
3. Purchasing-power gain or loss on monetary items
4. Current cost of inventory, property, plant, and equipment at year-end
5. Increases or decreases in the current costs of inventory, property, plant, and equipment minus general inflation effects

Additionally, the items below have to be reflected in a five-year summary in constant dollars:

1. Net revenues
2. General price-level adjusted data:
   a. Income from continuing operations
   b. Income per common share from continuing operations
   c. Net assets at fiscal year-end
3. Current-cost data:
   a. Income from continuing operations
   b. Income per common share from continuing operations
   c. Net assets at fiscal year-end
   d. Increases or decreases in the current costs of inventory, property, plant, and equipment minus the general price-level effects
4. Other data:
   a. Purchasing power gain or loss on monetary items
   b. Cash dividends declared per common share
   c. Market price per common share at year-end

It should be emphasized that neither complete financial statements prepared on a general price-level (constant-dollar) basis nor on a current-cost basis are mandated by FAS 33. However, firms are encouraged to provide additional information to assist users of financial statements in understanding the effects of changing prices on the firm.

On the basis of these disclosure requirements, it can be asserted that FAS 33 represents aspects of three different inflation-accounting models that have been proposed over the years: (1) historical-cost/constant-dollar or general price-level (GPL) accounting, (2) current-cost accounting (CCA), and (3) constant-dollar (GPL adjusted) current-cost accounting. In light of these disclosure requirements, this chapter presents a chronological development of the first two models individually. The third model is essentially the current-cost accounting model adjusted for changes in the unit of measurement. Hence, no separate discussion is given of this model.

HISTORICAL-COST/CONSTANT-DOLLAR ACCOUNTING

The historical-cost/constant-dollar (HC/CD) accounting model has a variety of names, such as general price-level adjusted accounting, GPLA, constant purchasing-power accounting, stabilized accounting or simply constant-dollar accounting.[1] Historical-cost/constant-dollar (HC/CD) accounting essentially is the conventional historical-cost accounting model, with the exception of the measurement unit used. Constant-dollar accounting recognizes the deficiencies of using the dollar as a unit of measure when the general price level fluctuates. Measuring financial information using dollars of different periods having different purchasing power is analogous to combining currencies of different countries in the same financial statements. To deal with this problem, constant-dollar accounting restates financial statements in terms of a stable purchasing-power unit. It must be emphasized, therefore, that HC/CD accounting is an extension of the historical-cost accounting system, producing no change in generally accepted accounting principles except that the unit of measure is restated into a common scale, thus rectifying the "stable dollar" assumption underlying the conventional accounting system. HC/CD and current-cost accounting are not substitutes. Only by remote coincidence would HC/CD and current-cost figures be equal for nonmonetary assets such as inventories and equipment. (Chapters 6 and 7 provide an analysis of the historical-cost/constant-dollar and current-cost models, respectively.)

It is interesting to note that the "stable-dollar" assumption in conventional accounting was criticized by Livingston Middleditch, an American writer, as far back as 1918.[2] L. Middleditch realized the difficulties in using the dollar as a unit of measure:

As the general purchasing price level fluctuates the dollar is bound to become a unit of different magnitude. To mix these units is like mixing inches and centimeters or measuring a field with a rubber tape-line.[3]

To overcome the problem of the fluctuating dollar, Middleditch recommended the restatement of "all accounts in terms of the same monetary unit." Such a restatement of accounts, Middleditch asserted, would "permit the true condition of affairs to be set forth."[4] This, however, may suggest that Middleditch confused general price-level restatements with current values. Although this misconception was pointed out in the same year by W. A. Paton,[5] there has been much confusion about these two models until very recently.[6] Middleditch is credited for his pioneering work in transplanting to accounting that constant purchasing power ideas developed by Irving Fisher (1911).[7] Paton called Middleditch's recommendation "an ingenious way of recognizing the changing value of money in the accounts."[8]

Though Middleditch is credited for his pioneering work, he is also criticized for his crude income statement and inadequate consideration of the dichotomy between monetary and nonmonetary items (in particular, nonmonetary current assets and long-term liabilities).[9] These shortcomings in Middleditch's work may be attributed to "a combination of an embryonic understanding of the concept of price-level accounting and the secondary importance of the income statement."[10] In the early 1900s, the balance sheet was the primary financial statement.

Price-Level Accounting in Europe

The evolution of inflation accounting in the United States has been influenced by developments in Europe. A brief review of these developments, therefore, is necessary. In Europe, the first comprehensive constant purchasing power (CPP), historical-cost financial statements appeared in Germany after World War I. This was a period when the German economy was severely affected by inflation culminating in the hyperinflation of 1923. Schmalenbach (1919) and his student Mahlberg (1921) are credited with developing the techniques and the theoretical basis for stabilized historical-cost financial statements that were soon used in other European countries at that time.[11]

The early approach of stabilizing financial statements was accomplished by restating the historical-cost data from nominal monetary units (the paper mark in Germany) to the gold standard. This practice was considered to be a natural response to the collapse in the value of the conventional measurement unit (the paper mark) in times of exceptional inflation.[12] As in the United States during this period, the income statement was not accorded much significance, and the emphasis was placed on stabilizing the balance sheet. It is reported that a law was enacted in Germany in 1923 requiring compulsory balance sheet stabilization in gold marks for certain business organizations.[13] The idea of using an index number instead of the gold standard to adjust financial statements is attributed to Irving Fisher, who in the early 1920s published index numbers in the United States for such purposes.[14]

Henry W. Sweeney

Sweeney was one of the early critics of the historical-cost principle and its underlying assumptions. In searching for a remedy for the defects of historical-cost accounting, Sweeney relied on the ideas of Fisher and Middleditch. Additionally, Sweeney was strongly influenced by the German literature of the early and middle 1920s, particularly the works of Schmalenbach and Mahlberg on this subject.[15] Although Sweeney may not be credited for originating the idea of stabilized accounting, he certainly deserves recognition for presenting the first comprehensive general price-level accounting model in the English literature.

Sweeney's misfortune was the timing of his major publication,[16] Stabilized Accounting (1936),[17] which was issued when inflation was not a major problem in the United States. In more recent years, as a result of significant inflation, Sweeney's ideas have been rediscovered.

There is one key difference between Sweeney's framework and the constant-dollar model outlined in FAS 33 as well as the FASB's 1974 proposed statement on this model and the Accounting Principles Board's Statement No. 3, "Financial Statements Restated for General Price-Level Changes" (1969). Contrary to later proposals, Sweeney considers monetary gains and losses to be "unrealized" until, for example, the debt is extinguished and the cash paid. Stated differently, monetary gains and losses from holding monetary items are viewed as "unrealized." It should be emphasized that Sweeney was wedded to the conservatism principle, and thus careful not to suggest early recognition of revenue. Adding together Sweeney's realized and unrealized monetary gains and losses furnishes the total monetary gains and losses similar to its computation in recent authoritative literature on constant-dollar accounting.

FAS 33 also requires disclosure of monetary or general purchasing power gains and losses from holding monetary assets and monetary liabilities during a period of general inflation. The key problem with monetary gains and losses in Sweeney and in FAS 33, among other writings, is that these gains and losses stem from the dubious assumption that general inflation is totally unanticipated.

It should be pointed out, however, that Sweeney favored stabilized replacement cost accounting rather than stabilized historical-cost statements. In expressing his preference for replacement cost, Sweeney remarked that "stabilized accounting, although primarily interested in homogeneous measurement, cannot refrain from giving more approval to replacement cost as a valuation base than to ordinary original cost."[18] It appears, however, that Sweeney's concern about the subjective nature of replacement cost led to his emphasis on the stabilized historical-cost system.[19]

American Accounting Association

The position of the American Accounting Association (AAA) in the 1940s was to ignore changes in price levels under the pretext that such changes were negligible. According to a statement on Accounting Principles Underlying Corporate Financial Statements prepared by the Executive Committee of the AAA and issued in June 1941:

> A marked change in the value of money might impair the usefulness of cost records; however, such changes in price levels as have occurred in this country during the last half century have afforded insufficient reason for the adjustment of asset values. [20]

The Accounting Concepts and Standards Underlying Corporate Financial Statements—1948 Revision—issued by the AAA also opposed any departure from historical cost, yet for the first time entertained the need to develop appropriate procedures in the event significant price-level changes were to occur:

> Readers of financial statements may be aided in their interpretations by considering the effect of fluctuations in the purchasing power of money. A marked, permanent change in price levels might impair the usefulness of statements reporting asset costs; however, price changes during recent years do not afford sufficient justification for a departure from cost. Accounting concepts and standards appropriate for the reflection of a drastic and permanent change in prices would need to be developed in the event of such a change. [21]

Shortly afterward, the AAA became more actively involved in the price-level debate. In 1951, the AAA Committee on Concepts and Standards Underlying Corporate Financial Statements, in its Supplementary Statement No. 2, Price Level Changes and Financial Statements, recommended "intensive research and experimentation" on the accounting effects of the changing value of the dollar, and a thorough test of financial statements stated in units of general purchasing power. [22] It also suggested, apparently to encourage experimentation, that during the period of development and experimentation of the supplementary general price-level adjusted statements, the statements need not be covered by the independent accountant's opinion. In December 1953, the AAA Committee on Concepts and Standards issued its Supplementary Statement No. 6, Inventory Pricing and Changes in Price Levels, in which it reiterated its recommendation for experimentation with the technique of price-level adjustments.[23] The committee was particularly concerned about the growing popularity of the "artificial LIFO" method, which it wanted to "abandon entirely in favor of a realistic flow assumption" if better techniques reflecting the impact of price-level changes could be developed.[24] Based on the committee's recommendation for a thorough study of the subject, the following projects were sponsored by the AAA.

1. Case Studies of Four Companies, by Ralph C. Jones (AAA, 1955).
2. Basic Concepts and Methods, by Perry Mason (AAA, 1956).
3. Effects of Price Level Changes in Business Income, Capital and Taxes, by Ralph C. Jones (AAA, 1956).

It is not clear what impact these studies had on the AAA. However, by 1957 the AAA had developed a more flexible approach to price-level accounting. In Accounting and Reporting Standards for Corporate Financial Statements—1957 Revision, published by the AAA, the Committee on Concepts and Standards reemphasized the need to reflect the impact of changing prices and recommended supplementary statements to show the effects of specific price changes (by means of specific indexes or replacement costs) and/or to reflect general price-level changes. It is stated that such a flexible approach was adopted by the committee, "until reasonably uniform principles of adjustment for price changes can be commonly accepted."[25] Since then the AAA has not been very active in promoting general price-level adjusted historical-cost statements. By the early 1960s, its position was shifting more toward current-value accounting—a subject that is discussed later in this chapter.

Official Pronouncements

In the aftermath of World War II, the United States economy was again experiencing inflationary pressures. Again the ability of the conventional historical-cost accounting system to portray "economic reality" was increasingly being questioned. Two of the largest companies, namely DuPont and U.S. Steel, attempted to reflect the impact of increasing prices by making supplementary charges to the historical-cost depreciation in their conventional income statements.[26] Such a move, however, was rejected by the SEC in light of the qualified audit opinion rendered due to departure from the generally accepted cost principle.[27] Because of the SEC's rejection, a number of firms had to pressure the American Institute of Accountants (AIA) the predecessor of the American Institute of Certified Public Accountants (AICPA), to permit higher depreciation charges in order to cope with rising costs.

In 1947, faced with increasing pressure to respond to the accounting problems stemming from rising prices, the AIA instructed its Committee on Accounting Procedures (predecessor of the Accounting Principles Board [APB]), to study the depreciation issue. In December 1947, the Committee on Accounting Procedures issued Accounting Research Bulletin (ARB) No. 33 dealing with depreciation and high costs. ARB No. 33 rejected the idea of increasing depreciation charges and recommended strict adherence to the generally accepted concept of depreciation based on historical cost. However, increased pressure from industry prompted a reconsideration of the committee's position. Perhaps the major reason that firms advocated a change in the generally accepted accounting policy was their opposition to paying taxes on "inflated profits."[28] Nevertheless, in October 1948, the Committee on Accounting Procedures, in a letter sent to the members of the AIA, reaffirmed the position it had taken in ARB No. 33 and indicated that no change in depreciation methods would be considered until the Study Group on Business Income, which had been formed in 1947, completed its project. In the meantime, the committee suggested that the problem of increasing prices should be administered by financial management through appropriations of earnings for plant maintenance. To help management communicate effectively with stockholders, the committee gave its full support "to the use of supplementary financial schedules, explanations or footnotes by which management may explain the need for retention of earnings."[29] In 1953, when the Committee on Accounting Procedure issued ARB No. 43, ARB No. 33—together with the letter of October 1948—was restated as part of ARB No. 43, which effectively confirmed the cost principle for a long time to follow.

The Study Group on Business Income, composed of more than 40 members of the AIA, was established in 1947. The AIA had received a $30,000 matching grant from the Rockefeller Foundation to launch a three-year study of business income, with particular attention to the effects of changing price levels. During this three-year period, the Study Group on Business Income produced the following five documents:[30]

1. Five Monographs on Business Income (New York: AICPA, 1950). This book contains five papers by leading economists on the nature of business income.
2. An Inquiry into the Nature of Business Income Under Present Price Levels, by Arthur H. Dean (privately printed, February 1949).
3. Business Income and Price Levels, an Accounting Study, by George O. May (privately printed, July 1949).
4. "The Case Against Price-Level Adjustments in Income Deter-

mination," by Howard C. Greer and Edward B. Wilcox, published both in The Illinois CPA (September 1950), and The Journal of Accountancy, (December 1950).
5. Changing Concepts of Business Income, Report of the Study Group on Business Income (New York: Macmillan, 1952).

The two main recommendations related to price-level accounting contained in the report of the Study Group were as follows:[31]

1. [I]n the longer view, methods could, and should, be developed whereby the framework of accounting would be expanded so that the results of activities, measured in units of equal purchasing power, and the effects of changes in value of the monetary unit would be reflected separately in an integrated presentation which would also produce a statement of financial position more broadly meaningful than the orthodox balance sheet of today.
2. For the present . . . the primary statements of income should continue to be made on the bases now commonly accepted. Corporations whose ownership is distributed should be encouraged to furnish information that will facilitate the determination of income measured in units of approximately equal purchasing power, and to provide such information wherever it is practicable to do so as part of the material upon which the independent accountant expresses his opinion.

Several members of the study group dissented to the foregoing recommendations, and this lack of consensus could have affected the enthusiastic acceptance of the study group's recommendations.

George O. May

In examining the evolution of inflation accounting in the United States, one should definitely not neglect the influence George O. May has had and the role that he played in shaping accounting practice. In Audits of Corporate Accounts (1934), published by the American Institute of Accountants and written by its Special Committee on Cooperation with the New York Stock Exchange chaired by May, one of the five basic recommendations set forth to eliminate the accounting abuses of the 1920s was to refrain from reflecting "unrealized profit" in the accounts. Moreover, May himself in 1936 adamantly opposed specific-price or appreciation accounting:

[I]n the 1920's accountants fell from grace and took to adjusting capital values on the books. . . . In extenuation they might plead unsound laws, unpractical economics and a widespread if unfounded belief in the new order of

things combined to recommend such a course but . . .
the wiser course is to admit the error and not be mis-
led again. [32]

May's bias toward general price-level adjusted financial statements is evident in his classic book Financial Accounting: A Distillation of Experience, published in 1943. [33] As a member of the AIA
Study Group on Business Income, May prepared in July 1949 a monograph—Business Income and Price Levels: An Accounting Study. In
this monograph, May proposed the use of LIFO to recognize the higher
costs of replacing inventories. He also argued that enterprises with
significant depreciation charges in their income statements—such as
railroads, public utilities, and capital intensive manufacturing firms—
ought to supplement the conventional depreciation expense with amounts
to reflect changes in general purchasing power. [34] Although his depreciation recommendation did not appear to have an impact then (as attempts by DuPont and U.S. Steel mentioned earlier would suggest),
his LIFO idea was soon widely accepted. In November 1949, the U.S.
Treasury Department approved the use of the dollar-value LIFO costing method by all taxpayers, a tax benefit that was previously limited
only to retailers. [35] In 1954, the Internal Revenue Code permitted the
use of accelerated depreciation methods for tax purposes. [36]

The adoption of LIFO and accelerated depreciation for tax purposes could have considerably eased the pressure emanating from the
business community for price-level accounting. At the same time, the
relatively stable prices that followed must have contributed to the lack
of interest in formulating inflation accounting pronouncements by the
standard-setting bodies of the time. For a period of ten years after
the issuance of ARB No. 43 in 1953, there were no official pronouncements.

Revival of Inflation Accounting in the 1960s

The publication by Edwards and Bell of The Theory and Measurement of Business Income (1961) engendered a revival of the inflation-
accounting debate. Edwards and Bell's book was followed by the publication of Sprouse and Moonitz's AICPA Accounting Research Study No.
3, "A Tentative Set of Broad Accounting Principles For Business Enterprises" (1962). Both publications, which are discussed in the section on the evolution of current-cost accounting, call for current-cost
accounting. While both writings advocate current costing, they also
seem to favor constant-dollar measurements. In October 1963, the
staff of the Accounting Research Division of the AICPA produced
Accounting Research Study (ARS) No. 6: Reporting the Financial Effects

of Price-Level Changes, after two years of work on the project. ARS No. 6 favored general price level adjusted historical-cost statements, and, in this regard, was instrumental in reviving HC/CD accounting.

ARS No. 6 was essentially designed to provide the necessary foundation before issuance of the pronouncement by the Accounting Principles Board. Accordingly, the study provides a justification of the need to reflect the impact of changes in the value of the dollar. The study proceeds with a discussion and illustration of adjusting historical-cost statements by application of a general price index. The major recommendations of ARS No. 6 are as follows:

1. General price-level restated statements should be presented as supplementary statements to conventional historical cost statements.
2. The Gross National Product Implicit Price Deflator Index should be used for purposes of restatement.
3. Gains and losses in purchasing power from holding monetary items should be recognized and reported (a) in the statement of changes in owners' equity, (b) as a component part of the calculation of net income for the period, or (c) in a statement of net income and inflation gain or loss.
4. The conventional financial statements should be restated in terms of the general price level of the end of the accounting period. In comparative presentations, statements of prior periods are to be rolled forward (restated) in the general price level of the end of the current year.

ARS No. 6 was essentially a restatement of Sweeney's stabilized historical cost-accounting model. In fact, in his review of ARS No. 6 for The Accounting Review (October, 1964), Sweeney wrote:

> The salient recommendations in this epoch-marking work arouse mixed emotions in this reviewer. For they arouse both gratification and frustration: Gratification because the basic recommendations of the Study are those of his own book, Stabilized Accounting; frustration because they have had to wait 28 years before receiving the respectability and acceptability that the Study is likely to confer on them ultimately. To review the Study's main concepts, therefore, places this reviewer in the anomalous position of practically reviewing his own work. [37]

ARS No. 6 was not officially approved by the AICPA since it was designed only to encourage discussion, prior to the issuance of any pronouncement on this subject, by the Accounting Principles Board

(APB). Based on ARS No. 6, in 1969 the APB issued Statement No. 3 "Financial Statements Restated for General Price-Level Changes." APB Statement No. 3 called for the presentation of supplementary financial statements in units of general purchasing power and provided detailed guidelines and procedures to be followed in their preparation. This statement was a long awaited official pronouncement on price-level accounting; however, it was not mandatory. Consequently, the statement was virtually ignored by the business community.

With significant inflation continuing into the 1970s, ASR No. 6 subsequently became the model for several general price-level proposals in many of the English-speaking countries. As the historical evolution of inflation accounting has shown thus far, the popularity of historical-cost/constant-dollar statements appeared to increase dramatically with the severity of the inflationary experience in a given period of time. In December 1974, the Financial Accounting Standards Board (FASB), which superseded the Accounting Principles Board in 1973 as the accounting standard-setting body, issued an exposure draft on Financial Reporting in Units of General Purchasing Power. The exposure draft was essentially an updated version of ARS No. 6, calling for mandatory general price-level adjusted supplementary statements.

While the FASB's Exposure Draft was under study, the Securities and Exchange Commission issued a new rule, Accounting Series Release No. 190 (ARS 190) in March 1976. The SEC rule required large firms to disclose particular replacement cost data. With the release of ASR 190, the FASB was forced to withdraw its 1974 Exposure Draft, Financial Reporting in Units of General Purchasing Power. Subsequent to considerable examination of the subject in relation to its Conceptual Framework Project, the FASB issued Statement of Financial Accounting Standards No. 33 (FAS 33), "Financial Reporting and Changing Prices" in 1979. FAS 33 requires historical-cost/constant-dollar, current cost, and current-cost/constant-dollar data. Let us briefly review the arguments for and against historical-cost/constant-dollar accounting as a prelude to our discussion of the evolution of current-cost accounting.

The historical-cost/constant-dollar model ought to appeal particularly to practicing accounting professionals. By its very nature, the constant dollar adjustment is a simple mechanical process involving the restatement of given accounts with a general price-level index. Since the process involves objectively determined data (both the historical-cost data, and a publicly available, objectively determined index), there is a low risk that the professional accountant faces relative to the subjectively determined current value measures. Viewed from this perspective, perhaps the preferred inflation accounting model to the accounting profession is historical-cost/constant-dollar.

On the other hand, some observers argue that the process of restating historical cost data results in statements that are neither interpretable nor relevant. [38] To such writers, the appealing aspect of FAS 33 is not its historical-cost/constant-dollar requirements, but its current-cost disclosure provisions. Although the HC/CD information may be criticized for lacking theoretical support, a recent empirical research study investigating the impact on security prices of the FASB's 1974-1976 deliberations on GPL accounting has led J. Sepe to conclude that "GPL-adjusted information is relevant information for security market participants."[39]

We now turn to current-cost accounting.

CURRENT-COST ACCOUNTING

This section provides an analysis of the historical evolution on current-cost accounting. (Chapter 7 furnishes a conceptual analysis of this model.) In tracing the history of current costing in the United States, it is interesting to note that it was during a period of deflation following the end of the Civil War (1865) that replacement cost was proposed as an appropriate cost for the purpose of calculating depreciation charges in the determination of railroad rates. The public utility regulatory agencies argued in favor of using replacement costs that were considerably lower than the historical-cost figures during those deflationary years. Not surprisingly, the railways argued against using replacement cost; Smyth vs. Ames became a landmark case in which the U.S. Supreme Court permitted the use of "fair value" to establish rates by public utilities. [40] When inflation appeared at the turn of the century, the situation reversed. Railways wanted to use replacement cost data in order to allow them to set higher rates, whereas the regulatory agencies fought for the use of historical costs, which tended to be lower. [41]

The use of current values was also widely favored in the United States, as Zeff's account illustrates. [42] Prior to the stock market crash of 1929, financial reporting in the United States was primarily geared to the creditor, particularly in relation to bank loans. Bankers during those days, as Zeff points out, were primarily concerned with liquidity and current values of assets. The balance sheet was considered the most important financial statement for conveying such information:

> Evidently an unquestioned axiom in financial circles was
> "the handsomer the balance sheet, the more prosperous
> the corporation," for both tangible and intangible assets
> were assigned values higher than cost in the balance sheets

of some of the most respected corporations. After all, if balance sheets were to be <u>statements of financial position</u>, they had to be revised to reflect current values. And these "current values" were not always based on the opinions of independent, expert appraisers.[43]

This attitude best explains the rationale for the asset write-ups witnessed during the 1910s and 1920s in the United States. This was followed by write-downs during and after the Depression.

W. A. Paton

One of the early American writers who argued in favor of current costs was W. A. Paton. In a 1918 article,[44] Paton launched the basic ideas of current-cost accounting, which were later to be expounded upon by Edwards and Bell. While Paton applauded Middleditch's "ingenious way of recognizing the changing value of money in the accounts," he emphasized that Middleditch's approach was only a solution to the measurement unit problem in financial reporting. Paton was primarily concerned with the objective of providing relevant information for decision making. For such purposes, he insisted that "it is not <u>general</u>, but <u>specific</u> price changes that the accounts should follow." These views were also reflected in a <u>Principles of Accounting</u> book that Paton coauthored with R. A. Stevenson in 1918.[45] In an appraisal of his contribution to current value accounting, Zeff describes Paton as "perhaps the first major American Accounting writer who persistently championed the cause of current values in preference to historical costs."[46] Yet it should also be pointed out that Paton's "pertinent publications [on this subject] are not as comprehensive as those of Schmidt," who is credited with developing a comprehensive current-cost accounting model in Germany in the early 1920s.

Fritz Schmidt

Fritz Schmidt published a comprehensive replacement cost-accounting framework in Germany as early as 1921, although his writings did not appear in U.S. journals until the 1930s.[48] At the same Schmidt's work was published, Germany was plagued by severe inflation, culminating in the hyperinflation of 1923. However, Schmidt's ideas were not implemented at that time. Instead, Schmalenbach's general purchasing-power accounting was favored as a logical solution to the deteriorating purchasing power of the German mark.

Schmidt (1930 and 1931) calls for valuation of assets and liabilities, cost of sales, and depreciation using current replacement costs. Additionally, Schmidt advocates the exclusion of holding gains from operating income, a recommendation later made by Edwards and Bell

(1961). However, Schmidt favors the inclusion of holding gains in a reserve within stockholders' equity rather than in the income statement, and completely disregards the purchasing-power gains and losses from monetary items."[49] It should be pointed out that Schmidt's income concept was identical to Edwards and Bell's "current operating income" and also very similar to FAS 33's current cost version of "income from continuing operations," and the "current operating profit" concept that was proposed by the Sandilands' Committee in Great Britain.

Although his work was not accepted in Germany during his lifetime, Schmidt appears to have contributed significantly to the ultimate popularity of CCA. He is credited, in particular, for having had "an important influence on the thinking of Limperg and the Dutch replacement cost school, which in turn served as a model for subsequent developments in current cost accounting elsewhere."[50]

Theodore Limperg, Jr.

A discussion on the evolution of current-cost accounting would not be complete without recognizing the contribution of Theodore Limperg and his influence in the actual implementation of replacement cost in the Netherlands. Limperg developed current-replacement-value accounting in the 1920s, and through his work the Netherlands has been identified with this model ever since. As Whittington observes:

> Limperg's achievement was not confined to developing a theoretical model. Perhaps his most important achievement for the development of accounting practice was to persuade the Dutch auditing profession to accept financial accounts based upon replacement values and to persuade some leading Dutch companies to adopt such methods.[51]

The fact that replacement cost was adopted by some large and successful companies, such as Phillips Industries, is viewed as "an important factor in the subsequent acceptance of CCA [Current-Cost Accounting] in the U.K. and the U.S. because it was impossible to dismiss this type of accounting as impractical."[52]

Limperg derived his ideas from Schmidt, yet their formulations were somewhat different. Schmidt's replacement cost was based on the idea of physical replacement, whereas Limperg advocated replacement value, a concept akin to "deprived value" (also called "value to the owner"), which is discussed later in this chapter, and is reflected in FAS 33 as well as Britain's recent CCA pronouncement SSAP 16.[53] Limperg's replacement value concept was further pursued by J. C.

Bonbright, an American academician, who developed the concept of "deprival value."[54]

J. B. Canning

An economist, J. B. Canning attempted to inject economic thought into accounting theory in his landmark book The Economics of Accountancy (1929).[55] Although he exposed the valuation of non-monetary assets by discounting future cash flows, Canning acknowledged that such a valuation basis was difficult to implement. Instead, he "proposed a method of indirect valuation by which an asset would be assessed at the current cost to reacquire by the least costly means."[56] If direct values are infeasible, Canning argued, then indirect valuation bases are justifiable. Canning was critical of the conventional historical-cost system, but his ideas were too radical for his time. In an annotated bibliography describing Canning's book, R. F. Vancil and R. L. Weil state: "If the profession had followed the principles set forth in this important book, we would have had a form of current value accounting long before now."[57]

Henry W. Sweeney

Although Henry W. Sweeney is generally known for his pioneering work on historical-cost/constant-dollar accounting, he has expressed his preference for replacement cost in lieu of historical-cost data. In a 1933 article, Sweeney declared: "[A]s a valuation base, replacement or reproduction cost must be judged both theoretically sounder and practically more desirable than actual original cost."[58] In his book Stabilized Accounting (1934), Sweeney devoted a chapter to the merits of replacement cost with an illustration of how to stabilize replacement cost data. Although Sweeney was influenced by Schmidt's work, he expanded Schmidt's version in proposing current-cost/constant-dollar data.

Kenneth MacNeal

An early critic of the historical-cost system, Kenneth MacNeal favored "economic values" rather than historical costs. His book Truth in Accounting,[59] published in 1939, had been neglected for a long time. Zeff presents a fascinating account of MacNeal's background, the circumstances that led MacNeal to write Truth in Accounting, together with a critical examination of the principal arguments contained in the book.[60]

According to MacNeal: "The economic value of anything is its 'power in exchange' which, measured in money, is its market price. The market price of a thing is the price at which it is actually being bought and sold."[61] In those situations where acceptable markets are not available for particular assets, he recommends the use of surrogates such as replacement costs for nonmarketable and reproducible assets.[62] MacNeal even accepts original cost as a surrogate for nonmarketable and nonreproducible assets, such as patents, copyrights, mines, and oil wells.[63]

MacNeal's income statement is composed of two sections. The "current" section of his income statement provides net profit from business operations, which includes the unrealized increases and decreases during the period in the market price or replacement cost of the current asset items such as inventories, raw materials, work in process, and finished goods. The second section of his income statement reflects the gains and losses on noncurrent assets resulting in net capital profit that is credited to capital surplus.[64] MacNeal's proposed balance sheet showed the assets of the firm at their economic values, or surrogates and liabilities at their face values, and the difference is shown as stockholders' equity.[65]

MacNeal's work was sharply criticized by his contemporary professionals and academics alike.[66] Although MacNeal did not attract immediate followers, his multiple valuation approach was adopted by later writers on the subject.

E. O. Edwards and P. W. Bell

The Theory and Measurement of Business Income by E. O. Edwards and P. W. Bell (1961),[67] as Mattessich rightly asserts, "has undoubtedly been the single internationally most influential work in the area of current cost accounting."[68] In terms of its content, Vancil and Weil have described it as "the classic statement on the integration of current value accounting and a constant dollar measurement unit."[69]

To elaborate on the development of current cost accounting, Edwards and Bell advocate income measurement using current cost.[70] Their concept of current cost is the cost of purchasing assets identical to those the firm possesses,[71] which is also the definition of current cost set forth in FAS 33. According to Edwards and Bell, holding gains and losses arising from the write-up of physical assets to their current costs should be reported as part of the total business income, though separately reported from current operating income. Edwards and Bell contend that reporting holding gains separately in the income statement is an important input in evaluating the performance of management. This view, however, has been disputed by, among others, D. F. Drake and N. Dopuch (1965),[72] who argue that it is difficult to distinguish between operating and speculative decisions of management; therefore, operating and holding gains ought to be viewed as interdependent. Still another view, which has been espoused by R. Gynther (1966),[73] is to treat holding gains as capital maintenance adjustments, not as income, on the grounds that this revaluation is needed to ensure the replacement of the assets consumed, and as such is undistributable without impairing the productive capacity of the firm.

FAS 33 calls for reporting of holding gains and losses from inventories, property, plant, and equipment, minus the general inflation component that produces a fictitious or illusory gain or loss. However, these net holding gains/losses, while appearing in the income statement, are excluded from the income stemming from continuing operations, thus echoing Edwards and Bell's position on this matter.

R. T. Sprouse and M. Moonitz

In a project commissioned by the AICPA, R. T. Sprouse and M. Moonitz prepared Accounting Research Study No. 3, "A Tentative Set of Broad Accounting Principles for Business Enterprise," (1962).[74] This monograph was hailed by some academic accountants for its advocacy of current replacement costs and net realizable values. The reaction of the AICPA to the Sprouse and Moonitz study, however, was decidedly different. The Accounting Principles Board immediately issued a statement saying that the Sprouse and Moonitz views were "too radically different . . . for acceptance at this time."[75]

Sprouse and Moonitz recommended measurement methods that included discounted present values (at historical-interest rates) for receivables and payables to be settled in cash, net realizable values for readily salable inventories, and replacement costs for other inventories and tangible fixed assets. In a significant departure from generally accepted accounting principles and procedures, they rejected the "realization" principle for lacking "analytical precision." In recognition of the impact of general price-level increases on the dollar as a measurement unit, Sprouse and Moonitz favored general price-level adjustments although their study did not devote much attention to this issue apparently because another study, ARS No. 6, was then underway to explore the general price-level problem.[76]

Exit-Value Accounting

Chambers, who has been writing on the subject since the 1960s, is the best-known proponent of exit-value accounting. In the 1970s, Sterling also began to advocate exit valuation. Proponents of exit-value accounting insist that the relevant attribute to be reported is the amount of cash that could be obtained currently by selling an asset under conditions of orderly liquidation. As Chambers observes, exit values reflect the firm's ability to adapt to a changing environment and thus represent conceptually correct measures of the firm's opportunity costs. (Chapter 8 provides an analysis of the exit-value model.)

Chambers calls his current-value accounting system "continuously contemporary accounting" because all reported balances on a given date are contemporary on that date. He recognizes the problems introduced by the fluctuating value of the dollar and recommends that purchasing power gains and losses arising from holding monetary items be reflected as "capital maintenance adjustments."[77]

R. R. Sterling[78] has been an enthusiastic proponent of exit valuation, especially exit-value/constant-dollar accounting. In Sterling's view, the relevant attribute that should be measured and communicated is "command-over-goods" because it reflects general and specific price changes. Although the exit-value balance sheet meets his criterion since this balance sheet reflects command-over-goods (i.e., the number of physical goods commanded in the market), the exit-value income statement needs to be adjusted for general price level changes in order to provide results that reflect command-over-goods.

AAA's Contributions to the Evolution of Current-Cost Accounting

In 1957, the American Accounting Association (AAA) for the first time had expressed mild support for the disclosure of either replacement-cost information or historical-cost/constant-dollar data or a combination of both types of data in Accounting and Reporting Standards for Corporate Financial Statements—1957 Revision. The AAA had made it clear then that its flexible approach was necessary "until reasonably uniform principles of adjustment for price changes are commonly accepted." Since then, however, various committees of the AAA have favored current-value accounting. This shift in the AAA position is evidenced by two reports of its Committee on Concepts and Standards dealing with (1) "Inventory Measurement," and (2) "Long Lived Assets," both issued in 1964.[79] These committee reports provided compelling arguments in favor of current-value accounting. In 1966, a separate AAA Committee issued A Statement of Basic Accounting Theory (ASOBAT).[80]

A Statement of Basic Accounting Theory (AAA, 1966) calls for financial statements reflecting historical and current costs, thus multivalues, to appear juxtaposed in columnar fashion. The basic philosophy underlying this document was expressed some thirty-nine years ago by Canning (1929), as previously discussed. The disclosure of multiple asset-valuation bases in financial statements, which Canning and ASOBAT have advocated, is based on the argument that current-value accounting should be flexible in applying different valuation bases that are relevant for given circumstances. Accordingly, such a system should report either historical cost, current cost, net realizable value, or discounted cash flow, among other values, whichever is more relevant for particular accounts under the circumstances.

Support for the multiple asset valuation was subsequently given by the AICPA's Trueblood Study Group on the Objectives of Financial Statements (1973). The Trueblood Objectives Report maintains that financial-statement objectives "cannot be best served by the exclusive use of a single valuation basis. Each of the valuation bases should be analyzed in terms of the stated objectives. Selection of the specific basis or communication of bases to be used is an implementation issue."[81] Nevertheless, the members of the Trueblood Study Group could not agree on whether value changes should be reflected in the bottom-line earnings figure. They did, however, agree that:

1. Changes in the values reflected in successive statements of financial position should also be reported, but separately, since they differ in terms of their certainty of realization.
2. Current values should also be reported when they differ significantly from historical cost.

The Trueblood Objectives Report also mentions the significance of utilizing dollars of the same purchasing power in the financial statements: "If the value of the unit of measure is unstable, that is, if inflation or deflation is so great that direct cash consequences are no longer comparable, such circumstances should be recognized in the financial statements."[82] Nevertheless, the report gives constant-dollar accounting very limited attention presumably because the Trueblood committee did not view this accounting model as relevant for forecasting such flows.

SEC's Accounting Series Release No. 190

The Securities and Exchange Commission (SEC) was granted statutory authority by the Securities Acts of 1933 and 1934 to ensure that financial reporting be consistent with the public interest. However, the SEC has relied on the accounting profession to establish generally accepted accounting principles. As inflation became a significant problem, there was increasing clamor for public action to remedy the deficiencies of the conventional financial statements. In response to this call, the FASB in 1974 issued an Exposure Draft on Financial Reporting in Units of General Purchasing Power, which proposed mandatory supplementary disclosure of general price-level adjusted (historical-cost) statements. Although this was a time when both current-value accounting and historical-cost/constant-dollar accounting were being reconsidered, the FASB, "merely dusted off ARS No. 6, condensed it, changed the title, and published it in the form of an exposure draft."[83] This exposure draft reflected no changes in thinking since 1963, despite a tremendous volume of writing on the subject.

It was while the 1974 Exposure Draft was pending that the SEC issued Accounting Series Release No. 190 in March 1976, an event that resulted in the FASB's withdrawal of the exposure draft and the subsequent issuance of FAS 33. The SEC's move was a landmark development in the evolution of inflation accounting in the United States and abroad. As Mattesich points out: "This event [the issuance of ASR 190] constituted the turning point at which the international preference for GPP Accounting changed into a preference for CCA."[84]

ASR 190, which has been rescinded since the issuance of FAS 33, was "designed to enable investors to obtain more relevant information about the current economics of a business enterprise in an inflationary economy," a rather general aim in contrast to the statement's more focused objective of providing assistance to users in terms of "assessment of future cash flows," "assessment of enterprise performance," "assessment of the erosion of operating capability," and "assessment of the erosion of general purchasing power."

ASR 190 required current-replacement cost disclosure for public companies whose inventories and gross property, plant, and equipment exceeded $100 million and 10 percent of their total assets. FAS 33, by contrast, requires compliance from firms having $1 billion of assets or $125 million of inventories and gross property, plant, and equipment. In FAS 33, the FASB desires information regarding the current cost of obtaining or reproducing an identical asset possessing the same service potential as the one on hand. The SEC, however, called for the current replacement cost of inventory and productive capacity, hence allowing for replacement by more efficient capacity.[85] Depreciation and cost of sales in terms of current replacement cost have also been required for SEC disclosure. The SEC did not mandate any aggregated income figures—like the FASB's income from continuing operations. Additionally, the SEC did not consider the problem of a stable measurement unit. The SEC had requested only current replacement-cost information, in contrast to the FASB, which also requires constant-dollar figures, but it should be emphasized that the SEC did not intend to provide a comprehensive solution to the problems associated with accounting for changing prices. To some extent, FAS 33 is a hybrid of the 1974 FASB exposure draft on supplementary constant-dollar information and the SEC's ASR 190, which required the disclosure of supplementary replacement-cost information.

FAS 33 requires current information together with the measurement of "real" holding gains, a measure that combines current-cost information with adjustments for general inflation. This enables interested users to determine both the real and the fictitious holding gains from nonmonetary items.

FAS 33 recommends the use of current costs or lower recoverable amount in the valuation of inventories, property, plant, and equipment. FAS 33 invokes the concept of "value to the business" in the measurement of an asset. It should be noted, however, that the concept of "value to the business" in FAS 33 is not well-defined. An appendix to FAS 33 notes that this value "is often called 'deprival value' because it can be assessed by assuming that the enterprise has been deprived of the use of an asset and by asking how much the enterprise would need to be paid to compensate it for the asset." The appendix, however, does provide the following guidelines for computing the value to the business, which constitutes the:

1. Current cost (current buying price or current production cost), or
2. Lower of the higher of net realizable (an exit value) or value in use (present value of cash flows).

FAS 33 does not give explicit consideration to the implications of adhering to the foregoing decision rule, which appears to emanate from the British Sandilands Report (1975), in turn derived from Bonbright (1937).[86] As Bonbright observes:

> The value of a property to its owner is identical in amount with the adverse value of the entire loss, direct and indirect, that the owner might expect to suffer if he were to be deprived of the property.[87]

Under this rule, there would be six conceivable cases, none of which is specified or even referred to by the FAS 33. The concept of deprival value is examined in Chapter 3.

SUMMARY AND CONCLUSION

This chapter has traced the historical evolution of inflation accounting in the United States, culminating in the official release of the first mandatory inflation-accounting pronouncement—FASB Statement No. 33.

A review of the historical American accounting literature leads to the roots of FAS 33. In substance, FAS 33 provides nothing really novel. What is now called historical-cost/constant-dollar accounting was proposed by Sweeney, who derived his ideas from German writers

Schmalenbach and Mahlberg, nearly fifty years ago. Similarly, current (replacement) cost accounting has long been advocated. The idea of using current costs was supported in the United States as early as 1865 in establishing rates for railroads. The current-cost requirements of FAS 33 reflect the current cost accounting model proposed by the German scholar Fritz Schmidt some sixty years ago. The concept of "profit (or loss) from continuing operations adjusted for changes in specific prices," as reflected in FAS 33, is analogous to the "current operating profit" concept proposed by Edwards and Bell (1961). The combination of constant-dollar and current-cost accounting in FAS 33 has also been suggested by Sweeney. What has been a controversial aspect of FAS 33 is its dual requirements to report in terms of historical-cost/constant-dollar and current-cost data. Yet this is only another manifestation of the perennial problem of accounting under inflationary conditions.

FAS 33 is based on a comprehensive synthesis of historical accounting thought and gradually accepted ideas about financial reporting that once were considered heretical (e.g., Sprouse and Moonitz, 1962). If the statement had been proposed in a period of insignificant inflation, it would probably have been unacceptable to preparers and users of financial statements alike. History shows that inflation-accounting recommendations in the 1950s and 1960s, two decades that were largely characterized by insignificant inflation, were generally ignored.

NOTES

1. We must hasten to add, however, that unless explicit reference is made that the historical-cost data are restated or adjusted for general price-level changes, abbreviated use of these terms could easily be misconstrued. The current-cost model, for example, can also be stabilized by restating the current-cost data in terms of constant dollars.

2. L. Middleditch, Jr., "Should Accounts Reflect the Changing Value of the Dollar?" The Journal of Accoutancy, (February 1918): 114-20.

3. Ibid., p. 115.

4. Ibid.

5. W. A. Paton, "The Significance and Treatment of Appreciation in the Accounts," Michigan Academy of Science, Twentieth Annual Report, ed. G. H. Coons (Ann Arbor, Mich., 1918); reprinted in S. A. Zeff, ed., Asset Appreciation, Business Income and Price-Level Accounting, 1918-1935, (New York: Arno Press, 1976), pp. 35-49.

6. See P. Rosenfield, "Confusion Between General Price-Level Restatement and Current-Value Accounting," The Journal of Accountancy (October 1972): 63-73.

7. I. Fisher, The Purchasing Power of Money (New York: Macmillan, 1911). For a discussion on the early history of inflation accounting, see G. Whittington "The Role of Research in Setting Accounting Standards: The Case of Inflation Accounting," in Accounting Standards Setting: An International Perspective, eds. M. Bromwich and A. Hopwood. London: Pitman, 1983. Also see R. Mattessich, "On the Evolution of Inflation Accounting—With a Comparison of Seven Major Models," working paper (University of British Columbia, Canada, 1981).

8. Paton, "The Significance and Treatment of Appreciation in the Accounts," p. 46.

9. For a review of Middleditch's article, see S. A. Zeff (1976), Asset Appreciation, pp. 3-6, and also D. Buckmaster, "Inflation Gains and Losses from Holding Monetary Assets and Liabilities, 1918-1936: A Study of the Development of Accounting Thought in the U.S.," International Journal of Accounting Education and Research, (Spring 1982): 1-22.

10. Buckmaster, "Inflation Gains and Losses," p. 3.

11. For a detailed discussion on the history of inflation in Germany, see Mattessich, On the Evolution of Inflation Accounting, and also Whittington, "The Role of Research in Setting Accounting Standards."

12. Whittington, "The Role of Research in Setting Accounting Standards," p. 13.

13. See H. W. Sweeney, "Effects of Inflation on German Accounting," The Journal of Accountancy, (March 1927): 180-191; reprinted in Zeff, Asset Appreciation, p. 13.

14. I. Fisher, The Money Illusion (New York: Macmillan, 1925), pp. 19-30.

15. Zeff, Asset Appreciation, contains an insightful collection and review of Sweeney's nine articles that were published between 1917-1934. See also Mattessich, On the Evolution of Inflation Accounting, and Whittington, "The Role of Research in Setting Accounting Standards," for an analysis of Sweeney's contribution to inflation accounting.

16. Mattessich, On the Evolution of Inflation Accounting, p. 6.

17. H. W. Sweeney, Stabilized Accounting (New York: Harper and Brothers, 1936); also reprinted in 1964 by Holt, Rinehart and Winston, with a foreword by S. A. Zeff, W. A. Paton, and Sweeney's own twenty-three page memoir, "Forty Years After: Or Stabilized Accounting Revisited."

18. Sweeney, Stabilized Accounting, p. 51.

19. There is some evidence suggesting that Sweeney's emphasis on stabilized historical cost was motivated by his desire for producing an acceptable dissertation. Sweeney, in a foreword to the 1964 edition of his book Stabilized Accounting, wrote, "Professor Kester [Sweeney's dissertation advisor] had . . . pointed out that a theory alone, no matter how intellectually stimulating and thorough, would not suffice. He had warned me that any corrective accounting plan I devised must be tested on actual accounts—and had to prove 'practical'. . . . I could theorize all I wished, in or out of armchairs, but, as Professor Kester continually warned me, if the theory could not be applied profitably, it would not be acceptable, and all my time on it would have been wasted." (p. xx).

20. Executive Committee of the American Accounting Association, Accounting Principles Underlying Corporate Financial Statements, June 1941; reproduced in American Accounting Association, Accounting and Reporting Standards for Corporate Financial Statements and Preceding Statements and Supplements, (Iowa City, Iowa: AAA, College of Business Administration, University of Iowa, undated), p. 54.

21. American Accounting Association, Accounting and Reporting Standards for Corporate Financial Statements and Supplements (Iowa City, Iowa: AAA, College of Business Administration, University of Iowa, 1957), p. 14.

22. Committee on Concepts and Standards Underlying Corporate Financial Statements, Supplementary Statement No. 2, Price Level Changes and Financial Statements, (Sarasota, Fla.: AAA, 1951). See p. 26 of source cited in note 21.

23. Committee on Concepts and Standards Underlying Corporate

Financial Statements, <u>Supplementary Statement No. 6, Inventory</u> <u>Pricing and Changes in Price Levels</u> (Sarasota, Fla.: AAA, 1953). See p. 36 of source cited in note 21.

24. Ibid. Also, see p. 40 of the source cited in note 20.

25. <u>Accounting and Reporting Standards for Corporate Financial</u> <u>Statements—1957 Revision.</u> See p. 9 in source cited in note 21.

26. S. A. Zeff, "Episodes in the Progression of Price-Level Accounting in the United States," in <u>Contemporary Studies in the</u> <u>Evolution of Accounting Thought</u>, ed. M. Chatfield. (Belmont, Calif.: Dickenson, 1968), p. 320.

27. Ibid.

28. See E. L. Miller, <u>Inflation Accounting</u> (New York: Van Nostrand Reinhold, 1980), p. 59.

29. See Committee on Accounting Procedures, Accounting Research Bulletin No. 43, <u>Restatement and Revision of Accounting Research Bulletins</u>, (AICPA, June 1953). Chapter 9A, par. 17, reproduced in Financial Accounting Standards Board, <u>Financial Accounting</u> <u>Standards</u> (Stamford, Conn.: FASB, 1981), pp. 33-5.

30. Zeff, "Episodes in the Progression of Price-Level Accounting," p. 321.

31. Report of Study Group on Business Income, <u>Changing Concepts of Business Income</u> (Houston, Tex.: Scholars Book, 1975), p. 105.

32. G. O. May, "The Influence of Accounting on Economic Development," <u>The Journal of Accountancy</u>, (January 1936): 11-22.

33. G. O. May, <u>Financial Accounting: A Distillation of Experience</u> (New York: Macmillan, 1943). In connection with the assessment earning capacity, May asserts: "It is advantageous to express revenues and charges against revenues in terms of a monetary unit of the same value." (p. 93).

34. Zeff, "Episodes in the Progression of Price-Level Accounting," p. 321.

35. Miller, <u>Inflation Accounting</u>, p. 60.

36. Ibid.

37. H. W. Sweeney, "Reporting the Financial Effects of Price-Level Changes: Accounting Research Study No. 6: A Critique," <u>The Accounting Review</u> (October 1964): 1100.

38. For a discussion on the shortcomings of general-price-level-adjusted historical-cost statements, see R. R. Sterling, "Relevant Financial Reporting in an Age of Price Changes," <u>The Journal of</u> <u>Accountancy</u>, (February 1975): 42-51.

39. J. Sepe, "The Impact of the FASB's 1974 GPL Proposal on the Security Price Structure," <u>The Accounting Review</u>, (July 1982): 484. Also see E. Noreen and J. Sepe, "Market Reactions to Account-

ing Policy Deliberations: The Inflation Accounting Case," The Accounting Review, (April 1981): 253-69.

40. See G. Boer, "Replacement Cost: A Historical Look," The Accounting Review, (January 1966): 92-7; and F. L. Clarke, "Inflation Accounting and the Accidents of History," Abacus, (December 1980): 81-2.

41. To Whittington, this episode is "a good illustration of how much self-interest has affected the inflation accounting debates." See Whittington, "The Role of Research in Setting Accounting Standards," p. 6.

42. Zeff, "Episodes in the Progression of Price-Level Accounting," p. 317.

43. Ibid.

44. W. A. Paton, "The Significance and Treatment of Appreciation in the Accounts," pp. 35-49.

45. W. A. Paton and R. A. Stevenson, Principles of Accounting. (Ann Arbor, Mich.: Ann Arbor Press, 1918), p. 461.

46. Zeff, "Episodes in the Progression of Price Level Accounting," p. 7.

47. Mattessich, On the Evolution of Inflation Accounting, p. 4.

48. See F. Schmidt, "The Basis of Depreciation Charges," Harvard Business Review, (April 1930): 257-64; "The Impact of Replacement Value," The Accounting Review, (September 1930): 235-42; "Is Appreciation Profit?" The Accounting Review, (December 1931): 289-93. Also, for a detailed analysis of Schmidt's contributions to the history of inflation accounting thought, see Mattessich, On the Evolution of Inflation Accounting, and Whittington, "The Role of Research in Setting Accounting Standards."

49. See Mattessich, On the Evolution of Inflation Accounting, p. 3.

50. See Whittington, "The Role of Research in Setting Accounting Standards," p. 8.

51. Ibid., p. 11.

52. Ibid.

53. Financial Accounting Standards Board, Statement of Financial Accounting Standards No. 33: "Financial Reporting and Changing Prices," (Stamford, Conn.: FASB, September, 1979); and Accounting Standards Committee, Statement of Standard Accounting Practice, No. 16, Current Cost Accounting (London: ASC, March 1980).

54. J. C. Bonbright, The Valuation of Property, Vol. I, (New York: McGraw-Hill, 1937), p. 71.

55. J. B. Canning, The Economics of Accountancy: A Critical Analysis of Accounting Theory, (New York: Ronald Press, 1929), pp. 195-247.

56. For an in-depth analysis of Canning's work, see AAA, Committee on Concepts and Standards for External Financial Reports, Statement on Accounting Theory and Theory Acceptance (AAA, 1977), p. 8.

57. R. F. Vancil and R. L. Weil, Replacement Cost Accounting: Readings on Concepts, Uses and Methods (Glen Ridge, N.J.: Thomas Horton and Daughters, 1976), p. 7.

58. H. W. Sweeney, "Capital," The Accounting Review (September 1933): 185-99; also reproduced in Zeff, Asset Appreciation.

59. K. MacNeal, Truth in Accounting, (Philadelphia, Pa.: University of Pennsylvania Press, 1939; new ed., Houston, Tex.: Scholars Book, 1970, pp. 86-87.

60. S. A. Zeff, "Truth in Accounting: The Ordeal of Kenneth MacNeal," The Accounting Review, (July 1982): 528-53.

61. MacNeal, Truth in Accounting, p. 87.

62. Ibid., p. 186.

63. Ibid., p. 188.

64. For a suggested format of an income statement a la MacNeal, see Truth in Accounting, p. 312.

65. Ibid., pp. 280, 288.

66. For a discussion on the criticisms of MacNeal, see Zeff, "Truth in Accounting," pp. 540-43.

67. E. O. Edwards and P. W. Bell, The Theory and Measurement of Business Income (Berkeley, Calif.: University of California Press, 1961).

68. Mattessich, On the Evolution of Inflation Accounting, p. 7.

69. Vancil and Weil, Replacement Cost Accounting, p. 8.

70. As Revsine observes: "Replacement cost, according to Edwards & Bell (E&B), was to be measured by using the current costs of the assets actually owned, even in the face of technological change. By contrast, in implementing Accounting Series Release No. 190, the Securities and Exchange Commission (SEC) . . . rejected their approach. The SEC instead required that replacement cost be measured by reference to the latest available technology, even though the firm may not own these latest technological assets. The SEC's more cumbersome approach was motivated, in part, by the belief that used asset prices do not impound technological change. E&B provide a terse argument to the contrary. . . . Subsequent analytics indicate that, under ideal conditions, the two approaches will often generate equivalent signals except that the E&B approach has the advantage of being less susceptible to measurement error. . . . The FASB . . . subsequently concurred with the original E&B approach to technological change." See L. Revsine, "The Theory and Measurement of Business Income: A Review Article," The Accounting Review, (April 1981): 342-54. For an expanded discussion of this issue, see Chapter 7.

71. See Edwards and Bell, The Theory and Measurement of Business Income, p. 79.

72. See D. F. Drake and N. Dopuch, "On the Case for Dichotomizing Income," Journal of Accounting Research, (Autumn 1965): 192-205; P. Prakash and S. Sunder, "The Case Against Separation of Current Operating Profit and Holding Gains," The Accounting Review, (January 1979): 1-22; and R. Samuelson, "Should Replacement-Cost Changes Be Included in Income?" The Accounting Review, (April 1980): 254-68.

73. R. S. Gynther, Accounting for Price-Level Changes: Theory and Procedures (London: Pergamon Press, 1966), pp. 64-79.

74. R. T. Sprouse and M. Moonitz, "A Tentative Set of Broad Accounting Principles for Business Enterprise," Accounting Research Study No. 3, (AICPA, 1962).

75. See Vancil and Weil, Replacement Cost Accounting, p. 13.

76. See Sprouse and Moonitz, A Tentative Set of Broad Accounting Principles, p. 18.

77. For a complete analysis of continuously contemporary accounting see R. J. Chambers, Accounting for Inflation: Methods and Problems, (Department of Accounting of the University of Sydney, Australia, 1975). This book contains Chambers' views on why he thinks CoCoA is superior to other accounting models.

78. R. R. Sterling, "Relevant Financial Reporting in An Age of Price Changes," The Journal of Accountancy, (February 1975): 42-51.

79. American Accounting Association, Committee on Concepts and Standards—Inventory Measurement, "A Discussion of Various Approaches to Inventory Measurement," The Accounting Review, (July 1964): 700-14; Committee on Concepts and Standards—Long Lived Assets, "Accounting for Land, Buildings, and Equipment," The Accounting Review, (July 1964): 693-99.

80. American Accounting Association, A Statement of Basic Accounting Theory (Evanston, Ill.: American Accounting Association, 1966).

81. Report of the (Trueblood) Study Group on the Objectives of Financial Statements, Objectives of Financial Statements (AICPA, October, 1973), p. 65. This document is generally referred to as the Trueblood Report, in memory of Robert M. Trueblood, who served as the chairman of the Study Group.

82. Ibid., p. 61.

83. Miller, Inflation Accounting, p. 8.

84. Mattessich, On the Evolution of Inflation Accounting, p. 8.

85. While the concepts of current replacement cost a la SEC and current cost in FAS 33 produce the same figures when technology is constant over time, under most circumstances the current replace-

ment costs for plant and equipment are different from the corresponding current costs. Thus, the FASB has neglected the issue of technological change in the statement.

86. Inflation Accounting Committee, <u>Inflation Accounting: Report of the Inflation Accounting Committee</u> (London: Her Majesty's Stationary Office, 1975).

87. Bonbright, <u>The Valuation of Property</u>, p. 71.

3

ANALYSIS OF FASB *STATEMENT NO. 33,* "FINANCIAL REPORTING AND CHANGING PRICES"

INTRODUCTION

FASB Statement No. 33, "Financial Reporting and Changing Prices,"[1] hereafter referred to as FAS 33, was issued in September 1979, on an experimental basis, in response to the financial-reporting problems arising from changing prices. Since then, the FASB has issued additional statements that cover accounting for changing prices in specialized industries. Appendix A to this chapter provides a listing of three statements with a brief description of their content. An analysis of FAS 33 is provided in this chapter, including an examination of the conceptual foundations and specific provisions of this statement. The chapter also evaluates FAS 33 as an experiment in financial reporting and presents suggestions for revising FAS 33. A brief discussion of FASB Statement No. 70, "Financial Reporting and Changing Prices, Foreign Currency Translation," (1982), is presented in Appendix B in this chapter.

BACKGROUND

In Chapter 2, we examined the evolution of inflation accounting in the United States. Before analyzing FAS 33 in this chapter, we will briefly review the immediate circumstances that led to the issuance of FAS 33, to achieve a better understanding of this statement.

Prior to issuance of Accounting Series Release (ASR) No. 190[2] by the Securities and Exchange Commission (SEC) in March 1976, requiring the disclosure of supplementary replacement cost data, the only authoritative pronouncement dealing with the effects of changing prices was <u>APB Statement No. 3</u>, "Financial Statements Restated For General Price-Level Changes" (June 1969). <u>APB Statement No. 3</u>, however, recommended, but did not require, the disclosure of supplementary historical-cost/constant-dollar data, stating:

> General price-level information may be presented in addition to the basic historical dollar financial statements but general price-level financial statements should not be presented as the basic statements. [3]

In December 1974, the FASB issued an exposure draft favoring historical-cost/constant-dollar financial statements as a supplement to the conventional accounting statements. While this exposure draft was pending, the SEC surprised the accounting profession and the business community by issuing ASR 190.

The SEC has the responsibility to ensure that financial reporting is consistent with the public interest. The commission, however, generally has relied on the accounting profession to establish accounting standards for financial reporting. That the SEC imposed its new regulation while the FASB was inviting comments on its exposure draft suggests the commission was dissatisfied with the FASB's approach. The SEC presumably believed that the public interest had been neither adequately served with the conventional statements nor with the FASB proposal. Therefore, it chose to impose its own standards without waiting for the profession to act. The SEC's action resulted in the FASB's withdrawal of the 1974 exposure draft and the subsequent issuance of FAS 33 in 1979. To some extent, the statement is a hybrid of the 1974 FASB exposure draft, which favored supplementary historical-cost/constant-dollar statements, and the SEC's ASR 190, which required the disclosure of supplementary replacement-cost information. Essentially FAS 33 calls for two types of supplementary disclosures—historical-cost/constant-dollar (HC/CD)[4] and current cost. Subsequent to the full implementation of FAS 33, ASR 190 was rescinded in 1980.

OBJECTIVES OF FAS 33

In issuing FAS 33, the intent of the FASB was to provide information on the effects of changing prices to users of financial reports. The FASB maintained that without such information users may experience difficulties in making investment and credit decisions, and resources, in general, may be inefficiently allocated. Thus, in issuing FAS 33, the objective of the FASB has been to improve the usefulness of financial reporting by improving the information content of financial statements. In short, FAS 33 is an attempt on the part of the board to achieve the objectives set forth in its Statement of Financial Accounting Concepts No. 1 [SFAC 1], "Objectives of Financial Reporting by Business Enterprises" (1978). According to SFAC 1, financial reporting aims to:

> provide information that is useful to present and potential investors and creditors and other users in assessing the amounts, timing, and uncertainty of prospective cash receipts. (p. viii).

In an effort to achieve the objectives of financial reporting as set forth in SFAC 1, FAS 33 establishes four specific objectives to assist users of financial statements in evaluating the impact of changing prices on their investment, lending, and other business decisions. The supplementary disclosures required by FAS 33 are specifically designed to provide users with information presumably useful for assessing:

1. Future cash flows
2. Enterprise performance
3. Erosion of operating capability
4. Erosion of general purchasing power

With the foregoing objectives in mind, FAS 33 requires supplementary disclosures by all publicly held firms having $1 billion of assets net of accumulated depreciation or $125 million of inventories and gross property, plant, and equipment. Other firms are also encouraged to disclose such data.[5] It must be emphasized, however, that FAS 33 does not require the presentation of full-fledged balance sheets and income statements on either a historical-cost/constant-dollar or current-cost basis, although firms are encouraged to provide such statements. In the meantime, no changes are to be made in the conventional, historical-cost financial statements.

NATURE OF REQUIRED DATA

FAS 33 requires the disclosure of the following data for the current year:[6]

1. Income from continuing operations under both historical-cost/constant-dollar and current cost bases.
2. The purchasing-power gain or loss on net monetary items. This amount is to be reported separately, and is not to be included in income from continuing operations.

3. The current-cost amounts of inventory and property, plant, and equipment at the end of current fiscal year.
4. Increases or decreases in the current cost amounts of inventory and property, plant, and equipment, net of inflation. Such changes are commonly referred to as holding gains or losses.

FAS 33 specifically recommends that (2), (3), and (4) above be excluded from the income from continuing operations.

In addition, the following items have to be reflected in a five-year summary, restated either in average-for-the-year, end-of-year, or base-year constant dollars:[7]

1. Net sales and other operating revenues
2. Income from continuing operations under both the historical-cost/constant-dollar (HC/CD) and current-cost bases, including earnings-per-share amounts
3. Net assets at the end of the fiscal year under both HC/CD and current-cost bases
4. Increases or decreases in the current-cost amounts of inventory and property, plant, and equipment, net of inflation
5. Purchasing-power gains or losses on net monetary items
6. Cash dividends declared, and the market price per common share at fiscal year-end
7. The average-for-the-year or end-of-year Consumer Price Index, whichever is used for restatement to constant dollars

FORMAT OF PRESENTATION

The income from continuing operations under both the HC/CD and current-cost bases may be presented using either the "income statement" format as shown in Exhibit 3.1 or the "reconciliation" format as shown in Exhibit 3.2. Exhibit 3.3 shows the format for the five-year summary of selected data.

HISTORICAL-COST/CONSTANT-DOLLAR DATA

FAS 33 calls for the application of the Consumer Price Index for All Urban Consumers (CPI-U) to provide for historical-cost/constant-dollar data. Unless a firm is presenting comprehensive financial statements, which may be prepared either in terms of average-for-the-year or end-of-year constant dollars, the current-year, minimum-required historical-cost/constant-dollar disclosures should reflect average-for-the-year dollars.

EXHIBIT 3.1

ABC Company, Inc., Statement of Income from Continuing Operations
Adjusted for Changing Prices for the Year Ended December 31, 19X1

	As reported in the primary statements	Adjusted for general inflation	Adjusted for changes in specific prices (Current Cost)
Net sales and other operating revenues	$253,000	$253,000	$253,000
Cost of goods sold	197,000	204,384	205,408
Depreciation and amortization expense	10,000	14,130	19,500
Other operating expense	20,835	20,835	20,835
Interest expense	7,165	7,165	7,165
Provision for income taxes	9,000	9,000	9,000
	244,000	255,514	261,908
Income (loss) from continuing operations	$ 9,000	$(2,514)	$(8,908)
Gain from decline in purchasing power of net amounts owed		$ 7,729	$ 7,729
Increase in specific prices (current cost) of inventories and property, plant, and equipment held during the year[a]			$ 24,608
Effect of increase in specific prices over interest in the general price level			18,959
			$ 5,649

Source: FASB Statement No. 33: "Financial Reporting and Changing
Prices," Appendix A, Schedule B, 1979. Copyright by Financial Accounting
Standards Board, High Ridge Park, Stamford, CT, 06905. Reprinted with
permission.
[a]At December 31, 19X1, current cost of inventory was $65,700; and
current cost of property, plant, and equipment, net of accumulated depreciation
was $85,100.

EXHIBIT 3.2

ABC Company, Inc., Statement of Income from Continuing
Operations Adjusted for Changing Prices for the Year Ended
December 31, 19X1 (In-end-of-year dollars)[a]

Income from continuing operations, as reported in the income statement		$ 9,000
Adjustments to restate costs for the effect of general inflation		
Cost of goods sold	(7,384)	
Depreciation and amortization expense	(4,130)	(11,514)
Income (loss) from continuing operations adjusted for general inflation		(2,514)
Adjustments to reflect the difference between general inflation and changes in specific prices (current costs)		
Cost of goods sold	(1,024)	
Depreciation and amortization expense	(5,370)	(6,394)
Loss from continuing operations adjusted for changes in specific prices		$(8,908)
Gain from decline in purchasing power of net amounts owed		$ 7,729
Increase in specific prices (current cost) of inventories and property, plant, and equipment held during the year[b]		$24,608
Effect of increase in general price level		18,959
Excess of increase in specific prices over increase in the general price level		$ 5,649

Source: Adapted from FASB Statement No. 33: "Financial
Reporting and Changing Prices, Appendix A, Schedule A, 1979.
Copyright by Financial Accounting Standards Board, High Ridge
Park, Stamford, CT, 06905. Reprinted with permission.

[a]This statement may also be prepared in average-for-the-
year dollars.
[b]At December 31, 19X1, current cost of inventory was $65,700;
and current cost of property, plant, and equipment, net of accumulated depreciation was $85,100.

EXHIBIT 3.3

ABC Company, Inc., Five-Year Comparison of Selected Supplementary Financial Data
Adjusted for Effects of Changing Prices
(In [000s] of average 1980 dollars)

	Years ended December 31				
	1976	1977	1978	1979	1980
Net sales and other operating revenues	265,000	235,000	240,000	237,063	253,000
Historical-cost information adjusted for general inflation					
Income (loss) from continuing operations				(2,761)	(2,514)
Income (loss) from continuing operations per common share				$ (1.91)	$ (1.68)
Net assets at year-end				55,518	57,733
Current cost information					
Income (loss) from continuing operations				(4,125)	(8,908)
Income (loss) from continuing operations per common share				$ (2.75)	$ (5.94)
Excess of increase in specific prices over increase in the general price level				2,292	5,649
Net assets at year-end				79,996	81,466
Gain from decline in purchasing power of net amounts owed				7,027	7,729

Source: FASB Statement No. 33: "Financial Reporting and Changing Prices, Appendix A, Schedule C, 1979. Copyright by Financial Accounting Standards Board, High Ridge Park, Stamford, CT, 16905. Reprinted with permission.

In the event the historical-cost/constant-dollar (HC/CD) amount significantly and permanently exceeds the "recoverable amount,"[8] which is the amount of cash expected to be recovered from the use or sale of an asset, FAS 33 requires the disclosure of the lower recoverable amount in lieu of the HC/CD data, and such reduction is to be reported as a loss in the computation of income from continuing operations. (See Exhibit 3.4 later in this chapter for the six cases underlying this valuation method.)

The mechanics of generating the historical-cost/constant-dollar data are discussed in Chapter 6 of this book, which deals with this model at greater length in both conceptual and practical terms.

CURRENT-COST DISCLOSURES

In reporting income from continuing operations on a current-cost basis, the cost of goods sold should be measured in terms of the current cost or lower recoverable amount of the goods sold at the time of sale.[9] Depreciation and amortization expenses should be reflected on the basis of the average current cost or lower recoverable amount of the asset's service potential during the period in use. Other revenues and expenses, gains, and losses are reflected at the amounts shown on the primary historical-cost statements, unless comprehensive current-cost/constant-dollar income statements are prepared using end-of-year constant dollars, in which case the revenues, expenses, gains, and losses would have to be restated to common dollars.

FAS 33 also requires the disclosure of current cost or lower recoverable amount for inventory and property, plant, and equipment at the end of the current fiscal year. The current cost of inventory is the current cost of replacing or manufacturing the inventory. For property, plant, and equipment, current cost refers to the "current cost of acquiring the same service potential (indicated by the operating costs and physical output capacity) as embodied in the assets owned" (par. 58). It should be emphasized that the FASB's intent is to reflect the current cost as opposed to the current replacement cost of property, plant, and equipment. Current-cost measures reflect the costs of assets owned and used by the firm—not other assets that might be acquired to replace the assets owned. By contrast, current replacement cost for such assets is the expected cost of replacing productive capacity whether in terms of identical assets or a more efficient and technologically superior configuration of assets. Guidelines are provided for measuring the current cost of used assets (par. 58):

a. By measuring the current cost of a new asset that has the same service potential as the used asset had when it was new (the current cost of the asset as if it were new) and deducting an allowance for depreciation; .

b. By measuring the current cost of a used asset of the same age and in the same condition as the asset owned;

c. By measuring the current cost of a new asset with a different service potential and adjusting that cost for the value of the differences in service potential due to differences in life, output capacity, nature of service, and operating costs.

Firms are also required to provide information, as part of the supplementary disclosures, on the methods of computing the current cost data. FAS 33 provides considerable flexibility in the approaches that can be used to determine the current-cost information. Firms are permitted to choose the methods they find appropriate in light of the availability, reliability, and cost of generating the data. The suggested approaches include: (1) internally or externally developed specific price indexes, (2) direct costing based on current invoice prices, vendors' price lists, and standard manufacturing costs (par. 60). Whichever method is used, the reported current cost should not "significantly and permanently" exceed the recoverable amount. This approach is analogous to the conventional "lower-of-cost-or-market" rule for inventory valuation.

In measuring the recoverable amount of an asset, firms use the higher of (1) the net realizable value of the asset (if the asset in question is about to be sold) or (2) the value in use of the asset (if the asset is expected to be used). The value in use of an asset represents the net present value of future cash flows expected to be derived from using the asset plus its salvage value.

EVALUATING CONCEPTUAL ISSUES

Considering the deficiencies of the traditional, historical-cost financial statements in periods of changing prices, the need to improve the quality and scope of financial reporting is crucial. In this regard, the issuance of FAS 33 was a significant development. However, a close examination of the supplementary disclosures reveals that particular requirements are of questionable relevance.

Irrelevance of Historical-Cost/Constant-Dollar Disclosures

Although the intent of the FASB was to provide supplementary disclosures to improve the information content of the financial statements, the required historical-cost/constant-dollar data do not seem to be consistent with this purpose. This contradiction had been pointed out by one of the dissenting board members:

> A major criterion that the Board has established for
> choosing among alternative disclosures is usefulness of
> the information for predicting earnings and cash flows.
> The evidence presented to the Board on usefulness in
> this sense was sketchy, but virtually all of it favored
> the current cost approach. In fact, usefulness for pre-
> dicting earning and cash flows was rarely associated
> with the historical cost/constant dollar approach, even
> by its supporters. (FAS 33, p. 26)

The historical-cost/constant-dollar model of accounting is identified by different names, such as "General Price-Level Account-ing (GPLA)," "Current Purchasing Power (CPP) Accounting," "Ac-counting for Changes in the Purchasing Power of Money," and "Finan-cial Reporting in Units of General Purchasing Power." As these vari-ous terms indicate, the aim of this model is to restate the unit of measure into a common scale (i.e., the general-purchasing-power unit) in order to improve the measurement system underlying the accounting process. This approach retains historical cost as a method of valuation, and the restatement is accomplished by application of index numbers that measure the general purchasing power of the dol-lar. It is obvious, therefore, that this accounting model does not con-vey "current values," although there appears to be some confusion in viewing historical-cost/constant-dollar and current-cost accounting as alternatives for inflation accounting. These two models are not substitutes. They examine different facets of the problem of accounting under inflationary conditions. It is generally understood that the need for a restatement in constant dollars is motivated by the desire to overcome the reporting problem arising from general inflation. What appears to be overlooked by the proponents of this proposal is that historical-cost/constant-dollar accounting deals with only one of the two problems in accounting for changing prices.

Part of the confusion in the inflation-accounting debate stems from the failure to isolate and deal separately with the two related problems arising from changing prices, namely: (1) the measurement problem resulting from the changing purchasing power of the monetary unit due to general inflation or deflation and (2) the valuation problem due to changes in the specific prices of goods and services.

The measurement problem of the conventional accounting system arises from the use of the dollar as the measurement unit under the assumption that it is a "stable unit" of measurement. Recent experi-ence has shown that the dollar has serious limitations as a means of communicating financial information. Unlike other units of measurement, such as the ounce or the meter, the dollar is an unstable unit. In fact, it is sometimes compared to a "rubber ruler" because the value of money, as a medium of exchange, is based on its ability to command goods and services (i.e., its purchasing power).

Inflation involves a decline in the purchasing power of the monetary unit and thereby introduces the measurement-unit problem of the conventional accounting model. But even if there were no inflation, variations in prices and values of individual assets would exist, casting doubt about the usefulness of historical-cost data. Consequently, historical-cost/constant-dollar accounting is only an attempt to deal with the problem of general inflation—the measurement problem— leaving the deficiency of the historical-cost records unresolved. There are no theoretical reasons for using historical-cost/constant-dollar accounting.

Purchasing-Power Gains and Losses

Generally, holding monetary assets during a period of inflation produces a loss of purchasing power. By contrast, holding monetary liabilities generates purchasing-power gains since borrowers are able to repay their obligations using cheaper dollars. The supplementary disclosure of purchasing-power gains and losses from holding monetary items, as required by FAS 33, is based on these assumptions.

The computation of purchasing-power gains and losses on short-term monetary items is straightforward and consistent with the above assumptions. The computation of purchasing-power gains or losses on holding interest-bearing, long-term debt is, however, far from simple. Apart from situations of unanticipated inflation, the loan interest rate generally includes an inflation factor, which is intended to compensate lenders for their loss of purchasing power during inflationary periods. Consequently, in situations where the inflation rate is perfectly anticipated, and thus the nominal rate fully embodies the anticipated inflation rate, there are no losers and no winners. Although lenders may be paid back in cheaper dollars, they are properly compensated through the interest rate on the loan. Likewise, although borrowers are repaying their debt obligation using cheaper dollars, their purchasing-power gain is offset by the higher interest rate they had to pay on the loan.

The FAS 33 approach of computing purchasing-power gains and losses on holding monetary items is based on the assumption that during an inflationary period borrowers gain at the expense of lenders by repaying their debt using cheaper dollars, that is, dollars with lower purchasing power. The existence of information-efficient capital markets and the theory of rational expectations suggests, however, that the nominal interest rate would fully impound the anticipated inflation rate so that lenders would be protected against the impact of inflation as long as the inflation rate was perfectly anticipated. Only when the actual rate of inflation differs from the anticipated rate would there be an economic gain or loss on holding debt, in the sense of a wealth transfer from lenders to borrowers, or vice versa. In efficient capital markets, anticipation errors are expected to be random, implying that debtors are as likely as creditors to gain or lose. Granted that there is no obvious rationale to expect that debtors would always gain from holding debt, it follows that the method of measuring purchasing power gains and losses required by FAS 33, is conceptually wrong. Consequently, the reported purchasing power gain or loss, although it is to be shown separately and not included in income from continuing operations a la FAS 33, can be highly misleading. However, it may be argued that the disclosure of the purchasing power gain or loss is consistent with the statement's stated objective of providing information useful for assessing the erosion of general purchasing power. FAS 33 asserts: "Financial information that reflects changes in general purchasing power can help in assessing whether an enterprise has maintained the purchasing power of its capital." How such information can be relevant to users of financial reports is unclear. Nevertheless, granted that one can justify the relevance of such data, its method of computation as prescribed by FAS 33 casts a cloud on the usefulness of such data.

Chapter 9 deals with the conceptual issues involved in accounting for monetary items during inflationary periods and provides a detailed analysis of the issue of purchasing-power gains and losses. The mechanics of computing purchasing-power gains and losses are illustrated in Chapter 6, in relation to the historical-cost/constant-dollar model.

Flexibility in the Application of Various Constant-Dollar Measures

FAS 33 requires the use of the average-for-the-year constant dollars for the current-year, minimum-required supplementary disclosures. However, firms that opt to provide comprehensive financial statements are allowed to use either the average-for-the-year or end-of-year constant dollars. In presenting the five-year summary of selected financial data, firms can use one of three options: average-for-the-year, end-of-year, or base-year constant dollars.

The use of average-for-the-year dollars in reporting the current-year, minimum-required supplementary data has significant computational advantages since revenues and expenses that occur uniformly throughout the year would not be restated, because such items already reflect the average dollar for the year. The board was concerned about simplifying the required disclosures, a factor that explains its choice of the average dollar for-the-year to disclose the minimum required supplementary data. The use of this average dollar, however, becomes inconvenient when comprehensive financial statements are prepared, primarily because the monetary items at the end of the year would have to be restated to the average dollar for-the-year. Confusion can arise when a company has to show two different cash balances, for example, in its conventional balance sheet in nominal dollars and its comprehensive average constant-dollar balance sheet as of the same date. Additionally, the flexibility in the selection of constant dollars in presenting the five-year summary of financial data, which is explained below, can be a source of confusion.

Problems with the Five-Year Summary of Selected Financial Data

FAS 33 requires the presentation of selected financial data of the five most recent years stated in constant dollars. The intent is to furnish data that could provide meaningful interperiod comparisons, by resolving the measurement problem inherent in using the dollar during periods of general price-level changes. Dollars of different time periods have varying degrees of purchasing power. Consequently, financial data of different periods should be restated in terms of a common unit of measure to enable meaningful trend analyses.

The requirement to report a five-year summary of selected data is unnecessarily flexible in permitting three constant-dollar options, which could make the data confusing. Firms may present the five-year summary either on (1) average-for-the-current-year, (2) end-of-current-year, or (3) base-year constant dollars. The use of base-year constant dollars has the advantage of ensuring that past data would not have to be restated every year. However, when using base-year dollars, different amounts would be shown in the current year's supplementary information and in the five-year summary for the current year. Therefore, the data could be confusing to some users. Moreover, the fact that firms may select any of the three options may make interfirm comparisons difficult.

This potential confusion notwithstanding, the constant-dollar five-year trend would facilitate users' assessment of the growth in sales, income, assets, and dividends as well as the trend in earnings and market prices. The disclosure of such data can enable users to compute "constant-dollar price-earnings ratios," and "constant-dollar market rates of return," thereby enhancing interperiod and interfirm comparisons.

Current-Cost Data: Pros and Cons

Aside from the fact that FAS 33 fails to provide a monetary working-capital adjustment based on specific price changes, the required supplementary disclosure of the current-cost income from continuing operations could be viewed as "distributable" or "substainable" income, in reflecting the amount that the firm can sustain in the future or distribute in dividends while maintaining its existing operating capacity. L. Revsine, among others, has argued that such an income measure, under certain restrictive conditions, is useful for assisting investors in predicting their cash flows and associated risks.[10] This point is amplified in Chapter 7, which is devoted to the discussion of the current-cost model.

FAS 33 also requires the current-cost amounts of inventory and property, plant, and equipment. In contrast to the historical-cost measures, which tend to be irrelevant during periods of changing specific prices, the disclosure of current-cost data, representing one method of reflecting current values, is expected to improve the information content of financial reports. We have presented an evaluation of current-cost accounting data for investment and credit decisions in Chapter 7.

FAS 33 also requires the supplementary disclosure of holding gains and losses net of inflation, resulting from increases or decreases in the current costs of inventory, property, plant, and equipment. However, FAS 33 intentionally avoids the term "holding gains and losses" in favor of a neutral description—"increases and decreases in the current costs," and specifically requires that these amounts be excluded, and shown separately, from income. The reason that FASB chose to take this stand is the lack of consensus on whether "holding gains and losses" on nonmonetary items constitute income.

One view suggests that "[t]he increase or decrease in current cost amounts of assets held by the enterprise may . . . provide a useful basis for the assessment of future cash flows" (par. 118). This view is based on the argument that separating normal operating income from results reflecting holding activities would enable users to make better predictions about future cash flows.[11] It is difficult, however, to separate operating results from holding activities because the two activities are not independent of one another.[12] Even if it were possible to separate holding gains and losses from operating income, a case could be made against the inclusion of holding gains and losses as components of income—based on the physical capital maintenance approach to measuring income. From this perspective, holding gains cannot be distributed as dividends without impairing the operating capability of the firm. It is because of this disparity of views between proponents of the financial capital maintenance concept, who consider holding gains as income, and proponents of physical capital maintenance, who would treat these amounts as direct adjustments to stockholders' equity, that the board elected to use the neutral description "increase or decrease in the current cost" instead of the more familiar term "holding gain and loss," and to require that these amounts be excluded from income.

Current Cost or Lower Recoverable Amount

FAS 33 specifies that whenever the "recoverable amount" of an asset is less than the current cost of this asset, the recoverable amount should be used to value the asset. Similarly, in measuring the current-cost income from combining operations, the cost of goods sold, depreciation, and amortization expenses are to be reflected in forms of the current cost or the recoverable amount. "Recoverable amount" represents "the current worth of the net amount of cash expected to be recoverable from the use or sale of an asset" (par. 62). The recoverable amount is equal to the higher of: (a) the net realizable value from the sale of the asset, assuming the asset concerned is to be sold, or (b) the "value in use" of the asset, assuming that the asset will continue to be used. FAS 33 defines value in use as "the net present value of future cash flows expected to be derived from the use of an asset, including the salvage value" (par. 63).

In valuing assets, the concept of "value to the business" is applied. Value to the business is defined as "the lower of (1) current cost or (2) recoverable amount, where recoverable amount is measured at the higher of net realizable value and net present value of future cash flows" (par. 99 [h]).

It should be emphasized that the concept of value to the business as described in the appendix to FAS 33 (par. 99 [h]) is ill-defined. In discussing this concept, the board asserts that this value is often referred to as " 'deprival value'[13] because it can be assessed by assuming that the enterprise has been deprived of the use of an asset and asking how much the enterprise would need to be paid to compensate it for the asset." Should management replace the particular asset in the normal course of business, its "value in use" or deprival value would be the current cost of the asset. If the asset were not to be replaced by management in the normal operations of the corporation, the value of the asset should be the higher of net realizable value or the present value of discounted cash flows (the discounted cash-flow figure being used under the assumption the asset would be utilized until it is worn out). As the FASB observes:

> The rationale for measurement of an asset should depend
> on the circumstances of the enterprise. Current cost is

the appropriate measure if purchase of the asset would be worthwhile in current circumstances, i.e., if the value of the earning power of the asset is at least equal to current cost. In some cases, however, current purchase of the asset would not be worthwhile and current cost would then overstate the worth of the asset.

There is, however, no explicit consideration in FAS 33 or its appendixes of the implications of adhering to the foregoing decision rule. Moreover, under this rule, there would be six conceivable cases, which are not even specified in FAS 33. The cases along with the presumed course of action for each as well as possible implications are shown in Exhibit 3.4. In effect, FAS 33 utilizes multiple valuation bases including current cost, exit values (i.e., net realizable values) and present values, in addition to historical-cost/constant-dollar (HC/CD) data. Exit values or present values are used in the event that they represent lower recoverable amounts.

EXHIBIT 3.4

Deprival Value

Valuation Case*	Presumed course of action and implications
1. PV > NRV > CC	Replace to use. It is unlikely for NRV to exceed CC.
2. CC > PV > NRV	Use until worn out.
3. CC > NRV $\geq$ PV	Sell. The firm, or its assets, seem(s) to be ready for liquidation.
4. PV > CC > NRV	Replace to use.
5. NRV > CC > PV	Buy to sell, which is an unlikely scenario.
6. NRV > PV > CC	Buy to sell, which is an unlikely scenario.

PV = Value in use. NRV = Net realizable value. CC = Current cost.

*Where HC/CD data are used in FAS 33, substitute HC/CD for CC in each of the valuation cases.

In its 1981 Annual Report, Anderson, Clayton & Company addresses this disclosure requirement:[14]

> Because one of the purposes of this information is cash flows of the Company when property, plant and equipment and inventories are replaced at higher costs, the statement recognizes that the value of an asset to a business cannot exceed the maximum that an enterprise would be willing to pay to acquire an asset.
>
> Accordingly, the amount of cash recoverable from use of an asset may be so small that the enterprise would not wish to buy the asset at its current cost if the asset were not already owned. This concept of lower recoverable amount was required to prevent serious overstatement of asset values.

Nevertheless, as previously asserted, the concept of deprival value or value to the business is flawed. It mixes present valuation with two of its surrogates—current (replacement) costing and exit valuation (i.e., net realizable value). S. Agrawal points out the fallacy involved in finding the deprival value:[15]

> On the one hand, it is being asserted that it is not easy to determine the present value of net receipts. Because of this difficulty a surrogate needs to be used. But then it is being stated that the surrogate itself requires the determination of the present value of the net receipts as an essential part of its computation. Thus the argument seems to run as follows:
> (i) First determine the real value
> (ii) Then use the real value in the computation of a surrogate
> (iii) Finally, use the surrogate as an approximation of the real value.

Additionally, deprival valuation is intended to determine whether the owner should buy, use, or sell the asset(s) in question. However, according to FAS 33, the application of either net realizable value or present value as the lower recoverable amount is determined beforehand by the owner's decision to sell immediately or to continue to use, respectively. As Agrawal contends:[16]

> This modification seems to go contrary to the basic reasoning for using the deprival value. The underlying assumption is that we are trying to determine the maximum loss

that the owner will suffer if the asset had been lost.
After . . . such deprival, the owner must decide that if
he still had the asset, what would have been rational for
him—to sell the asset . . . or to continue using it; only
after getting the pertinent data about the net realizable
value and present value, could he have made a rational
decision. If we are assuming instead that the owner could
have made the decision without comparing these two figures, then we are treating him as irrational.

Finally, FAS 33 calls for the use of historical–cost/constant–
dollar data in finding the deprival value where HC/CD data is used in
lieu of current cost. However, the FASB does not clearly indicate why
HC/CD data should be considered in deprival valuation.[17] In addition,
no other authoritative pronouncement in this country or abroad calls
for the inclusion of HC/CD data in deprival valuation. Moreover, the
use of HC/CD data in finding the deprival value has never before been
advocated in accounting literature—to the best of our knowledge.

Need for Improvement in Accounting for Monetary Items

FAS 33 is deficient in its treatment of monetary items. As previously discussed, the required disclosure of purchasing-power gains
and losses on holding monetary items is based on dubious assumptions
and is misleading. FAS 33 does not require the disclosure of a monetary working capital adjustment. In order to maintain the corporation's
operating capacity during periods of increasing prices, adjustments
reflecting the purchasing power loss due to increases in monetary
working capital items may well be needed because of higher specific
prices. As the board asserts: "[A]n enterprise may need to increase
its net monetary working capital to maintain operating capability and
that factor is ignored in the measurement of current cost income."
Furthermore, FAS 33 does not require a "gearing" or financial-leverage adjustment to reflect the presumed benefit or cost to equity shareholders from realization of specific price changes on productive assets
that have been debt-financed. The rationale for a gearing adjustment
is that the financing required for capital maintenance is partly debt-
oriented, and, therefore, income need not be reduced by the total
capital maintenance requirement (for items such as cost of goods
sold, depreciation, and net monetary working capital assets). It
should be noted that the board acknowledged omission of a "gearing"
disclosure requirement (FAS 33, Appendix C, par. 2):

an enterprise may be able to obtain some of the capital

required to maintain operating capability by borrowing
or by raising new equity capital from external sources:
that possibility is ignored in the measurement of current
cost income.

Yet, the FASB asserts, some observers view the purchasing-
power gain or loss on net monetary items as precluding to some
extent the necessity for monetary working capital and gearing adjustments because a loss on holding receivables, for example, may be
considered tantamount to the additional monetary working capital required for receivables, while a gain on holding debt may lessen the
need for additional investments to maintain operating capability.
Nevertheless, monetary working capital adjustments and gearing
adjustments may well reflect specific price changes inherent in the
purchasing-power gains and losses on monetary items. Chapter 9
provides an examination of monetary working capital and gearing
adjustments.

Income Tax Considerations

According to FAS 33, in regard to income taxes the actual provision from the conventional financial statements is to be repeated in
the historical-cost/constant-dollar and current-cost analyses of income from continuing operations. This requirement appears to be
inconsistent. Should not the tax be computed based on historical-cost/
constant-dollar income and current-cost income instead of utilizing
the income tax figure from the conventional income statement since
these figures could be significantly different, and, therefore, could
have significantly different tax effects?

In annual reports, a footnote such as the following regarding
the income tax provision in FAS 33 is often found:[18]

Present tax laws do not allow deductions for the higher
depreciation and cost of sales resulting from the constant dollar or current cost adjustments. Even though
expenses reported in the restated financial statements
are substantially higher than those reflected on the historical basis, there is no reduction allowed in the income
tax provision for higher depreciation. In other words,
income taxes are levied . . . in real terms at rates
which exceed established statutory rates, the net effect
of which is the imposition of a tax on shareholders' investment . . . during periods of rapidly increasing
inflation.

Thus, the tax law does not allow the higher costs to be deducted, and so there is no additional tax shield from such costs. As Colt Industries observes:[19]

> [We] . . . emphasize the need to reconsider national tax policies in order to give recognition to the reality of inflation which has adverse effects on a company's ability to retain earnings to meet the escalating costs of replacing and expanding its productive capacity.

The tax issue is a sensitive and complex topic area. There are those who contend that the computation of income taxes should not be based on current-cost accounting on the grounds that tax measurement is a socioeconomic and political issue. Regardless of which accounting system prevails, the government will find it necessary to raise tax revenues to pay for its expenditures. Moreover, in view of the subjective nature of current-cost accounting, it is inconvenient for measuring taxable income.

Depreciation Issue

In FAS 33, no particular method is specified for computing depreciation under both the historical-cost/constant-dollar and current cost approaches. It is presumed that the method of depreciation, estimates of useful lives, and salvage values will be the same as applied in the traditional historical-cost model. FAS 33 recognizes, however, that different depreciation methods could be used for the current cost and historical-cost/constant-dollar disclosures if the conventional method used were chosen to allow for expected price changes.[20] Any changes in depreciation method vis-a-vis the conventional financial statements should be reflected in the supplementary disclosures.

FAS 33: AN EXPERIMENT IN FINANCIAL REPORTING*

FAS 33 constitutes a break with tradition. Prior to its issuance, the FASB as well as its predecessors—the AICPA's Accounting Principles Board and Committee on Accounting Procedure—has been direc-

---

*Professor Hans Heymann of Illinois Institute of Technology collaborated with the authors on this section of the chapter.

tive in its approach: Accounting standards were promulgated based on the concept that the FASB knew what was best for everyone. Stated differently, financial accounting standards were formulated in a non-experimental fashion.

In requiring both historical-cost/constant-dollar and current cost supplementary disclosures, the intent of the FASB was to provide a basis for studying the usefulness of both types of information. The comments that the FASB received from its Exposure Draft revealed a difference of opinion regarding the perceived usefulness of the two approaches.[21] There was strong support from preparers and auditors of financial statements for historical-cost/constant-dollar disclosures, while other parties favored current-cost disclosures. Faced with opposing views from its constituents, the FASB found it necessary to conduct further experimentation by requiring both types of data:

> The Board intends to study the extent to which the information is used, the types of people to whom it is useful, and the purpose for which it is used. (par. 115)

In rationalizing its decision to require a dual-reporting approach on an experimental basis, the FASB states:

> Preparers and users of financial reports have not reached a consensus on the general, practical usefulness of constant dollar information and current cost information. It seems unlikely that a consensus can be reached until further experience has been gained with the use of both types of information in systematic practical applications. This Statement, therefore, requires certain enterprises to present information both on constant dollar basis and on a current cost basis. (par. 13)

In conducting this experiment, the FASB has made clear its intent to review the FAS 33 requirements on an ongoing basis and to amend or withdraw the requirements whenever sufficient evidence is gathered to warrant such action. Consistent with this position, the FASB has recently amended its requirement dealing with financial reporting of foreign operations by issuing FAS 70, "Financial Reporting and Changing Prices and Foreign Currency Translation," in December 1982. FAS 70 is briefly reviewed in Appendix B to this chapter.

The FASB plans to review FAS 33 comprehensively within a period of five years. It is believed that by that time the FASB will have gathered sufficient evidence to assess the usefulness of the required disclosures and to select the type of information that should be required.

Another reason that prompted the FASB to release FAS 33 on an experimental basis was that the FASB did not believe that it had resolved all the implementation problems, which it felt could only be examined in the context of the reporting process per se. To this end, the FASB decided to encourage experimentation within broad guidelines designed to provide more flexibility than is customarily the case with FASB statements. In this manner, the FASB seeks to encourage the development of techniques to achieve its objective of objectively communicating the impact of price changes on financial statements. The FASB's intentions notwithstanding, the question still arises as to whether FAS 33 can be considered an experiment in financial reporting—a question that is addressed next.

There are two kinds of experiments: (1) scientific, which is concerned with ascertaining what is being done, and (2) exploratory, which is an information-gathering exercise to find out what can be done and what consensus there is for alternative approaches. The experiment contained in FAS 33 appears to illustrate the second type. Even though the board is the standard-setter in the private sector, it is attempting to find out what its constituents wish to see reported. In seeking to develop a new standard on inflation accounting, the FASB is searching for a consensus.

In conformity with the experimental method, FAS 33 specifies various size criteria (already provided above) for companies that are required to adhere to its provisions. The experimental sample, however, appears to be biased on the following counts: (1) reliance essentially on preparers of financial statements to provide the data fairly, (2) reliance on auditors to report on an "exception-only" basis, (3) excessive flexibility in its provisions (thereby providing too much latitude and inadequate guidance to preparers), (4) cost involved in developing the required data, (5) lack of confidentiality in disclosure, and (6) involuntary compliance by firms. Furthermore, there are no clear-cut experimental objectives, hypotheses, or experimental procedures provided in the statement.

FAS 33 is designed to be a "field experiment" required of all companies meeting the specified criteria. It is different from prior experiments by the FASB and AICPA, as P. L. Defliese observes:[22]

> Previous experimentation in financial reporting was voluntary and was understandably conducted under the cloak of secrecy because companies, on a selective basis, didn't want to publicize any but their official results. Now under FAS 33 everyone will have to let it all hang out one way or the other.

Defliese mentions two previous experiments that were voluntary, in contrast to the experiment mandated by the FASB in FAS 33:[23]

> In 1975 the FASB conducted a voluntary field test of its
> general purchasing power exposure draft. . . . In 1977
> the AICPA conducted a test of four types of accounting
> models designed to reflect changing prices; 23 companies
> participated voluntarily. . . . Both tests were on a con-
> fidential basis.

Ironically, the firms seem to be in control of the results in this
experiment. Auditors are just checking the disclosures for major
deficiencies and omissions. While the FASB is the standard-setter,
a question could be raised as to whether the board is shirking its
responsibility as the standard-setter by requiring this experiment.

The experiment contained in FAS 33 is not so well conceived
and designed as it could have been. Accordingly, what the FASB expects to learn from FAS 33 and how it intends to evaluate the results
are unclear. As the board's most recent research director, Michael
Alexander, has asserted:[24]

> It is just possible that we may find ourselves at the end
> of a five-year period still debating and deliberating—not
> knowing any more than we do today about the usefulness
> of information on changing prices—unable to determine
> whether the objectives of FAS 33 were ever achieved.

It might appear that voluntary, confidential rather than mandated,
public experiments should be more valid and less biased, since companies would participate on their own volition in a voluntary experiment. An involuntary experiment could be subverted by firms that do
not believe in it, thereby impairing its credibility. As FASB member
Ralph Waters, who dissented from FAS 33, has asserted:

> This experimentation should be conducted with volunteer
> companies working through professional organizations of
> business executives, accountants, and financial analysts.
> Regulators mandate experiments in financial reports;
> standard setters should not. (FAS 33, p. 28)

However, the results of voluntary experiments may conceivably be
questionable, since those firms that voluntarily participate may well
show more favorable outcomes than firms that do not participate.

If refined, the use of the experimental approach to setting standards could provide a vehicle to facilitate the introduction of major
changes in financial reporting. The experimental approach may be
useful in mitigating opposition to, and forging a consensus on, new
accounting methods. As the chairman of the FASB recently said:[25]

> We [the Board] all agree on one major point: If any sig-
> nificant change is ultimately concluded to be necessary,
> that change must be accomplished through a gradual,
> minimally disruptive process.

By issuing FAS 33 with its dual-reporting requirement, the FAS
has demonstrated its concern for achieving a consensus on supplementary disclosure requirements. It appears, however, that the board
fully recognized the difficulties it created in attempting to establish
standards by consensus. The chairman of the FASB asserted:[26]

> It is clear . . . that a conceptual approach best serves
> the public interest and that standard setting by consensus,
> compromise or consequences does not serve that public
> interest. The objective of our due process procedure is
> to build a consensus for a solution prior to its adoption.
> Building a consensus does seem more feasible than search-
> ing for and finding a consensus. It does put the initiative
> and responsibility where it belongs—with the standard
> setter. . . . We must explain our conclusions, but it is
> unrealistic to expect that all or more of our constituents
> will become believers in the specific solutions to particu-
> lar problems.

The board appeared to be using the experimental nature of FAS 33 as
a means of building a consensus among the parties concerned with the
scope and quality of financial reporting—perhaps as a "political"
compromise—an issue that we pursue below.

Among the statements issued by the FASB, FAS 33 could rank
at the top for generating so much heated debate. As D. Solomons has
observed:[27]

> Numerous other politically sensitive accounting issues
> could be cited, but none has received as much attention
> as accounting for inflation, for none has such widespread
> potential repercussions throughout the business world.

As the background discussion accompanying FAS 33 indicates,
the board in its deliberations was confronted with two opposing views.
Preparers and public accounting firms indicated a strong preference
for the historical-cost/constant-dollar, while users generally preferred current-cost information. Such a difference in views can be
explained perhaps by the underlying motivations and interests of each
group. Preparers and public accounting firms understandably gave
more weight to the ease and cost of generating the data, and the ob-

jectivity and verifiability of the disclosed information. Comments received from preparers and public accounting firms "typically emphasized the lower cost and higher verifiability and representational faithfulness of historical-cost/constant-dollar accounting."[28] On the other hand, users expressed their preference for current-cost information because of the relevance and usefulness of the data despite increased subjectivity.

It is apparent, as an appendix to the statement indicates, that the FASB recognizes that "[c]onstant dollar accounting and current cost accounting are methods for dealing with the different problems, and that it is inappropriate to view them as competing alternatives" (par. 110). One can also assume that the FASB was aware of the abundant literature dealing with the deficiencies of the historical-cost/constant-dollar model. Yet the FASB rationalized its dual-reporting requirement as an experiment, on the grounds that it did not have sufficient evidence to choose one method in preference to the other, apparently heeding C. T. Horngren's advice that "the setting of accounting standards is as much a product of political action as of flawless logic or empirical findings."[29]

In promoting a better understanding of the FASB's dilemma, D. L. Gerboth's remark is also pertinent:

> When a decision-making process depends for its success on public confidence, the critical issues are not technical; they are political. . . . In the face of conflict between competing interests, rationality as well as prudence lies not in seeking final answers, but rather in compromise—essentially a political process.[30]

Faced with opposing views from its constituents, the FASB had to capitulate, departing from a conceptually defensible standard to one that can be perceived as a political compromise. It can be argued, therefore, that the FASB has presented FAS 33 as an experiment with a view to allaying the fears of politically opposing groups, who might otherwise be inclined to view its disclosure requirements as revolutionary. As M. Moonitz observes:[31]

> The . . . use of the label "experiment" was simply a device to defuse the opposition of the accounting firms and their clients to a new and untried method. As an "experiment" each firm could help clients make some adjustment to account for inflation, but neither accountant nor client had to take a strong stand in favor of the soundness of the results.

In light of the "politicization" of the accounting standards in the United States, [32] FAS 33 can be seen as one step in the right direction. In spite of conceptual deficiencies underlying particular disclosure requirements, FAS 33 may well be instrumental in improving the information content of financial reporting.

In spite of the apparent irrelevance of historical-cost/constant-dollar information, the incomplete nature of the current-cost data, and other shortcomings of its provisions, FAS 33, nevertheless, may be instrumental in providing heretofore unavailable information to investors and other interested parties.

FAS 33 is also consistent with the efficient market hypothesis, which asserts that the market as a whole is efficient in processing publicly available information. This hypothesis also recognizes that in view of the cost of generating current-cost data and the inside information required to do so, capital market agents (e.g., investors and portfolio managers) will not be able to fully and correctly estimate the current-cost data on a firm-by-firm basis. Accordingly, the disclosures probably could contain new information, i.e., not anticipated by the market.

In the context of the efficient market hypothesis, capital market agents are expected to develop their own current-cost estimates for each company and formulate their own assessment of the economic consequences of the data. This implies that stock prices have impounded the current-cost information as estimated by capital market agents. Such estimates, however, are subject to error inasmuch as such data is firm-specific; generating such data requires inside information to which outsiders are assumed to have little access, and the information is expensive to generate. Thus far, empirical studies have not generally reflected market efficiency in regard to inside information, i.e., the strong form of market efficiency. Assuming that current cost data is theoretically relevant information for investors, then FAS 33 may be instrumental in conveying relevant information to capital markets.

This argument says nothing about the relevance of historical-cost/constant-dollar information. It may well be true that FAS 33 is capable of creating considerable confusion among the uninitiated, who might find it difficult to sift the relevant from the irrelevant data. Yet, from the capital market's viewpoint, which assumes the existence of few sophisticated investors and the opportunity for arbitrage (i.e., the purchase and sale of a security at the same time to take advantage of price differences), it is conceivable that the market in the aggregate would benefit from FAS 33 regardless of how confusing the presentation of the data may appear to be to various individual users. Whether FAS 33 conveys relevant information to capital market agents is an empirical issue. Chapter 11 reviews empirical research studies dealing with this topic.

Proponents of the efficient market hypothesis also argue that it is redundant to adjust current-value statements using publicly available, general purchasing-power indexes on the grounds that the market is efficient in processing publicly available information. Stated differently, this viewpoint holds that what is needed is current-cost information without general price-level adjustments.

An implication of the efficient market hypothesis is that the benefits versus costs of accounting disclosures, in particular reporting media, should be evaluated. FAS 33 gives only lip service to this implication, which would be difficult to measure. Whether the disclosures called for in FAS 33 have relevant, new informational content, which becomes impounded into security prices instantly after being released to the market, is a question that Chapter 11 addresses.

The foregoing discussion assumes that capital markets are generally efficient in processing information and in establishing equilibrium stock prices. The efficiency of capital markets, however, has been recently questioned by Modigliani and Cohn, who suggested that "Because of inflation-induced error, investors have systematically undervalued the stock market by 50 percent."[33] F. Modigliani and R. A. Cohn specifically contend that financial analysts have been inefficient in analyzing the impact of inflation on levered firms. In presenting their startling findings, they stated that:[34]

> we readily admit that our conclusion is indeed hard to
> swallow—and especially hard for those of us who have
> been preaching the gospel of efficient markets. It is
> hard to accept the hypothesis of a long-lasting, system-
> atic mistake in a well organized market manned by a
> large force of alert and knowledgeable people.

As pointed out earlier, one of the weaknesses of FAS 33 is the accounting treatment of the impact of inflation on monetary liabilities. In this regard, it appears that FAS 33 is not contributing to the efficiency of the capital markets.

CONCLUSION AND SUGGESTIONS FOR REVISING FAS 33

In light of serious deficiencies in the traditional, historical-cost financial statements during periods of changing prices, FAS 33 constitutes a significant step toward improving the information content of financial reporting in the United States—its deficiencies notwithstanding.

It is interesting to note that the United States apparently is currently alone in giving the "historical-cost/constant-dollar" statement serious consideration. It is true that this approach has been proposed at one time or another by several authoritative accounting organizations abroad. In Britain, the Accounting Standards Steering Committee issued in 1974 its "Provisional Statement of Standard Accounting Practice" (SSAP 7), which was somewhat similar to the FASB's Exposure Draft of 1974. In Australia, too, a proposal for a "Method of Accounting for Changes in the Purchasing Power of Money" was released in December 1974. Parallel moves also have been taken in various other countries. However, in Britain, Statement of Standard Accounting Practice No. 16 was issued in March 1980, favoring current-cost accounting. The Institute of Chartered Accountants in Australia and the Australian Society of Accountants have also issued a proposed standard favoring current-cost disclosures with no provision for historical-cost/constant-dollar information. In December 1982, the Canadian Institute of Certified Accountants issued an accounting standard dealing with reporting the effects of changing prices.[35] The Canadian standard is similar to FAS 33 in many respects—one exception being that the Canadians do not require historical-cost/constant-dollar supplementary information. That the United States is currently the only major industrialized, English-speaking country requiring historical-cost/constant dollar data should make it easier for the FASB to eliminate this requirement in revising the statement.

In revising FAS 33, the FASB should clarify its position and resolve the controversial issues with respect to: (1) the computation and the reporting of purchasing-power gains and losses on holding monetary items, (2) the accounting treatment of holding gains and losses on nonmonetary items. (Should these items be treated as income or direct adjustments to stockholders' equity?), and (3) the clarification of the capital maintenance concept.

FAS 33 has not adequately dealt with the accounting treatment for monetary items. We suggest that a revision of the statement should consider the provision for a monetary working capital adjustment. We also suggest that the FASB study the need for a gearing (or financing) adjustment. Such issues are related to the conceptual framework of financial reporting and cannot be addressed in isolation. We, therefore, suggest continued emphasis by the FASB on completion of its conceptual framework as a means of resolving the financial-reporting issues arising from changing prices.

In view of the experimental nature of FAS 33, the FASB has been unusually flexible in some of its provisions. Such flexibility in the application of constant dollars, as previously discussed, would only create more confusion and inconvenience to users. The FASB should seriously examine the possibility that there are "perhaps . . . too many alternatives permissible in its provisions, which may open up a Pandora's box of loopholes and subterfuges to circumvent its spirit and intent."[36] Unlike other statements issued by the FASB, this one is experimental, and the FASB has announced its intention of undertaking a comprehensive review of the statement within the five-year experimental period. There is no doubt that the experience gained and the evidence gathered shall have contributed significantly toward improving financial reporting in the face of changing prices in the United States.

APPENDIX A: FASB SUPPLEMENTAL INDUSTRY STATEMENTS
ON FINANCIAL REPORTING AND CHANGING PRICES

This appendix provides a synopsis of FASB statements designed
to supplement FAS 33 for particular industries. FASB Statement 39,
"Specialized Assets—Mining and Oil and Gas," (1980) calls for disclosure of the current costs (or lower recoverable amounts) of mineral resources. Firms having mineral reserves aside from oil and
gas are required to provide the following additional information for
each of their five most recent fiscal years: (1) estimates of significant
quantities of proved and probable mineral reserves, (2) the estimated
quantity of those reserves produced in the year, (3) the amount of
reserves bought and sold during the year, and (4) the average market
price of the mineral.

FASB Statement 40, "Specialized Assets—Timberlands and
Growing Timber," (1980) deals with the forest products industry. It
allows firms in this industry to measure the current cost of timberlands, growing timber, and related expenses at the historical-cost/
constant-dollar amounts or current costs (or lower recoverable
amounts).

FASB Statement 41, "Specialized Assets—Income-Producing
Real Estate," (1980) concerns the measurement of income-producing
real estate and also calls for the disclosure of either historical-cost/
constant-dollars or current costs (or lower recoverable amounts).

FASB Statement 46, "Motion Picture Films" (1981) is concerned
with the reporting of supplemental inflation-accounting disclosures by
the motion picture film industry. Again the disclosures may be in
terms of historical-cost/constant-dollars or current costs (or lower
recoverable amounts).

FASB Statement 54, "Investment Companies," exempts investment companies from compliance with FAS 33. FAS 54 specifies that
investment companies are not required to provide supplementary information regarding the effect of changing prices.

APPENDIX B: FASB STATEMENTS 52 and 70

There has been a substantial increase in foreign operations by U.S. firms in recent years. We have also witnessed a very unstable international monetary situation with fluctuating exchange rates and several currency revaluations, including that of the U.S. dollar. This situation has given rise to several problems in international business dealings. One of these problems is accounting for the different monetary systems in different countries. More specifically, accountants have to deal with at least two major accounting problems: (1) how to account for international business transactions denominated in foreign currency in light of changing foreign exchange rates and (2) how to prepare financial statements that would provide information useful for evaluating multinational corporations. Since useful comparisons and calculations can only be made if measures of the firm's profitability and financial position are expressed in a common unit of measurement—domestic currency—foreign monetary measures have to be converted into domestic units through a process of foreign currency translation.

The accounting procedures dealing with these problems have been subjected to considerable opposition and have generated a great deal of controversy. Multinational firms had strongly opposed FAS 8, "Accounting for the Translation of Foreign Currency Translations and Foreign Financial Statements" (1975), on foreign currency translations, in view of the sensitivity of their reported earnings to the translation adjustments and the concern about the potential impact on their stock prices.

In light of the deficiencies of FAS 8, the Financial Accounting Standards Board has issued <u>Statement of Financial Accounting Standard No. 52</u>, "Foreign Currency Translation," (December 1981). This statement was also subjected to considerable opposition, having generated a great deal of controversy when first issued as an exposure draft. The fact that the final statement was released with only a four-to-three vote and with the board's own chairman opposing it is indicative of the controversial nature of the statement.

Among the key provisions of FAS 52 on foreign currency translation are the following:

1. The financial position and operating results of an entity should be reflected prior to translation in its functional currency—i.e., the currency of the primary economic environment in which the entity functions.
2. If the entity's local currency constitutes its functional currency, the financial statements of the entity should be translated into U.S. dollars using the current closing exchange rate for assets

and liabilities and the current weighted-average rate for most income flows. Gains and losses stemming from such translation are to be reported in stockholders' equity rather than the income statement.

3. The gains and losses from foreign currency translation referred to in (2) above are realized upon sale or liquidation of the investment in the foreign entity.

4. If the functional currency of a foreign entity is the U.S. dollar, then the financial statements of the entity should be translated into the dollar using the procedures outlined in FAS 8. The gains and losses would, accordingly, be recognized in the income statement.

5. If the local currency of a foreign entity has had a cumulative three-year inflation rate of 100 percent or more (and is, thus, a "highly inflationary" economy), the reporting currency becomes the functional currency—typically, the U.S. dollar.

FASB Statement No. 70, "Financial Reporting and Changing Prices: Foreign Currency Translation," was issued by the board in 1982. This standard includes the following provisions:

1. FAS 33 still applies to companies using the U.S. dollar as the "functional currency."

2. If a firm uses a functional currency other than its own local currency for a significant percentage of its operations, it is not required to conform to the historical-cost/constant-dollar requirements prescribed in FAS 33 provided that current-cost information is presented. However, a firm that lacks significant physical operating resources, which has used historical-cost/constant-dollars to approximate current-cost data, in conformity with FAS 33, may continue to do so.

3. Current-cost data for firms using a functional currency other than its own should also be measured in this functional currency. To reflect the current-cost figures in terms of constant dollars, firms may use either the U.S. Consumer Price Index for All Urban Consumers or a general price index based on the functional currency. Thus, the impact of general inflation on the current-cost data can be measured either after translation (i.e., translate-restate, using the CPI-U) or before translation (i.e., restate-translate, using a foreign general price-level index).

Either the translate-restate or restate-translate method may be used, but the FASB does not provide criteria for choosing between these two methods. Additionally, this choice is bound to impair comparability in financial reporting among firms.* Furthermore, this standard leaves a number of significant questions unanswered:†

1. Should [the] purchasing power gain or loss be calculated based on U.S. purchasing power or foreign purchasing power?
2. Should the item called "excessive increase in specific prices over increase in general level" be based upon a measurement that compares current cost to U.S. inflation or foreign inflation?
3. Should the translation adjustment caused by fluctuating exchange rates be calculated based on current cost equity as it is done under the translate-restate method or based upon current-cost equity adjusted for local inflation as it is done under the restate-translate method?
4. If restate-translate is chosen by the board, should a parity adjustment be required? . . . A parity adjustment would serve to readjust from foreign restatement into U.S. restatement.

Additionally, it is unclear how inflation impacts foreign operations from FAS 33, 52, and 70. FAS 52 is largely based on the somewhat nebulous concept of a "functional currency"—i.e., the currency of the primary economic environment in which the entity functions. It is not necessarily obvious which currency "functions" for a particular enterprise.‡ Firms may conceivably use different currencies for different purposes. Also, FAS 52 states that if the entity's local currency constitutes its functional currency, then the financial statements of the entity are to be translated into U.S. dollars (using the current closing exchange rate for assets and liabilities, and the current weighted-average rate for most income items). In this case, gains and losses are reported in stockholders' equity, not in the income statement. The rationale given in FAS 52 is unconvincing that translation adjustments in the case of a foreign functional currency be made to stockholders' equity while adjustments in the case of the U.S. dollar as the functional currency be made to income. In the first case, it is assumed that the exchange rate changes affect the net assets of the reporting enterprise, not its cash flows. In the second case, it is

---

*See Report of the Subcommittee of the Committee on Financial Accounting Standards, "Response to 'Financial Reporting and Changing Prices: Foreign Currency Translation, An Amendment of FASB Statement No. 33,'" American Accounting Association, October 1982, p. 4.
†Ibid., p. 4-5.
‡Ernst and Whinney, Foreign Currency Translation: The FASB's New Rules, An Executive Summary, 1981.

assumed, however, that the exchange rate changes impact the cash
flows of the reporting enterprise, and so the gains and losses should
appear in the income statement. According to most empirical evidence
on the efficient market hypothesis, whether gains and losses appear
in the income statement or in stockholders' equity does not matter,
for the market is concerned with the substance, not the geography,
of disclosure.

NOTES

1. Financial Accounting Standards Board, Statement of Financial Accounting Standards No. 33 (FAS 33), "Financial Reporting and Changing Prices," (Stamford, Conn: FASB, 1979).

2. Securities and Exchange Commission, Accounting Series Release No. 190, "Notice of Adoption of Amendments to Regulation S-X Requiring Disclosure of Certain Replacement-Cost Data," SEC Docket. Vol. 9, No. 5 (Washington, D.C.: U.S. Government Printing Office, April 6, 1976).

3. Accounting Principles Board, "Financial Statements Restated for General Price-Level Changes," APB Statement No. 3 (New York: AICPA, 1969), par. 20.

4. The term "historical-cost/constant-dollar" has become more popularly used after the issuance of FAS 33. This concept has been more commonly referred to as "General-price-level-adjusted accounting" (GPLA).

5. FAS 33, par. 25.

6. FAS 33, pars. 29, 30.

7. Ibid., pars. 35, 65.

8. This term is explained later in this chapter.

9. "Cost of goods sold measured on a LIFO basis is considered an acceptable measure of current cost, provided that the effect of any decrease in inventory layers is excluded." (FAS 33, fn. 3, p. 20). This flexibility was permitted in order to simplify the computations—a factor that was of concern to the board.

10. L. Revsine, Replacement Cost Accounting (Englewood Cliffs, N.J.: Prentice-Hall, 1973), pp. 86-138.

11. E. O. Edwards and P. W. Bell, The Theory and Measurement of Business Income (Berkeley, Calif.: University of California Press, 1961). Although Edwards and Bell were not the first to suggest the need to separate income into operating income and holding gains/losses, their book has contributed to popularizing this notion of measuring income as a means of providing a better basis for predicting a firm's long-run income.

12. This point has been convincingly presented by D. F. Drake and N. Dopuch, "On the Case for Dichotomizing Income," Journal of Accounting Research, (Autumn 1965): 192-205. Also, see P. Prakash and S. Sunder, "The Case Against Separation of Current Operating Profit and Holding Gain," The Accounting Review, January 1979, pp. 1-22.

13. Baxter characterizes deprival value very lucidly by analogy: "If a thief threatens to make off with one of your assets, but offers to refrain if you pay enough, what is the highest sum he can prise from you? Usually your ceiling will be replacement cost—i.e., this is de-

prival value. But sometimes you will stick at a lower figure, because you do not deem the asset worth replacing; here the lower figure takes over as deprival value." See W. T. Baxter, <u>Accounting Values and Inflation</u>, London: McGraw-Hill, 1975), pp. 125-26.

14. Quoted in <u>Accounting Trends and Techniques</u> (AICPA, 1982), p. 91.

15. S. P. Agrawal, "Use of Recoverable Amounts in the Valuations Required Under FASB #33." Paper presented at the Southeastern Regional Meeting, American Accounting Association, April 1983, pp. 6-7.

16. Ibid., pp. 5-6.

17. Ibid., p. 3.

18. Textron Annual Report 1980.

19. Colt Industries Annual Report, 1980.

20. In contrast to FAS 33, ASR 190 required the computation of current replacement-cost depreciation <u>only</u> on a straight-line basis.

21. See FAS 33, par. 112.

22. P. L. Defliese, "Inflation Accounting: Pursuing the Elusive," <u>The Journal of Accountancy</u>, (May 1979): 63.

23. Ibid., p. 63, fn. 4.

24. M. O. Alexander, "FAS 33 and the Future—Research and Decisions." Presentation at American Accounting Association Annual Meeting, Chicago, August 1981.

25. Speech by Donald Kirk quoted in <u>The Week in Review</u>, Deloitte, Haskins and Sells, February 25, 1983, p. 1.

26. Quoted in <u>The Week in Review</u>, Deloitte, Haskins and Sells, September 5, 1980. [Emphasis added]

27. D. Solomons, "The Politicization of Accounting," <u>The Journal of Accountancy</u>, (November 1978): 61.

28. FAS 33, par. 112.

29. C. Horngren, "The Marketing of Accounting Standards," <u>The Journal of Accountancy</u>, (October 1973): 61.

30. D. L. Gerboth, "Research, Intuition, and Politics in Accounting Inquiry," <u>The Accounting Review</u>, (July 1973): 481.

31. M. Moonitz, Correspondence with the authors, February 16, 1982.

32. The articles by Solomons, Horngren, and Gerboth in notes 28, 30, and 31, respectively, are notable references on the subject of the "politicization" of accounting.

33. F. Modigliani and R. Cohn, "Inflation, Rational Valuation and the Market," <u>Financial Analysts Journal</u>,(March–April 1979): 24-44.

34. Ibid., p. 35.

35. Canadian Institute of Chartered Accountants, <u>CICA Handbook, Reporting the Effects of Changing Prices</u>, Section 4570, December 1982.

35. Canadian Institute of Chartered Accountants, CICA Handbook, Reporting the Effects of Changing Prices, Section 4570, Canadian Institute of Chartered Accountants, December 1982.

36. R. Bloom and A. Debessay, "A Critique of FAS 33," Management Accounting, May 1981, p. 53.

4

INCOME AND CAPITAL MAINTENANCE

INTRODUCTION

In conventional accounting, the key concept underlying the income measurement process is the principle of matching costs against revenues. Very little attention is given to the capital maintenance concept associated with income measurement. The matching principle, however, provides only a vague standard and does not furnish a sufficient conceptual basis for the income measurement process.[1]

A logical starting point in the process of income measurement would be to define capital, which would serve as a benchmark. Capital must be maintained before income can be measured. To understand why capital maintenance is perceived to be central to the income measurement process, let us consider the following definition of income.

INCOME DEFINED

Over 200 years ago, Adam Smith defined income as the amount that can be consumed without encroaching upon capital.[2] This definition was later expanded by the English economist J. R. Hicks, who defined an individual's income as "the maximum value which he [the individual] can consume during a week, and still expect to be as well off at the end of the week as he was at the beginning."[3] Alexander applied the Hicksian definition to the corporation: "the amount that the corporation can distribute to the owners of equity in the corporation and be as well off at the end of the year as at the beginning."[4] In order for a corporation to remain as well off at the end of the year as at the beginning, the corporation has to maintain its capital intact. For this reason, the "capital maintenance concept" is important. The above definition establishes the significance of capital maintenance in income measurement but leaves a number of unanswered questions. There is no precise meaning of the term "well-offness," or the capital that needs to be maintained intact before income can be distributed. A review of the economics literature provides some clarification.

Capital is perceived as a stock of wealth at an instant of time, while income is considered the flow of wealth in excess of that necessary to maintain a constant capital.[5] Stated differently, capital represents the "tree," which should remain intact; income, the "fruit" on the tree, which can be consumed. We can also view capital as "the amount in the reservoir at any one time, and [income] as the amount flowing out of the reservoir during a period of time."[6]

Based on the above exposition, the income of a given corporation can be measured by comparing the ending capital and beginning capital, assuming that no additional capital is introduced or withdrawn from the firm during the year. This assertion makes two key assumptions. First, it is taken for granted that the ending and beginning capital can be adequately measured. This is, however, where the problem lies. There is no unique approach to measuring capital. There are different concepts of "well-offness" and capital. Well-offness can be viewed as wealth, which may be psychic or monetary. Capital, in turn, can represent wealth, in terms of monetary units or the amount of goods and services one can buy. The second assumption is that there is a stable unit of measurement. A meaningful comparison of a firm's beginning and ending capital can only be possible if one uses a stable unit of measurement. In conventional accounting, the dollar is the unit of measure. Such a unit of measurement is, however, unstable, and thus unsuitable in a period of general price-level changes. In order to be able to measure income by comparing the ending and beginning capital figures, it is necessary (1) to agree on what constitutes capital and (2) to ensure that such capital, however defined, is measured in a constant unit of measurement to facilitate comparability.

Concepts of Capital

To apply the Hicksian definition of income, the wealth or capital at the end of a year should be measured in order to determine the amount that can be distributed without impairing the capital that the firm had at the beginning of the year. The issues to be considered are what concept of capital to maintain and how this concept should be measured.

Essentially, there are two concepts of capital: (1) financial capital and (2) physical capital. Each of these concepts of capital can be measured either in monetary units, which would be acceptable under a stable monetary situation, or in terms of "constant dollars," which would be appropriate in periods of general price-level changes. Before we analyze the two principal concepts of capital, let us first consider the measurement-unit problem.

Before we can measure the income for the year, we have to confront the measurement-unit problem. Let us proceed with an example to illustrate the significance of the measurement-unit problem. Suppose that the capital of the firm at the end of the year is $13,000. Given the beginning capital of $10,000, which serves as our benchmark of well-offness, and an ending capital in monetary units of $13,000, and assuming there were no capital transactions, it appears that the income for the year (the amount that the firm can distribute and still be as well off at the end of the year as at the beginning) is $3,000 (i.e., the excess of the ending capital over the beginning capital). It should be emphasized that we are using the dollar as the unit of measurement. During periods of general price-level changes, the dollars of such periods are not comparable, and any mathematical manipulations with such dollars of different years is tantamount to adding or subtracting oranges and apples. The point is that a constant (stable) unit of measure is desirable in order to determine the income by comparing the end-of-the-year capital with the beginning capital. One approach is to use general purchasing-power units, which would involve measuring both the beginning and ending capital of the firm in terms of general purchasing-power units of the dollar, either as of the beginning, the average-for-the-year, or end-of-the-year.[7] Let us assume, in our example, that the rate of inflation during the year was 10 percent. To measure income, the initial $10,000 invested capital is adjusted to reflect the end-of-year dollars. Accordingly, the $10,000 beginning-of-year dollars reflect $11,000 end-of-year dollars. Thus, for the firm to be as well off at the end of the year as at the beginning, the capital that needs to be maintained intact is $11,000, giving an income measure of $2,000 that can be distributed without encroaching upon the capital of the firm. This discussion has demonstrated that in order to measure income using the Hicksian approach, one has to be cognizant of the measurement-unit problem that arises in a period of unstable general price-level conditions. Instead of comparing the capital in units of money, it is desirable to compare beginning and ending capital, measured in units of the same purchasing power.

It should be pointed out again that the issue of capital maintenance is separate from the valuation problem. For instance, to determine the capital at the end of any given year, the assets of a firm could be valued either at historical cost, current-(replacement) cost, exit value, and so on.

If current cost were used as the relevant attribute in valuing the assets of a firm, the income for a given period could be measured by comparing the beginning and ending capital measured by taking the current cost of the assets of the firm at the two points in time. Let us illustrate this point by the following simple example. Assume XYZ Company is established by cash investment of $10,000 on January 1, 19X2. The cash is immediately used to buy land valued at $10,000. Assume now that the current cost of the land at December 2, 19X2 is $12,500. Using current cost as the attribute for asset measurement would result in $12,500 capital on December 31, 19X2. Assuming a stable monetary situation, XYZ Company would report an income of $2,500 ($12,500 - 10,000), which conforms to the Hicksian definition of income (since the company can distribute the $2,500 as dividends and still be as well-off as it was at the beginning of the year in terms of maintaining its initial $10,000 capital intact).

Financial Capital Maintenance

Financial or money capital maintenance pertains to the original cash invested by the stockholders in the firm. Financial capital maintenance emphasizes the ability of the firm to generate cash flows from using its resources. Put another way, cash is used to acquire production assets that, in turn, are used to generate cash flows for the firm. Using our previous example, if the firm is established by an investment of $10,000 by the owners, this $10,000 becomes the benchmark—the financial capital that is to be maintained intact, and any excess above this amount at the end of the year (assuming that there were no capital transactions) is considered a measure of income that can be distributed without encroaching upon the financial capital of the firm. Let us continue with our example and measure the annual income. To do so, we need to know the financial capital of the firm at the end of the year. This leads to the problem of the valuation of the assets and liabilities of the firm at the end of the year in question. It is important to emphasize that the issue of capital maintenance is independent of the asset valuation problem.

The valuation problem is a matter of choosing the attributes of assets and liabilities to be measured. Depending on the attribute chosen, different measures of financial capital can be developed. There are several models that have been proposed, at one time or another, in the accounting literature as the basis for financial accounting maasurement. These include the following:

1. Present value of expected cash flows
2. Historical cost
3. Current-cost or current-replacement cost
4. Current-exit value (e.g., net realizable value)

From a theoretical standpoint, the present value model provides an ideal measure of the economic value of an asset. According to this model, the value of an asset is determined by discounting the expected net cash inflows from the use and/or disposition of the asset. Economists have also used the present value model in valuing a business entity as a whole.[8]

The present value model assumes that the amounts and timing of future cash flows as well as the discount rates and inflation rates are all known with certainty. To the extent that these factors are uncertain, the model presents implementational problems.

There are also conceptual problems in applying the present value model. For example, the cash flows generated by a firm's plant assets are produced through joint utilization of operational assets. Any allocation of total benefits among jointly used individual assets is arbitrary. It is because of this allocation problem that individual machines are valued indirectly in the conventional accounting model by using the historical-cost principle, which provides a basis for reliable valuation under the assumption that exchange values are determined by arm's-length negotiation. The valuation of assets on the basis of sacrifices incurred to secure them is considered more reliable than the valuation of expected benefits from using those assets. Thus, the present value model, albeit ideal, is difficult to implement. The other models are all considered to be alternatives to present valuation.

Apart from the present value model, each of the alternative models has particular advantages and disadvantages. A discussion of these issues is pursued in subsequent chapters. For our purposes in this chapter, it is sufficient to note that the financial capital of a firm can be measured using any of the above models.

A principal criticism of the concept of financial capital maintenance is that the resulting bottom-line income figure includes holding gains as a component of periodic income. Reflecting holding gains in the income statement may indicate: (1) the success of the firm in buying inventories and equipment at prices which have subsequently increased and (2) a surrogate of an increase in the exit value or the present value from selling or using the assets in question. On the other hand, inclusion of such holding gains may raise two serious problems. First, the reported income figure, if distributed as dividends, could impair the firm's ability to maintain its current level of operations. Such holding gains can only be available for distribution if the company is liquidated. In the absence of evidence to the contrary, the firm is assumed to be a going concern and, as such, any holding gains should not be considered income that can be distributed as dividends. The second criticism of the bottom-line income measure is that it may not be useful to investors interested in normal operating results as a basis for predicting future normal operating income.

Physical Capital Maintenance

The concept of physical capital maintenance views capital as a physical phenomenon in terms of the capacity to produce goods or services. Under this concept, cash is used to acquire assets in order to generate cash flows, and the concern is, therefore, with the firm's ability to replace its physical productive assets. By contrast, financial capital maintenance is concerned with the original cash invested in the firm, and the firm is viewed as a reservoir of cash, which is used to acquire production assets that, in turn, are used to generate cash flows for the firm. The excess of cash over the original cash invested is viewed as the income that can be consumed, leaving the firm as well-off as it was at the beginning of the year in terms of keeping the original financial capital intact.

Proponents of physical capital maintenance argue that in applying the Hicksian approach to measuring income, the capital the firm needs to keep intact is not the financial capital but the physical productive capacity. This view is based on the following rationale. Firms produce certain goods or services. To ensure a firm's ability to produce such goods and services, at least at its present operating levels, it is necessary for the firm to maintain its prevailing physical operating capacity. This implies that the income should represent the maximum dividend that could be paid without impairing the productive capacity of the firm. [9] In fact, the income measure that is associated with the physical capital maintenance concept is often referred to as "distributable income," implying that such income can be distributed without impairing the firm's ability to maintain its operating level. The "distributable income" is also perceived as "sustainable" income, implying that the firm can sustain such income as long as the firm ensures the maintenance of its present physical operating capacity. It should be emphasized, therefore, that the concept of physical maintenance accents the firm's ability to replace its physical productive capacity, if not also its monetary productive assets. In short, physical capital maintenance is concerned with sustaining the operating capability of the firm.

There is, however, a difference of opinion regarding the meaning of maintaining physical productive capacity. At least three different interpretations are suggested:[10]

1. Maintaining identical or similar physical assets that the firm presently owns
2. Maintaining the capacity to produce the same <u>volume</u> of goods and services
3. Maintaining the capacity to produce the same <u>value</u> of goods and services

The second interpretation accommodates technological improvements and in this respect is superior to the first interpretation, which essentially assumes the firm will maintain and replace its identical assets, an untenable assumption in light of technological improvements. The third interpretation not only reflects technological changes but also the impact of changes on the selling prices of outputs. Although this might be a highly refined approach, it may well be difficult to implement.

On the balance sheet, the physical capital maintenance concept requires the valuation of the physical assets of the firm at their current cost or lower recovery value (i.e., the higher of present value or net realizable value). (See Chapters 3 and 7 for a further discussion of this subject.) To compute income that preserves the physical capital intact, the holding gains and losses resulting from the increases or decreases in the current costs of the productive capacity of the firm are treated as "capital maintenance adjustments." Once the necessary capital maintenance adjustments are made, the difference between the beginning and ending capital would represent (assuming the ending capital is greater, and in the absence of any capital transactions by the owners) the amount that could be distributed while maintaining the physical capital of the firm intact. In the income statement, the income of the period, under the physical capital maintenance approach, is measured by matching the realized revenues with the current cost of the assets sold or consumed. Such a direct comparison, we must hasten to add, is only possible under a stable monetary situation. When changes in the general level of prices occur, the respective monetary measures of the physical capital amounts must be restated in units of the same purchasing power.

The fundamental difference between the financial and physical capital maintenance concepts using current (replacement) cost is in the treatment of "holding gains and losses." Under the concept of financial capital maintenance holding gains are reflected as income of the given period, whereas under the concept of physical capital maintenance holding gains are shown in the stockholders' equity section of the balance sheet as "capital maintenance adjustments."

To be consistent with the physical capital maintenance concept, some would argue in favor of requiring backlog depreciation—i.e., catch-up depreciation if current cost were increasing over several periods. If the current cost increases from period to period, the accumulated capital adjustment would not equal the replacement cost needed to maintain productive capacity, which might justify the need for backlog depreciation. A comprehensive discussion of this topic is presented later in this chapter.

Generally, the concept of physical capital maintenance is consistent with the going-concern assumption—by maintaining the firm's ability to continue its normal operations—and the entity theory of the firm. However, it has been criticized as an "unnecessary abstraction."[11] Nevertheless, it appears that the physical capital maintenance concept could serve as a basis for providing information that would assist users in predicting the amounts, timing, and risks associated with future cash flows that could be expected from the firm. The reason is that the resulting income figure is the income that the firm is expected to sustain in the future, and can thus serve as a suitable basis for predicting future cash flows. This point is discussed further in Chapter 7.

Backlog Depreciation

With the recent emphasis on current-cost accounting in the authoritative literature, the concept of "backlog" or "catch-up" depreciation has assumed more prominence. Backlog depreciation represents the difference between the accumulated depreciation that would have been recorded, based on the latest current-cost or current-replacement cost[12] and the accumulated depreciation actually recorded. For example, assume there is an asset costing $2,000 having an estimated useful life of two years. Assume also that the current cost of the asset increases by 10 percent each year. The depreciation expense based on the current cost in each year would be $1,100 in Year 1 and $1,210 in Year 2;[13] the total accumulated current cost depreciation, $2,310. The latter amount is less than the current cost of the asset, which is expected to be $2,420 at the date of replacement. This example demonstrates that if current cost were increasing continuously over periods of time, the cumulative depreciation would be less than the current cost of the asset.

This phenomenon has led to the debate regarding the necessity for backlog or catch-up depreciation in order to equate the accumulated depreciation total to the amount needed to replace the asset. We present a discussion on the significance of the backlog issue and the alternative views on the necessity for reflecting backlog depreciation, as well as the proposed alternative methods of accounting for backlog. In addition, the appendix to this chapter provides a comparative analysis of the treatment of backlog depreciation in selected international inflation-accounting pronouncements.

The Case of Backlog Depreciation

If one accepts the premise that an objective of current (replacement) cost accounting is to preserve or maintain the operating capability of the firm, then consistency would demand that a solution be found to the backlog issue, which arises when current (replacement) cost increases, as shown in the preceding example. In line with this thinking, it has been argued that "unless the cumulative capital maintenance adjustment equals the current cost of present productive capacity, productive capacity has not been maintained."[14] A proposed solution to overcome this problem is that "current depreciation expense must include not only an amount based on current replacement cost but also an amount sufficient to compensate for expense based on lower replacement costs in previous periods."[15] Stated differently, in order for the firm to be able to replace its physical assets, using funds retained through depreciation charges, additional amounts for backlog depreciation should be included.

To sum up, the case for disclosure of backlog depreciation rests on cash-flow implications. To the extent that depreciation charges based on current cost would not enable the firm to replace the assets from funds retained through depreciation charges, an amount representing the shortage ought to be provided for in one form or another. The next question is whether backlog depreciation should appear as an expense, distorting the normal current operating results of the firm and violating the conventional matching principle, or whether it should be treated as an adjustment to retained earnings. Treating backlog depreciation as an adjustment to retained earnings implies that the reported income for the period can be distributed without impairing the operating capability of the firm. Assuming there is a deficit in the retained earnings account, reflecting backlog depreciation in this account would create a greater deficit and an additional impairment of the capital of the firm. There is a similar problem with the procedure of treating backlog depreciation as an adjustment to holding gains.

The Case against Backlog Provisions

If a firm has a regular asset replacement pattern, no backlog depreciation should be necessary as long as the depreciation is based on the current cost of the asset at the end of the period. This can be illustrated by the following example. Assume that the firm owns two identical assets, which were acquired in two consecutive years, each at an original cost of $2,000 and an estimated useful life of two years. Let us assume, as before, that the current cost of these assets increases by 10 percent per year. At the end of the second year, when the first acquired machine is to be replaced, its current cost would be $2,420 [($2,000 x (1.10)^2$]. Assuming that depreciation is computed on the basis of the end-of-year current cost of the asset, then the accumulated depreciation for the two assets for the year would be $2,420, an amount equal to the current cost of the asset at the time the asset is to be replaced. In this situation, there is no need for backlog depreciation.

In support of the foregoing argument, the FASB has asserted:

> [C]atch-up [backlog] additions to current expenses are unnecessary as long as an enterprise regularly replaces assets. Thus, if the enterprise . . . has five assets instead of one and replaces on the average one each period, current depreciation expense for each period equals the replacement cost of the asset being replaced, and that is all that is required to maintain productive capacity in a going-concern. [16]

In a similar vein, Vancil and Weil contend that "so long as the firm's acquisitions to maintain physical capacity are made in an amount at least equal to depreciation based on replacement costs, and are made at least as often as that depreciation is computed, then the net assets retained by depreciation based on current costs will be sufficient to maintain physical capacity."[17] This argument is based on the assumption that all funds retained through depreciation are invested in a similar asset with an after-tax return at least as large as the rate of increase in prices of the firm's specific plant assets.[18] Vancil and Weil present this argument in defense of replacement cost accounting, which has been criticized by Chambers[19] for its failure to ensure the maintenance of physical capacity, as its proponents claim.

According to Gynther, there would be no need for any backlog depreciation under a complete current-cost model that provides current-cost adjustments both for "monetary working-capital" and non-monetary items. An attempt to specifically account for backlog would constitute double-counting in Gynther's view.

Gynther argues that there would be no need to specifically show backlog depreciation in the income statement:[20]

> [t]o the extent that:
> a. the non-monetary assets in which the funds retained in the business over the years by those depreciation charges have been reinvested in other non-monetary assets—and
> b. losses are being recognized on holding those monetary assets that have <u>not</u> been reinvested in other non-monetary assets.

Put another way, if the funds stemming from accumulated depreciation are invested in goods rather than retained as monetary assets, the firm benefits. The value of the goods will increase as their specific prices increase. On the other hand, if the funds arising from depreciation were to be invested in monetary assets, the monetary working capital adjustment would show a holding loss.

An analysis of the treatment of backlog depreciation in inflation-accounting pronouncements from four countries is provided in the appendix to this chapter.

CONCLUSION

The whole issue of backlog depreciation revolves around the concern to ensure the availability of sufficient funds to replace physical productive assets. A study of this subject, however, suggests that there is little justification for this concern for several reasons. First, as long as the firm replaces its assets on a regular pattern, the problem of backlog depreciation should not arise. Second, as long as the funds retained from depreciation charges are prudently invested, there should be no need for backlog depreciation.

Finally, it is important to recognize what might be achieved by adopting a system of current-cost accounting. It is apparent that an objective of current-cost accounting in the measurement of periodic income is to match against revenues the current costs of the assets consumed in earning revenues with a view toward maintaining the operating capability of the firm. Having accomplished this objective, concern about whether there are sufficient funds available for replacing certain assets should be a financing problem and not an accounting issue.

APPENDIX: THE ISSUE OF DEPRECIATION IN SELECTED
INFLATION ACCOUNTING PRONOUNCEMENTS ABROAD

United States

The latest authoritative price-level accounting pronouncement
in the United States, FASB Statement 33, does not deal with backlog
depreciation. By the FASB's own admission, this is one of those items
on which the board has deferred action in order to reduce the complexity of the statement.[1]

Australia

According to the latest authoritative price-level accounting
statement in Australia, Proposed Statement of Accounting Standard
on Current Cost Accounting (1982), depreciation charges are to be
based on the average current cost for the period (which is also the
requirement in FASB Statement 33). According to the proposed
standard, no provision is necessary for backlog depreciation. It is
argued that the funds retained from depreciation charges are expected
to be reinvested and, therefore, to yield sufficient returns to offset
the need for any backlog provisions. Interestingly enough, the National
Council of the Australian Society of Accountants and the Institute of
Chartered Accountants in Australia, the two organizations responsible
for the issuance of the proposed standard, appear less concerned about
ensuring the availability of sufficient funds to finance the replacement
of specific assets, as the following statement demonstrates:

> [W]here funds are reinvested as a result of a non-cash
> charge, the resources generated will also be subject to
> normal CCA procedures. Then procedures will measure
> profit based on total operating capability as it exists after
> making reinvestments. Whether or not they ensure suffi-
> cient funds are available to finance the replacement of
> specific assets is irrelevant, since CCA is not designed
> for this purpose (although it may assist). [Emphasis
> added.][2]

According to an Omnibus Exposure Draft issued in March 1980
by the Australian Accounting Research Foundation, the Australian
Current Cost Accounting (CCA) System is "not concerned with replacing assets but rather with the determination of profit in a way
that, in meaningful economic terms, measures increments or decre-
ments in operating capability."[3] This position is reaffirmed in the

1982 proposed statement. It should be pointed out, however, that according to an earlier Statement of Provisional Accounting Standard (DPS 1.2), backlog depreciation was to be reflected as an adjustment to the "current cost adjustment account."[4]

Support for the current position of the Australian accounting profession, which entirely ignores any provision for backlog depreciation on the grounds that CCA is not designed to ensure availability of sufficient funds for asset replacement, is also provided by Clarke, who argues that: "The problem of funding asset replacements or repairs to existing assets so that physical capital may be maintained is a financial matter, not an accounting one. The financial consequences of inflation may well make . . . asset replacement more costly. But that does not mean that accounting to incorporate the financial effects of inflation need pay any particular attention to those problems, as such."[5]

It should be noted, however, that the argument that CCA is not designed for the purpose of ensuring availability of sufficient funds for asset replacement could be challenged for lack of consistency. Chambers, for instance, maintains that it is "hypocritical" to justify CCA on the basis of sustaining operating capacity and then to assert (regarding the issue of the need for backlog depreciation) that capital maintenance is the concern of financial managers, not of accountants.[6]

The stated objectives of the Australian Proposed Current Cost Accounting statement do not contain any explicit reference that would make backlog depreciation relevant information. Paragraph 4 of the 1982 Australian proposed statement asserts that: "The objective of CCA is to ensure that, having regard to changes in specific prices, the results and resources of an entity are realistically measured so as to be of maximum value to users." This statement says nothing about ensuring sufficient funds for asset replacement, and to the extent that the periodic income is measured using current cost, one can contend that the objective of communicating realistic measures of the firm's performance has been accomplished. There is still, however, one troublesome point. Another objective (par. 7) of the proposed standard states that the "CCA assists investors, managers and other users in better assessing . . . the financial viability of the entity." Granted that backlog depreciation represents potential cash outflow at the time of replacement, does it not constitute relevant information in assessing the financial viability of the entity? It can be argued that users who are interested in making future cash-flow projections would find information pertaining to backlog depreciation relevant. However, as discussed earlier, there would be no need for any backlog depreciation if all pertinent data were already impounded in a comprehensive current-cost income model that provides current cost adjustments both for "monetary working capital" and nonmonetary working-capital items. As Gynther has pointed out, any attempt to specifically account for backlog would constitute double-counting. [7]

Canada

On the subject of backlog depreciation, the 1982 Canadian Accounting Pronouncement on "Reporting the Effects of Changing Prices" states:

> When an enterprise has a pattern of asset replacements that is subject to significant irregularities, backlog depreciation may become a material factor to be considered by users in assessing maintenance of operating capability. In such circumstances, management may wish to comment on the significance of backlog depreciation in its narrative discussion of the supplementary information. [8]

The Canadian approach considers only current-cost depreciation in arriving at income (loss) on a current-cost basis. Thus, although interested users can determine the backlog depreciation from the supplementary information, no attempt is made to retain an amount equal to the backlog depreciation from the income attributable to common shareholders in order to ensure the availability of sufficient funds for the replacement of physical productive assets.

United Kingdom

According to Statement of Standard Accounting Practice No. 16: "Current Cost Accounting" (SSAP 16), the amount of depreciation charge applied in computing the "current cost operating profit" reflects the amount of fixed assets consumed during the period, based on the value of these assets to the business. No provision is made for any backlog depreciation in arriving at the current operating income.

Although SSAP 16 is not specific on how backlog depreciation is treated, according to the Sandilands' Report, which advocated the adoption of CCA in the United Kingdom in 1975, backlog depreciation should be treated directly as an adjustment to the "fixed assets revaluation reserve with the corresponding credit to the cumulative depreciation." The Sandilands' Report admits that adjusting backlog depreciation to the revaluation reserve account instead of charging it to the income statement does not serve to retain funds to provide for the full replacement cost of the physical assets unless, of course, the assets are replaced on a regular, revolving basis. [9]

NOTES

1. For a critique of accounting income, see E. S. Hendriksen, Accounting Theory, 4th ed. (Homewood, Ill.: Richard D. Irwin, 1982), p. 137.

2. A. Smith, An Enquiry into the Nature and Causes of Wealth of Nations (London: George Routledge, 1890) quoted in FASB's Conceptual Framework for Financial Accounting and Reporting: Elements of Financial Statements and Their Measurement, (Stamford, Conn.: FASB, 1976), p. 124.

3. J. R. Hicks, Value and Capital, 2nd ed. (Oxford, England: Clarendon Press, 1946).

4. S. S. Alexander, "Income Measurement in a Dynamic Economy," revised by D. Solomons, Studies in Accounting, eds. W. T. Baxter and Sidney Davidson (London: The Institute of Chartered Accountants in England and Wales, 1977), p. 44.

5. I. Fisher, The Nature of Capital and Income (New York: Macmillan, 1906), p. 52, quoted in E. S. Hendriksen, Accounting Theory, p. 142.

6. Hendriksen, Accounting Theory, p. 142.

7. It should be noted that since the intent is to express the amount of the capital reported at different points in time in terms of a common unit of measurement, one can restate the nominal dollar amounts of capital for any given period in terms of their equivalent purchasing-power units relative to the beginning, ending, or average for-the-year dollars. One may even restate all amounts to the base-year dollars. FASB Statement No. 33, "Financial Reporting and Changing Prices" (1979), for instance, calls for the use of average-for-the-year adjustments unless comprehensive financial statements are presented in which case the end-of-year, average-for-the-year, or base-year index may be used.

8. Once capital is determined by discounting future expected flows, income for a given period can be measured by comparing the beginning and ending capital of the period. Three different income measures are possible under the present value model: (1) ideal income, which is possible under the assumption of perfect certainty, where future flows, and interest rates are perfectly known; (2) ex ante income, which is derived by considering a world of uncertainty and imperfect knowledge in which future flows and interest rates are subjectively determined in predicting income for the period; (3) ex post income, which is measured at the end of the period. Ex post income measurement also involves a world of uncertainty and imperfect knowledge. The beginning capital would be adjusted for changes that have taken place until the end of the period, whereas the capital at the end of the period is measured by using subjectively determined

future flows and interest rates. For further discussion in these measures, see T. A. Lee, Income and Value, Measurements: Theory and Practice, (Baltimore, Md.: University Park Press, 1975), chapter 3.

9. A persuasive argument in support of the physical capital maintenance concept is given by L. Revsine and J. J. Weygrandt, "Accounting for Inflation: The Controversy," The Journal of Accountancy, (October 1974): 72-8.

10. These ideas are elaborated upon in the British Sandilands' Report. See Inflation Accounting Committee, (Sandilands Committee), Inflation Accounting: Report of the Inflation Accounting Committee, (London: Her Majesty's Stationery Office, 1975), p. 35.

11. See J. R. Grinyer and T. W. Symon, "Maintenance of Capital Intact: An Unnecessary Abstraction?" Accounting and Business Research (Autumn, 1980): 403-13. R. J. Chambers is also opposed to the physical capital maintenance concept and contends that "[t]he maintenance of capital does not, . . . mean the maintenance of any given physical good." R. J. Chambers, Accounting, Evaluation and Economic Behavior (Englewood Cliffs, N.J.: Prentice-Hall, Inc., 1966), p. 114. For further discussion on the criticisms of the physical capital concept, read FASB's Conceptual Framework, pp. 140-43.

12. Current-cost and current-replacement cost are often used interchangeably, although there is a subtle but important distinction between them. Current cost is defined as the current purchase price of an asset owned, whereas replacement cost is the current purchase price of assets that will replace existing assets. For a detailed discussion of this distinction, see Chapter 7.

13. This is computed as follows: With a ten percent increase in the replacement cost of the asset, the cost of the asset will be $2,200 ($2,000 x 1.10) at the end of the first year and $2,420 ($2,200 x 1.10) at the end of the second year. Using the straight-line method, the depreciation for the first year is $1,100 and for the second year $1,210.

14. Financial Accounting Standards Board, FASB Discussion Memorandum: Conceptual Framework for Financial Accounting and Reporting: Elements of Financial Statements and Their Measurement, Stamford, Conn.: FASB, December 2, 1976, p. 128.

15. Ibid.

16. D. T. Tweedie, "Current Cost Accounting: U.K. Controversies and Overseas Solutions," in P. T. Wanless and D. A. R. Forrester, eds., Readings in Inflation Accounting, (Chichester, Great Britain: Wiley, 1979), pp. 446-8.

17. R. F. Vancil and R. L. Weil, "Current Replacement Cost Accounting, Depreciable Assets and Distributable Income," in Vancil and Weil, eds., Replacement Cost Accounting: Readings on Concepts, Uses and Methods, (Glen Ridge, N.J.: Thomas Horton and Daughters, 1976), p. 58.

18. Ibid.

19. R. J. Chambers, "NOD, COG and PuPu: See How Inflation Teases!" The Journal of Accountancy, (September 1975): 62.

20. R. S. Gynther, "CCA: Its Expected Effects," Part 1, The Australian Accountant (April 1978): 158.

NOTES TO APPENDIX

1. Financial Accounting Standards Board, Statement of Financial Accounting Standards No. 33, "Financial Reporting and Changing Prices," (Stamford, Conn.: FASB, September 1979), p. 28.

2. Paragraph 66 of the Guidance Notes to the Australian Proposed Statement of Accounting Standards in Cost Accounting, Melbourne, Australia: Australian Accounting Research Foundation, February 1982.

3. Australian Accounting Research Foundation, Exposure Draft, "Current Cost Accounting—Omnibus Exposure Draft" (Melbourne, Australia: AARF, March 1980), par. 25.

4. See The Institute of Chartered Accountants in Australia and Australian Society of Accountants, "Explanatory Statement: The Basis of Current Cost Accounting," (DPS 1.2/309.2, issued October 10, 1976, amended August 1978), pars. 13.25 and 13.26.

5. F. L. Clarke, "CCA: Progress or Regress?" in Current Cost Accounting: Identifying the Issues, eds. G. W. Dean and M. C. Wells. Second ed., (Lancaster, England: International Center for Research in Accounting, University of Lancaster, and Sydney, Australia: Department of Accounting, University of Sydney, 1979), p. 70.

6. Ibid.

7. R. S. Gynther, "CCA: Its Expected Effects," Part 1, The Australian Accountant, (April 1978): 158.

8. The Canadian Institute of Chartered Accountants, CICA Handbook, Section 4510, Reporting the Effects of Changing Prices, (October 1982), par. 4510A.15.

9. Inflation Accounting: Report of the Inflation Accounting Committee, 480-2.

5

CRITERIA FOR EVALUATING
ALTERNATIVE ACCOUNTING MODELS

INTRODUCTION

The conventional accounting model, although credited for verifiability of its data,[1] has been criticized for failing to convey relevant
information for economic decision making. The inadequacy of the conventional model, which is a direct consequence of the weaknesses of
its underlying assumptions and principles, becomes more pronounced
during periods of instability in the general price level, as discussed
in Chapter 1. In view of these shortcomings, several alternative
accounting models have been proposed.

The principal alternative models, namely—(1) historical-cost/
constant-dollar (also known as general price-level adjusted historical
cost), (2) current cost, and (3) current exit price—are analyzed and
evaluated in Chapters 6, 7, and 8, respectively. A brief overview of
these models is given at the end of this chapter. The primary objective of this chapter is to present a framework for evaluating the proposed models.

PROBLEMS IN EVALUATING
ALTERNATIVE ACCOUNTING MODELS

It may be asserted that the information needs of the various
financial-statement users are different. Accordingly, it may not be
possible to agree on what accounting data should be conveyed in financial reports. This implies that it is not possible for one accounting
model to satisfy all potential users. The appropriate accounting model
would be one that satisfies the particular information needs of the

given financial statement user. Therefore, it can be stated that no single accounting model is always superior or inferior to all other models for all users. Thus, any attempt to evaluate the proposed alternative models should be concerned with comparing and contrasting the inherent differences in the alternative accounting models without attempting to rank the models.

In contrast to the foregoing argument, a case can be made to evaluate the proposed alternative accounting models in order to demonstrate the preferability of one over another. In this endeavor, it is recognized that no meaningful assessment of the proposed alternative accounting models can be made without first establishing a framework for evaluating the proposed alternative accounting models.

OBJECTIVES OF FINANCIAL REPORTING

We rely upon the objectives of financial reporting set forth in the FASB's SFAC 1, "Objectives of Financial Reporting by Business Enterprises" (1978), and the "qualitative characteristics" in SFAC 2, "Qualitative Characteristics of Accounting Information" (1980), for a framework to evaluate each model.

The principal objectives of financial reporting as stated in SFAC 1 are as follows:

To provide information useful in making rational business and economic decisions by investors, creditors, managers, and other users.

To provide information useful in assessing the amounts, timing, and uncertainty of prospective cash flows.

To provide information useful in assessing the performance of management in the discharge of its stewardship responsibility.

In discussing the objectives of financial reporting and the type of information that should be conveyed to potential users, it is important to realize that certain external users, who may have specialized information needs, such as tax authorities and regulatory agencies, have the authority to mandate the type of financial information they need. Likewise, management is in a position to generate whatever information is needed for internal decision making. Therefore, the major focus of external financial reporting should be to satisfy the information needs of external users who lack the authority to demand the type of information they want. Such external users include investors, creditors, suppliers, employees, customers, labor unions, the financial press, and financial analysts. The users are assumed to be interested in the future performance of the firm—its ability to generate future cash flows. The information needs of lenders are considered similar to those of investors, since lenders are also interested in assessing the prospective net cash inflows of the borrowing firm. The ability of the firm to meet its obligations is dependent on the firm's net cash inflows. Of the external users, investors and creditors are considered to be the prominent groups and the primary beneficiaries of financial reporting.

QUALITATIVE CHARACTERISTICS OF ACCOUNTING INFORMATION

Having stated the principal objectives of financial reporting, the question that needs to be addressed is how to evaluate the data generated by the proposed alternative accounting models. One approach is to identify certain desirable attributes—qualitative characteristics—that can be associated with accounting information in order to enhance its usefulness to potential users.

In SFAC 2, the FASB has identified the key attributes of relevance and reliability as desirable qualitative characteristics of accounting information. By and large, the qualitative characteristics identified in SFAC 2 provide a comprehensive set of attributes that has been developed over the years by the various authoritative accounting bodies.[2] A discussion is presented on the nature and significance of the attributes set forth in SFAC 2 and on the problems involved in applying these attributes to alternative accounting models.

Information Needs of Investors. In the context of investment decision making, a rational investor should choose an investment alternative that promises the highest return for a given risk, or one that entails the minimum risk for a given expected return, other things being equal. For such decisions, information is considered relevant if it assists the investor in making predictions about future returns and associated risks, or in revising or confirming prior beliefs about expected returns and risks of available investment opportunities.

The relevance of a given set of accounting information to an investor depends on a number of factors including wealth, attitude toward risk, and portfolio strategy. Portfolio theory suggests that specific security information is relevant only to the extent that it impacts the expected return and risk of the investor's portfolio.[3] By holding a well-diversified portfolio, an investor can reduce much of the risk associated with holding a single security. In this regard, the relevant information to a well-diversified investor is that which helps the investor in assessing the expected return and risk at the portfolio level. Similarly, the relevance of accounting information also depends on whether the investor is pursuing an "active" or "passive" trading strategy. An investor who is actively involved in trading a given stock would be interested in accounting information that could help in predicting short-run movements in security prices as opposed to a passive investor who buys and holds the stock for long-term ownership.[4]

In any case, to be relevant, accounting information should assist the investor in making predictions about the amounts, timing, and related uncertainties of prospective cash flows.

Predictive Ability. Given that expected returns and related risks are assumed to be relevant variables in investment decision making, then, an important criterion in evaluating accounting models is the "predictive ability" of the information generated by a given model. The assumption used here is that investors prefer the accounting model that calls for information useful for predicting expected cash flows and the degree of uncertainty involved in such forecasts.

There are serious problems, however, in applying the predictive-ability criterion to deciding among alternative accounting models:

> Though much of the relevance of accounting information
> may derive from its value as input to a prediction model,
> the probability that it will lead to correct predictions does
> not determine its reliability as a set of measurements.
> The correctness of predictions depends as much on the
> predictive model used as on the data that go in to the
> model. Thus, the result of a predictive process cannot
> be used to assess the reliability of the inputs into it.[5]

A predictive model that uses data that is related in a cause-effect sense to the variable to be predicted should be superior to a corresponding model that uses inputs having no causal relationship to the variable of interest. It should be emphasized, however, that improving the input data without changing the predictive model is not necessarily expected to provide better predictions, as illustrated by the following example:

> The econometric models now used for economic forecast-
> ing are designed to use . . . financial aggregates (among
> other things) as those aggregates are compiled at present.
> They might work less well if price-level adjusted data
> were used. However, it might be possible to revise the
> model for use with that kind of data so that even better
> predictions could be made (SFAC 2, par. 54).

In choosing among alternative accounting models, a criterion that should be used is whether the model generates information that logically pertains to the variables that the potential user wishes to predict.

Relevance

Relevant information makes a difference in assisting users who are predicting the results of future actions or confirming previous expectations (SFAC 2, pars. 46-55). There are three factors affecting relevance: (1) predictive value, (2) feedback value, and (3) timeliness. Predictive value reflects the quality of information to correctly forecast the outcome of particular events. Feedback value is concerned with the ability of information to confirm or correct prior expectations. If the information is not timely, it cannot be relevant for decision making.

With respect to relevance, there is no unambiguous definition of what should be considered relevant information for particular users, since users' needs are unknown. Moreover, although in an abstract sense, one can argue that in order to be relevant, accounting information should assist users in assessing the amounts, timing, and related uncertainties of expected cash flows, that objective does not tell us what types of accounting information are appropriate. In addressing this issue, the FASB has admitted that this is an unanswered question, awaiting completion of the conceptual framework project (SFAC 2, par. 50). Although the board did not specify financial-accounting standards, forms of financial statements, or the measurement of the elements of financial statements in order to satisfy the objectives of financial reporting as stated in SFAC 1, the FASB does provide some useful insights about the type of information that may be conveyed. To be relevant for decision making, information must be future-oriented.

The FASB, at this stage, however, neither requires nor prohibits "management forecast information." (SFAC 1, footnote 6, p. 16.) Instead, it calls for: (1) information about resources and obligations of an enterprise. This information is expected to enable the interested user "to identify the enterprise's financial strengths and weaknesses and assess its liquidity and solvency." On the basis of such information, users are expected to be able to formulate expectations about cash inflows and outflows of the firm (SFAC 1, par. 41), (2) information about an enterprise's financial performance. The FASB suggests that the primary focus of financial reporting should be to provide information about an enterprise's performance. An earnings statement containing disaggregated information about the components of the reported earnings should aid users in assessing the enterprise's cash-flow prospects. Although the FASB does not specify how the enterprise's earnings should be measured, it clearly prefers earnings on an accrual basis to a cash basis (SFAC 1, par. 44). On the basis of past performance, interested users may be able to assess the firm's earnings prospects and the attendant risks (SFAC 1, par. 42). Information about a firm's performance may also be used as a basis for assessing management's effectiveness and efficiency in the discharge of its stewardship responsibilities (SFAC 1, par. 52), and (3) information about uses and sources of cash. The FASB asserts that information about an enterprise's sources and uses of cash is "useful in understanding the operations of an enterprise, evaluating its financial activities, assessing its liquidity or solvency, or interpreting earnings information" (SFAC 1, par. 49).

To summarize, as reflected in SFAC 1, information pertaining to an enterprise's economic resources and obligations and earnings performance as well as information about sources and uses of cash is relevant to achieving the objectives of financial statements. The FASB's position on this matter is best described as follows:

> Investors, creditors, and others may use reported earnings and information about the elements of financial statements in various ways to assess the prospects for cash flows. They may wish, for example, to evaluate management's performance, estimate "earning power," predict future earnings, assess risk, or to confirm, change, or reject earlier predictions or assessments. Although financial reporting should provide basic information to aid them, they do their own evaluating, estimating, predicting, assessing, conforming, changing, or rejecting (SFAC 1, p. ix).

Reliability

Reliability of accounting information depends on three factors: (1) representational faithfulness, (2) verifiability, and (3) neutrality. Representational faithfulness reflects the validity of the information in question—i.e., whether it represents what it purports to represent (SFAC 2, par. 63). For example, does the reported value of an asset represent its economic value? Consider the asset whose specific prices have declined during an inflationary period. For such an asset held during a period of significant general inflation, the historical-cost/constant-dollar figure will not be representationally faithful.

A second factor affecting reliability is verifiability, which refers to the availability of supporting evidence regarding the measurement of the information. That the information provided can be confirmed by independent parties enhances its reliability. Verifiability of accounting data is demonstrated by the degree of consensus that can be obtained among independent parties using the same measurement methods.

Reliability also involves freedom from bias and neutrality. Bias in accounting measurement is the tendency for data to be too high or low. Bias may be introduced either in the measurement method used or in misrepresentation (unintentional or intentional) by the measurer. In this regard, freedom from bias should enhance the reliability of the accounting information. Likewise, to be reliable, information should be neutral in the sense that it is not designed to favor one interest group over another.

In summary, reliability of the accounting information is an important qualitative characteristic that should be considered in evaluating alternative accounting models. Information that is perceived to be completely unreliable would simply be ignored even if such information were relevant. However, a trade-off may be needed. To increase the relevance of accounting information, it may be necessary to sacrifice reliability to some extent. The use of subjectively derived current value data falls in this category.

Comparability

Another criterion that should be applied in evaluating alternative accounting models is the ability to generate accounting data suitable for comparison purposes. Decision making involves a comparison among alternatives. To be useful for decision making, accounting information should facilitate intrafirm or interfirm comparisons over time. In evaluating competing accounting models, an important factor that should be considered is the ability of the model to generate comparable data for firms that are similar. Stated differently the accounting model should possess the ability to make similar economic situations look alike, and unlike situations appear different.

In making intrafirm or interfirm comparisons, it is important to ensure consistency of the accounting methods used. Likewise, in making a comparative analysis of time-series, financial-accounting data, the measurement unit used should remain constant. Otherwise, a valid comparison cannot be made between different time periods. In this regard, an accounting model that uses a constant unit of measurement is preferable to one that uses nominal dollars in an economic environment where the general price level is unstable.

The foregoing discussion has identified several qualitative characteristics of accounting information, including: (1) relevance, (2) reliability, and (3) comparability. In evaluating the proposed alternative accounting models, the extent to which a given model possesses these criteria is examined. Our evaluation also considers the "cost-benefit" constraint. To the extent that the cost of providing these attributes exceeds the benefits, then the accounting model under consideration would not be selected.

Based on the principal objectives of financial statements (as described earlier), the assumed information needs of potential users, and the desirable attributes of useful accounting information, we can proceed with the discussion and evaluation of the proposed alternative accounting models.

SUMMARY

The objective of this chapter has been to present a discussion of the criteria for evaluation of the alternative accounting models. One approach that has been suggested is to simply compare the inherent characteristics of each model without attempting to rank the models. This approach is based on the contention that since the information needs of potential financial statement users are varied, no single accounting model will always prove superior or inferior in satisfying the information needs of particular users. Although they may well be some truth to this contention, a case is established for the need to assess the ability of each proposed model to satisfy the information needs of the primary users of financial statements—namely, investors and creditors. It is argued that most other potential users who may conceivably have special information needs, such as managers, tax authorities, and government agencies, probably have the power to obtain the type of information they need directly from the firm. Accordingly, in line with the approach suggested by the FASB, as set forth in SFAC 1, the primary objective of financial reporting is to meet the information needs of investors and creditors.

The assumed information needs of investors are derived from portfolio theory. According to portfolio theory, rational investors make investment decisions based on the expected future returns and risks of alternative investment opportunities. In order to satisfy the information needs of investors, the accounting information that is generated from an alternative model should enable investors to make predictions about future expected returns and associated risks of available investment alternatives. Assuming that one agrees to the principal objectives of financial reporting, then a set of desirable attributes—qualitative characteristics—can be identified to serve as a basis for evaluating the quality of the data generated by alternative accounting models. SFAC 2 has identified relevance, reliability, and comparability, among other attributes, as desirable qualitative attributes that should be present in accounting data. The relevance of the accounting data is judged by whether the data satisfies the assumed information needs of investors. Although relevany is certainly an important factor, it is equally important that such data also be perceived as reliable. Unless the data are considered reliable, investors may very well not utilize the data. Likewise, investors need to compare investment opportunities. Thus, accounting data should enhance comparability among firms. Investors may also be interested in evaluating the performance and financial trends of a given firm over time. In this regard, the accounting data should make it possible for investors to compare the financial data of a given firm on a time-series basis. Viewed in this manner, the principal qualitative attributes of relevance, reliability, and comparability can be used as criteria for evaluating alternative accounting models.

The proposed alternative accounting models are, therefore, evaluated in the subsequent three chapters, based on the objectives of financial statements as presented in SFAC 1 and the qualitative characteristics set forth in SFAC 2. A brief overview of the proposed models is presented below.

Overview of the Proposed Alternative Accounting Models

In general, the proposed accounting models can be classified in two ways: (1) those that entail a modification of the conventional, historical-cost accounting model, by restating the historical-cost data to reflect changes in the general price level, and (2) those that call for a departure from the historical-cost model in favor of current valuation. The historical-cost/constant-dollar model, also referred to as the general price-level-adjusted historical-cost model, essentially involves the restatement of the conventional, historical-cost financial statements to reflect changes in the general purchasing power of the dollar. This model is discussed in the next chapter.

Current value accounting is a term used here to encompass a broad classification of accounting models that represent a significant departure from the conventional model. Unlike the conventional model, which is fundamentally based on the cost principle, current value models are based on different versions of market-exchange values. Proponents of current-value models contend that the use of current-value models, rather than historical costs represents a significant improvement in the financial-reporting system irrespective of whether inflation prevails or not.

Cost generally represents the "fair market value" at the time of a transaction. As time passes, however, specific price changes occur for various reasons, including changes in demand and supply, technological improvements, and other factors. Adherence to original cost, despite specific price changes, results in balance sheets that fail to reflect the economic values of the resources owned by a firm, and in income statements that provide distorted measures of operating performance. Current-value models are intended to overcome the valuation problem caused by adherence to the historical-cost principle. It is argued that the departure from the historical-cost principle will result in more useful balance sheets and income statements.

It must be noted, however, that current-value models like the historical-cost model do not reflect the impact of changing price levels (i.e., the effect of general inflation or deflation) on financial reporting. Thus, current-value models, strictly speaking, cannot be considered "inflation-accounting" models.

Inflation, which by definition means a general price-level increase, reflects a decrease in the general purchasing power of the monetary unit. In an inflationary period, dollars of different time periods do not convey the same economic meaning. It is not, therefore, suitable to compare financial statements of different time periods denominated in nominal dollars, even if such statements were derived from current-value models. For purposes of meaningful interperiod comparison, current-value financial statements should be presented in terms of a constant unit of measurement. Given the state of the art in financial reporting today, the use of constant dollars—i.e., dollars with equivalent purchasing power—is considered an acceptable solution to the measurement-unit problem. In a period of general price-level changes, the current-value/constant-dollar model would address both the valuation problem as well as the measurement-unit problem inherent in the conventional historical-cost model.

One problem with current-value accounting is that the concept of "current value" is not well-defined. A review of the literature reveals that the term has different meanings to different people, which poses the problem of which current value to use. As a result of market imperfections, such as transaction costs, the market-exchange value of an asset depends on whether one takes the point of view of the buyer or the seller. From the buyer's point of view, the current value of an asset is determined by its current entry price, whereas from the seller's point of view, the value of an asset is represented by its current exit price. A disparity of views among proponents of current-value models regarding the appropriate current value to be used in financial reporting has led to the emergence of two major alternative current-value models: (1) current cost, reflecting the current purchase prices and (2) current exit value, reflecting the current selling price or the cash equivalent of the item in question. The current-cost model, along with its more comprehensive version—the current-cost/constant-dollar—is analyzed in Chapter 7. An analysis of the current exit value and current exit-value/constant-dollar models is provided in Chapter 8.

Multiple Valuation Approach. It is noted that strict adherence to any of the foregoing alternative models poses theoretical and practical problems. Therefore, it is suggested that a satisfactory current-value accounting framework should be flexible in applying different valuation bases in order to achieve greater relevance.[6] Accordingly, such a system would report, for example, either historical cost, replacement cost, or net realizable value for particular assets, whichever is presumed to be more relevant under the circumstances. For instance, the valuation of discontinued inventories in terms of exit values, and plant and equipment in terms of current replacement cost, would be considered more appropriate than the strict application of either valuation method to all assets.

One version of a multivaluation framework would present both historical- and current-value measures in parallel columns, as advocated in A Statement of Basic Accounting Theory.[7] Although multivaluation seems intuitively appealing, and the disclosure of several measures may satisfy the information needs of users of financial reports, multivaluation has been opposed on the grounds of information overload.[8]

NOTES

1. Although the conventional accounting model is essentially based on verifiable, arm's-length transactions, there is considerable subjectivity involved in conventional accounting. For example, depreciation is based on a subjectively measured estimate of an asset's useful life and an estimated salvage value. Additionally, the estimation of bad debt expense is essentially judgemental.

2. Perhaps the first of such attempts was made by Moonitz in 1961. [See M. Moonitz, Accounting Research Study No. 1, "The Basic Postulates of Accounting," (New York: AICPA, 1961)]. Since then, the American Accounting Association in 1966 [see American Accounting Association, A Statement of Basic Accounting Theory (Evanston, Ill.: AAA, 1966)], the Accounting Principles Board (APB) of the American Institute of Certified Public Accountants (AICPA), in 1970 [see American Institute of Certified Public Accountants, APB Statement No. 4, "Basic Concepts and Accounting Principles Underlying Financial Statements of Business Enterprises," (New York: AICPA, 1970)], and the AICPA (Trueblood) Study Group on Objectives of Financial Statements in 1973 [see Report of the Study Group on the Objectives of Financial Statements, Objectives of Financial Statements. (New York: AICPA, 1970(] have addressed the question of developing desirable qualitative characteristics of accounting information.

3. See W. Sharpe, "Capital Asset Prices: A Theory of Market Equilibrium Under Conditions of Risk," Journal of Finance, (September 1967): 425-42; J. Lintner, "Security Prices, Risk and Maximum Gains from Diversification," Journal of Finance, (December 1965): 587-616; J. Mossin, "Equilibrium in a Capital Asset Market," Econometricia, (October 1966): 768-83. See also W. H. Beaver, "Current Trends in Corporate Disclosure," Journal of Accountancy, (January 1978), pp. 44-52.

4. See W. H. Beaver, Financial Reporting: An Accounting Revolution, (Englewood Cliffs, N.J.: Prentice-Hall, 1981), chapter 1, for a discussion on the information needs of investors.

5. Financial Accounting Standards Board, Statement of Financial Accounting Concepts No. 2, "Qualitative Characteristics of Accounting Information," (Stamford, Conn.: FASB, May 1980), par. 75.

6. See, as examples, American Accounting Association, A Statement of Basic Accounting Theory (Evanston, Ill.: AAA, 1966); and Report of the Study Group, Objectives of Financial Statements (New York: AICPA, 1973).

7. See the first listing in the preceding note. Backer has also proposed a multiple-reporting approach: M. Backer and R. Simpson,

<u>Current Value Accounting</u>. (New York: Financial Executives Research Foundation, 1973).

8. A detailed consideration of this approach is beyond the scope of this book.

6

THE HISTORICAL-COST/
CONSTANT-DOLLAR MODEL

INTRODUCTION

The historical-cost/constant-dollar (HC/CD) model has been identified by different names—such as "general price-level accounting (GPLA)," "current purchasing-power (CPP) accounting," "accounting for changes in the purchasing power of money," "financial reporting in units of general purchasing power," and "inflation accounting." As these names suggest, the objective of this method of financial reporting is to restate the unit of measurement in terms of dollars having the same purchasing power. This model recognizes the problems inherent in using the dollar as a unit of measurement. The value of the dollar as a unit of measure depends on its command over goods and services. When prices rise or fall, the purchasing power of the dollar fluctuates in the opposite direction. That the dollar fluctuates with price-level changes makes it unsuitable as a unit of measurement in financial reporting during periods of significant price-level changes.

The conventional accounting model treats the dollar as a stable unit of measurement. Therefore, the conventional balance sheet contains assets that were acquired at different times using dollars of varying purchasing power. Yet these nonhomogeneous dollars are added together, which is analogous to combining different currencies. The summation cannot be meaningfully interpreted.

The motivation for restating historical financial statements to constant dollars, i.e., dollars that represent the same units of purchasing power, is to recognize that dollars of different periods are not comparable. Thus, by restating the original reported amounts for changes in the general purchasing power of the dollar, the financial statements would reflect the original amounts in terms of a common current dollar, which, if spent today, would command the same general purchasing power as the original dollars.

RESTATEMENT PROCESS

To restate the original dollars to constant dollars, an acceptable general price-level index is needed. Such an index is constructed by taking the average price of a set of goods and services in successive periods, and expressing the successive average prices as a percentage of the average price of the same set of goods and services as of a given base year. The base year is assigned an index number of 100. Several general price-level indexes are available in the United States, such as the Consumer Price Index and the Wholesale Price Index, prepared by the Bureau of Labor Statistics of the U.S. Department of Labor, and the Gross National Product Implicit Price Deflator, prepared by the Office of Business Economics of the U.S. Department of Commerce. The Consumer Price Index for All Urban Consumers (CPI-U) is required by FASB Statement No. 33, "Financial Reporting and Changing Prices," as the index for restating historical-cost statements into constant-dollar statements. Among the advantages of using the CPI-U is that it is published monthly and is not revised after its initial publication.

In preparing historical-cost/constant-dollar financial statements, average-for-the-year or end-of-year dollars can be used.[1] However, for the sake of simplicity, restatement of comprehensive financial statements should be done in terms of end-of-the-current-year dollars. Prior statements would be "rolled-forward" to reflect the purchasing power units in terms of dollars of the latest balance sheet date.[2]

However, before restating the items of the historical-cost financial statements into constant dollars, the accounts have to be classified into monetary and nonmonetary items.

Monetary and Nonmonetary Items

Monetary items are those accounts reflecting a fixed quantity of the monetary unit regardless of the changes in the general purchasing power of that unit. Examples of monetary assets are cash, accounts receivable, notes receivable, and other forms of contractual claims to a fixed amount of cash in the future. Likewise, monetary liabilities, such as accounts and notes payable and long-term debts, are obligations to pay a fixed quantity of the monetary unit, regardless of the changes in the general purchasing power of the monetary unit.

Thus, by their very nature, monetary items are already stated in current end-of-year dollars and, therefore, should not be restated (except for comparative purposes with statements at different points in time).[3]

Purchasing-Power Gains and Losses

Holding monetary assets during a period of increasing general price levels involves a loss of general purchasing power, because a given amount of money could buy fewer goods and services. For example, assume that ABC Company had $10,000 in a checking account in the bank on January 1, 19X1, which remained intact until December 31, 19X1. Assume that 10 percent inflation occurred during the year. This situation implies that ABC Company would need $11,000 on December 31, 19X1 to maintain the same general purchasing power that it had on January 1, 19X1. The fact that the company only holds $10,000 results in a loss of general purchasing power of $1,000. The same purchasing power loss would also stem from holding accounts receivable or notes receivable or any claim to a fixed quantity of money since the amount of money expected to be received commands a diminishing amount of general purchasing power during periods of general price-level increases. Similarly, holding a monetary liability would entail the opposite effect. If we assume, for the sake of simplicity, that the company had a noninterest-bearing accounts payable (and no implicit interest) of $10,000 on January 1, 19X1, which is paid on December 31, 19X1, then one can argue that the company is settling its obligation by an amount that has less general purchasing power than the original obligation. Therefore, a claim can be made for a reported purchasing power gain from holding monetary liabilities during inflationary periods.

How purchasing power gains and losses on holding monetary items should be computed—particularly with regard to interest-bearing, long-term liabilities—and whether such gains and losses represent elements of income in a given period constitute a complex and controversial topic. We have devoted Chapter 9 to a discussion of the conceptual issues in the treatment of monetary items.

Whatever their nature, purchasing-power gains and losses from holding monetary items are the unique product of constant-dollar accounting, (whether based on historical cost, current cost, or exit value). Most of the literature on the HC/CD model tends to treat purchasing-power gains and losses on holding monetary items as realized components of income. It should be noted, however, that the HC/CD requirements of FAS 33 call for the exclusion of purchasing-power gains and losses from the computation of income. Such gains and losses are separately reported.

Nonmonetary Items

All assets and liabilities that lack the properties of monetary items are classified as nonmonetary. Nonmonetary assets include inventories, building, plant, and equipment, and claims to cash in amounts dependent on future prices. Unlike monetary assets, nonmonetary assets do not represent a fixed claim to receive cash, and thus their prices in terms of the monetary unit may change over time. While most liabilities are monetary, nonmonetary liabilities include obligations to furnish given amounts of goods or services irrespective of the changes in prices or obligations to pay cash in amounts dependent on future prices of specific goods or services. Thus, nonmonetary liabilities do not represent fixed claims to pay cash, e.g., deferred revenues.

As of the balance sheet date, the monetary assets and liabilities are already stated in dollars of current purchasing power as of the end of the year; consequently, the monetary items will appear at the same amounts, whereas nonmonetary items are reported at their restated amounts, in the constant-dollar-adjusted balance sheet. It should be noted, however, that in preparing comparative balance sheet amounts, the monetary items from previous balance sheets should be restated to reflect the current end-of-the-year dollars. A discussion of the procedures for restating historical-cost statements to constant dollars is illustrated at the end of this chapter.

EVALUATION OF THE HISTORICAL-COST/ CONSTANT-DOLLAR MODEL

To the extent that this model is essentially the historical-cost model, except for the unit-of-measurement modification, it enjoys much the same degree of verifiability found in the conventional historical-cost model.

Since specific price movements are not necessarily synchronized with movements of the general price-level index, the restatement in terms of constant dollars does not reflect the current economic value of the resources of the firm. In fact, it is difficult to interpret the restated amounts. As Hendriksen observes:[4]

[The restatement to constant dollars] is not intended to represent current values, but merely the historical cost restated for changes in general purchasing power. However, interpretation remains difficult because historical cost represents the number of dollars paid for a specific item, but the restated amount does not represent the

amount that would have been paid for the item if the
current price-level and the current price structure
were then known. And since it is not intended to be
a surrogate for current value, there is difficulty in
attaching any current market or utility valuation
interpretation to it.

It is apparent, therefore, that this model is not designed to
convey current values although there has been some confusion about
its significance.[5] It is generally understood that the need for such a
restatement is motivated by the desire to overcome the reporting
problems arising from inflationary conditions. What seems to be
overlooked by the proponents of this proposal is that it deals only
with the conventional historical-cost accounting model. However,
even if there were no inflation, there would still be variations in the
prices of individual assets, hence leaving the deficiency of the historical-cost records unresolved. Similarly, the general price-level
adjusted income statement may conceivably not reflect upon the performance of the firm. Under a stable pricing system, the conventional
income statement serves as a measure of the operating performance
of the firm, which can provide a basis for predicting future operating
income, with a view to assessing the firm's cash-generating ability.
In a period of changing prices, however, the conventional income
statement fails to match the current cost of operations against its
revenues. To the extent that the general price-level index does not
reflect the specific price-level changes of particular goods and services sold by the firm, the restated income statement provides a
measure of income that is difficult to interpret, even though it may
serve to reduce the "paper profit" from using the conventional historical-cost model in a period of general inflation. Because of the
dubious assumptions underlying the computation of purchasing power
gains and losses on holding monetary items, the inclusion of such
gains and losses would only produce a more confusing and potentially
misleading measure of performance.

SUMMARY

The historical-cost/constant-dollar model does not adequately
satisfy the key qualitative characteristics of relevance and reliability.
As pointed out earlier, because the restated historical-cost data
seldom reflects current costs or values, the HC/CD balance sheet
does not provide relevant data about economic resources of the firm.
Moreover, there is no conceptual basis to consider the HC/CD income
statement relevant. Because the purchasing-power gains and losses

on holding monetary items are improperly computed (see Chapter 9), such gains and losses are misleading. This is demonstrated by the fact that highly leveraged firms on the brink of bankruptcy wind up "looking good" under this model by showing substantial purchasing-power gains from holding debt.

To the extent this model is historical cost-based, it displays a high degree of verifiability. On the other hand, it fails the test of "representational faithfulness." It is not a valid indicator of financial position or operating performance. In this regard, there is reason to question the reliability of the model despite its high degree of verifiability.

The historical-cost/constant-dollar model enhances the time-series comparability of accounting data, by eliminating the measurement-unit problem inherent in the historical-cost model. In this regard, it is an improvement over the conventional historical-cost model. But, to the extent that the model still retains the historical-cost principle, the fundamental nature of the model still leaves much to be desired.

Considering the questionable relevance of HC/CD data, it appears that the cost of producing the data would exceed the benefits. In spite of its shortcomings, however, the HC/CD model has been seriously considered and sponsored by several authoritative accounting organizations. Both in the United States and abroad, it has been viewed as a supplement to historical-cost accounting and as an alternative to current-value accounting. In the United States, constant-dollar accounting has been advocated as a historical-cost supplement by APB Statement No. 3 (1969). In December 1974, the FASB issued an exposure draft which, had it been adopted, would have required supplementary financial statements in terms of general purchasing power. In England, the Accounting Standards Steering Committee issued in 1974 the "Provisional Statement of Standard Accounting Practice" (SSAP 7), which was similar to the FASB's exposure draft on constant-dollar accounting. In Australia, too, a proposal for a "Method of Accounting for Changes in the Purchasing Power of Money" was released in December 1974. However, in more recent years advocacy of constant-dollar financial statements has diminished in authoritative accounting pronouncements notwithstanding the required disclosures of FASB Statement 33, "Financial Reporting and Changing Prices," issued in 1979. It appears that there is some understanding today that constant-dollar accounting is no panacea for the problems of contemporary accounting. In England, the Statement of Standard Accounting Practice No. 7 was withdrawn in favor of current value accounting; in 1980, the Statement of Standard Accounting Practice No. 16, "Current Cost Accounting," was issued. In Australia, a 1974 proposal on "Accounting for Changes in the Purchasing Power of Money" was also dropped. Instead, the trend in Australia is now toward current-cost accounting as evidenced by the Statement of Provisional Accounting Standards, "Current Cost Accounting," which was issued in 1976 and amended in 1978, and the 1982 proposed standard on current-cost accounting. In Canada, an exposure draft on current-cost accounting was first issued by its Institute of Chartered Accountants in 1979 and later revised and reissued in 1981. Although the first Canadian Exposure Draft recommended exclusively current-cost-data disclosures to supplement the conventional financial statements, the second exposure draft and the 1982 Canadian Standard—"Reporting the Effects on Changing Prices"—also called for supplementary disclosure of the general purchasing-power gain or loss incurred from holding monetary items during a period of inflation. It should be emphasized that the Canadian standard does not require the restatement of nonmonetary historical costs into constant dollars.

PROCEDURES FOR RESTATING HISTORICAL-COST STATEMENTS TO CONSTANT DOLLARS

In preparing historical-cost/constant-dollar statements, the first step is to classify the accounts into monetary and nonmonetary items. Because monetary items are already stated in current end-of-year dollars, they should not be restated, except when comparative statements are prepared, in which case the monetary as well as the nonmonetary items from the preceding balance sheets should be restated to constant dollars at the end of the year. Also, if the balance sheet is to be prepared in terms of average-for-the-year-dollars, all end-of-year monetary items would have to be restated.

Nonmonetary items are restated by multiplying each amount by the following conversion factor: index for end of current year/index at the time nonmonetary items is acquired.

When the restatement to constant dollars is done for the first time, the process can be time-consuming. Each amount should be analyzed carefully to determine the amounts and the dates of transactions. In subsequent years, however, the restatement process becomes easier since the previously restated financial statements can readily be converted to the end-of-the-current-year dollar.

To illustrate the process of conversion to constant dollars, we present the simplified balance sheets and an income statement for ABC Company, Inc. We use the same statements to illustrate the application of the current-cost model and the current exit-value model. (See Exhibits 6.1 to 6.5.) The reader should refer back to this section when dealing with these models in subsequent chapters.

EXHIBIT 6.1

ABC Company, Inc., Balance Sheets
as of December 31, 19X1 and 19X2
(Historical-cost-basis)

| | December 31 | |
	19X1	19X2
Assets		
Cash	$12,000	$34,400
Inventory	19,200	29,520
Equipment cost	20,000	20,000
Less: accumulated depreciation	4,000	8,000
Net book value	16,000	12,000
Total assets	$47,200	$75,920
Liabilities and Stockholders' Equity		
Accounts payable	$ 7,200	$ 6,000
Stockholders' equity:		
Common stock	40,000	40,000
Retained earnings	-0-	29,920
Total liabilities and stockholders' equity	$47,200	$75,920

EXHIBIT 6.2

ABC Company, Inc., Income Statement for the
Year Ended December 31, 19X2
(Historical-cost basis)

Sales		$82,800
Cost of goods sold		38,880
Gross margin		43,920
Operating expenses:		
Depreciation expense	$ 4,000	
Other expenses	10,000	14,000
Net income		$29,920

128

EXHIBIT 6.3

ABC Company, Inc., Historical-Cost/Constant-Dollar Comparative Balance Sheets
as of December 31, 19X1 and December 31, 19X2
(In December 31, 19X2 dollars)

	December 31			
	19X1		19X2	
Assets				
Cash		$14,571.43		$34,400.00
Inventory		27,200.00		32,376.77
Equipment cost	$28,333.33		$28,333.33	
Less: accumulated depreciation	5,666.67		11,333.33	
Net book value		22,666.66		17,000.00
Total assets		$64,438.09		$83,776.77
Liabilities and Stockholders' Equity				
Liabilities:				
Accounts payable		$ 8,742.86		$ 6,000.00
Stockholders' equity:				
Common stock		55,666.67		56,666.67
Retained earnings		(971.44)		21,110.10
Total liabilities and stockholders' equity		$64,438.09		$83,776.77

129

EXHIBIT 6.4

ABC Company, Inc., Historical-Cost/Constant-Dollar Income
Statement for the Year Ended December 31, 19X2
(In December 31, 19X2 constant dollars)

Sales		$90,812.90
Cost of goods sold		48,784.52
Gross margin		42,028.38
Operating expenses:		
Depreciation expense	$ 5,666.67	
Other expenses	10,967.74	16,634.41
Current operating income/		
HC basis		25,393.97
Purchasing-power loss		
(see Exhibit 6.5)		(3,312.44)
Historical-cost/constant-dollar		
net income		$22,081.53

Note 6A: Basic Information

6A-1 ABC Company, Inc. was established on January 1, 19X1,
by issuing $40,000 of common stock, at par.

6A-2 Comparative historical-cost balance sheets as of December
31, 19X1, and December 31, 19X2, are given in Exhibit 6.1,
and Exhibit 6.2 presents the historical-cost income statement for the year ending December 31, 19X2. Additional
explanatory notes and supporting computations for these
statements are given in Notes 6-1 and 6-2, respectively.

6A-3 Assume that there was a steady general price-level increase
in 19X2. The Consumer Price Index (CPI-U) steadily increased from 140 in December 19X1 to 170 in December
19X2. The CPI-U in December 19X0 was 120.

6A-4 Assume that the ABC Company sales are all cash and that
purchases are also made in cash. For simplicity, assume
that there is no income tax and that the ABC Company has
not declared any dividends in 19X2.

6A-5 Assume that ABC Company uses the first-in, first-out
(FIFO) method of inventory valuation.

6A-6   6,000 units of inventory were purchased on June 30, 19X2, at a unit cost of $8.20.

6A-7   7,200 units were sold in 19X2, generating sales revenue of $82,800. Sales were made evenly throughout the year, during which time selling prices were adjusted to reflect increasing inventory prices.

6A-8   Operating expenses amounting $10,000 were incurred uniformly throughout the year.

6A-9   ABC Company acquired its equipment in January 1, 19X1, at a cost of $20,000. The equipment has an expected life of five years and no salvage value. The equipment is to be depreciated on a straight-line basis.

EXHIBIT 6.5

ABC Company, Inc., Computation of Purchasing-Power Gain or Loss for the Year Ended December 31, 19X2 (In December 31, 19X2 constant dollars)

Net monetary items, January 1, 19X2 (cash–accounts payable):		
($12,000 – 7,200) x 170/140		$ 5,828.57
Add: (sources of monetary items)		
Cash receipts from sales $82,800 x 170/155		90,812.90
		$96,641.47
Deduct: (uses of monetary items)		
Cash payments for purchases		
$6,000 x $8.20 x 170/155	$53,961.29	
Cash payments for other expenses		
$10,000 x 170/155	10,967.74	64,929.03
Net monetary item balance required to keep up with inflation		31,712.44
Actual net monetary item balance on December 31, 19X2		
($34,400 cash – $6,000 accounts payable)		28,400.00
Net purchasing-power loss from holding a net monetary asset position during inflation		$ (3,312.44)

Note 6-1: Explanatory Notes and Supporting Computations
for the Historical-Cost Balance Sheet Presented in Exhibit 6.1.

6-1-A. Cash
(a) The December 31, 19X1, cash balance is given.
(b) The December 31, 19X2, cash balance is derived as
follows:

Beginning cash balance, January 1, 19X2	$12,000
Add: Cash receipts from sales in 19X2	82,800
	94,800

Deduct: Cash payments for purchases in 19X2 (6000 x 8.20)	$49,200	
Cash payments given for accounts payable	1,200	
Cash payments given for operating expenses	10,000	60,400
Ending cash balance December 31, 19X2		$34,400

6-1-B. Inventory
(a) The December 19X1 inventory is composed of 4,800 units
that were purchased at the start of 19X1 at a unit cost of
$4.00. Thus, the ending inventory is 4,800 units at
$4.00 = $19,200.
(b) The December 31, 19X2, inventory is computed as follows:

December 31, 19X1, inventory	4,800 units @ $4.00
Add: Purchases in 19X2	6,000 units @ 8.20
Less: Units sold in 19X2	7,200 units
December 31, 19X2, inventory on FIFO basis	
(i.e., last-in costs are still here)	
3,600 units @ 8.20 = $29,520	

6-1-C. Depreciation for 19X1 and 19X2 is computed by taking one-
fifth of the original cost $20,000, hence $4,000 per year.
The accumulated depreciation is $4,000 and $8,000 by the
end of 19X1 and 19X2, respectively.

Note 6-2: Supporting Computations for the Historical-
Cost Income Statement Presented in Exhibit 6.2.

6-2-A. Cost of goods sold in 19X2, historical basis:

From beginning inventory	4,800 units @ $4.00 = $19,200
From 19X2 purchases	2,400 units @ 8.20 = 19,680
7,200 units total cost of goods sold	$38,880

Note 6–3: Explanatory Notes and Supporting Computations for the Historical-Cost/Constant-Dollar Balance Sheets Presented in Exhibit 6.3.

6–3–A. Restatement of Balance Sheet Items for the ABC Company

(a) Monetary items: Since the December 31, 19X2, monetary items are already stated in end-of-year dollars, these amounts are not changed. However, because we are presenting comparative balance sheets, the monetary items that appear in the December 31, 19X1, historical-cost balance sheet of ABC Company should be restated in terms of the December 19X2 dollars. The computation involved here is straightforward. Each monetary amount as of December 31, 19X1, is multiplied by the following conversion factor:

$$\frac{\text{End-of-current-year index} \quad (12/31/X2) = 170}{\text{End-of-previous-year index} \quad (12/31/X1) = 140}[6]$$

Thus, the cash on December 31, 19X1, is restated to $12,000 x 170/140 = $14,571.43, and the accounts payable on December 31, 19X1, is restated to $7,200 x 170/140 = $8,742.86.

(b) Restatement of nonmonetary items:

Inventory—December 31, 19X2. We have assumed that the ABC Company is using the FIFO method of inventory valuation; the ending inventory on December 31, 19X2, is composed of those units that were purchased on June 30, 19X2, when the CPI-U was 155. Therefore, the December 31, 19X2, inventory is restated to $29,520 x 170/155 = $32,376.77.

Inventory—December 31, 19X1. The December 31, 19X1, inventory is composed of the 4,800 units that were purchased at the beginning of 19X1, when the CPI-U was 120. Accordingly, the December 31, 19X1, inventory is restated to $19,200 x (170/120) = $27,200.

Equipment. The equipment was purchased at the beginning of 19X2, when the CPI-U was 120. Thus, the restated amount at December 31, 19X2 = $20,000 x (170/120) = $28,333.33.

Accumulated depreciation, December 31, 19X2 = 2/5 ($28,333.33) = $11,333.33. Accumulated depreciation, December 31, 19X1 = 1/5 x ($28,333.33) = $5666.67.

Common stock. Since the common stock was issued at the beginning of 19X1, the restated amount = $40,000 x (170/120) = $56,666.67.

Retained earnings. December 31, 19X2, and December 31, 19X1, on a constant-dollar basis can be derived as a balancing residual amount. The accuracy of the retained earnings balance can, however, be checked as follows:

Beginning retained earnings (HC/CD) balance December 31, 19X1	$ (971.44)
Add: HC/CD Net income for 19X2	22.081.53
Retained earnings (HC/CD) balance December 31, 19X2	$21,110.09[7]

Note 6-4: Explanatory Notes and Supporting Computations for the Historical-Cost/Constant-Dollar Income Statement of ABC Company Presented in Exhibit 6.4.

6-4-A. Restating of the Historical Income Statement in Constant Dollars

(a) In restating the income statement in terms of end-of-year dollars, those items such as revenues and operating expenses that are assumed to be incurred evenly throughout the year are restated using the average-of-the-year index. Hence, the appropriate conversion factor of the ABC Company is 170/155. Thus,

$$\text{sales} = \$82,800 \times 170/155 = \$90,812.90.$$
$$\text{other expenses} = \$10,000 \times 170/155 = \$10,967.74.$$

(b) The cost of goods sold amount can be restated to end-of-year (December 31, 19X2) dollars as follows:

Beginning inventory: 19,200 x 170/120	$27,200.00
Purchases (6,000 x 8.20) x (170/155)	53,961.29
Cost of goods available for sale	81,161.29
Ending inventory 29,520 x 170/155	32,376.77
Cost of goods sold	$48,784.52

(c) Depreciation expense: Since the equipment was purchased at the beginning of 19X1, depreciation expenses is restated to December 31, 19X2, dollars as follows:

$$\$4,000 \times (170/120) = \$5,666.67$$

6-4-B. Computation of Purchasing-Power Gain or Loss
on Monetary Items

The computation of the purchasing-power gain or loss on
monetary items involves a careful analysis of the beginning-
of-the-year monetary items and transactions related to
monetary items during the year. Although the amounts of
monetary items are, by definition, fixed, their value in
terms of general purchasing power changes. This requires
a restatement of the net monetary items at the beginning of
the year in terms of the purchasing power of the dollar at
the end of the year. All monetary receipts and payments are
then restated to the end-of-year dollars. It is generally
assumed, as in this example, that most sales revenues and
operating expenses occur uniformly throughout the year. In
converting such items, therefore, the average general price-
level index for the year is used. The purchasing-power gain
or loss for the year is, thus, determined by deducting the
actual net monetary assets at the end of the year from the
adjusted net monetary assets at the end of the year, the latter consisting of the restated beginning-of-the-year position
and the net monetary transactions during the year, all items
in end-of-year dollars.

The computation of the purchasing-power gain or loss
for the ABC Company is presented in Exhibit 6.5 on p. 131.

NOTES

    1. Comparative financial statements can also be restated to reflect base-year dollars. This means that current and prior statements would be "rolled backward" to show the purchasing-power units of the base year.

    2. It should be emphasized that FAS 33 calls for restatement of historical-cost data on a piecemeal basis, using the average-for-the-year CPI-U index. If comprehensive financial statements are optionally provided, then either the end-of-the-year or average index may be used.

    3. However, if average-for-the-year dollars are used, even the monetary items would have to be restated.

    4. E. S. Hendriksen, Accounting Theory, 4th ed. (Homewood, Ill.: Richard Irwin, 1982), p. 223. See also P. Rosenfield, "GPP Accounting, Relevance and Interpretability," The Journal of Accountancy, (August 1975): 52-9; R. R. Sterling, "Relevant Financial Reporting in an Age of Price Changes," The Journal of Accountancy, (February 1975): 42-51.

    5. See P. Rosenfield, "Confusion Between General Price-Level Restatement and Current-Value Accounting," The Journal of Accountancy, (October 1972): 63-8.

    6. See Note 6-3-A. for index information.

    7. $0.01 difference due to rounding error.

7

THE CURRENT-COST ACCOUNTING MODEL

INTRODUCTION

The current-cost accounting (CCA) model is a modified version of the familiar replacement-cost accounting (RCA) model.[1] However, the term "current replacement cost" (CRC) has at times been used to encompass both models.

The essential characteristic of the current replacement-cost model is the use of current entry prices as the basis for income measurement and balance sheet valuation. The RCA model has a long history dating back to the early 1900s, as our discussion on the historical evolution of inflation accounting in Chapter 2 shows. Despite its historical background, there are unresolved issues regarding the measurement and interpretation of current replacement cost.[2] There are also different views on the measurement of income using this model because of differences in the underlying capital maintenance concepts. These complications arise because of the need to account simultaneously for the impact of specific price changes and changes in the general purchasing power of the monetary unit.

This chapter presents a background discussion on the essential differences between CCA and RCA, followed by a description of the underlying conceptual basis of the current (replacement) cost model. Apart from the differences that are pointed out, the CCA and RCA models are identical. For ease of exposition, reference is made only to the CCA model in the remainder of the chapter. In those instances where a specific reference is essential, we identify the particular model in question. After presenting the conceptual basis of the CCA model, illustrative numerical examples, showing the CCA income statement and balance sheet are presented covering the different approaches that have been suggested by proponents of the CCA model. This is followed by a critical evaluation of the CCA model.

DIFFERENT INTERPRETATIONS OF REPLACEMENT COST

Differences in the interpretation of replacement cost accounting first surfaced in the early 1920s between Schmidt's and Limperg's models. In 1921, Schmidt developed a comprehensive replacement-cost model in Germany, which was based on the idea of physical asset replacement.[3] At about the same time, Limperg developed a replacement accounting model in the Netherlands. However, Limperg's concept of replacement cost was different from Schmidt's. Limperg advocated replacement of productive capacity, a concept which was based on the concept of "value to the owner" or "deprival" value.[4] Limperg's ideas on replacement cost are currently reflected in FASB Statement No. 33, "Financial Reporting and Changing Prices" (1979), and the United Kingdom's recent price-level accounting pronouncement, SSAP 16 (1980), as well as the Canadian pronouncement (1982).[5]

Although it has been suggested that "among accountants, the current entry price of a resource is usually referred to as its current replacement cost,"[6] there are at least two possible interpretations of the current entry price of assets:

(1) Replacement cost of existing assets. This cost is defined as the amount of cash or equivalent that would have to be paid to replace the assets currently employed by the firm using identical assets. The replacement cost model first introduced by Schmidt and later developed by Edwards and Bell is based on this notion of replacement cost—i.e., current cost. Edwards and Bell argue against using the replacement cost of an equivalent asset that could provide similar service potential: "It is not the current cost of service provided by fixed assets . . . we wish to measure, but the current cost of using the particular fixed assets which the entrepreneur chose to adopt and is still using."[7] Although they recognize the problems involved in measuring the current cost of assets that are no longer manufactured, Edwards and Bell contend that "it will be misleading to use the price of the new, improved substitute product as a basis for determining the current cost of using the old one."[8] Instead, they have proposed the following solution:[9]

> Where no market exists for new fixed assets of the type used by the firm, two means of measuring current costs are available: (1) appraisal, and (2) the use of price index numbers for the like fixed assets to adjust the original cost base to the level which would now have to be paid to purchase the asset in question.

This interpretation of current replacement cost is essentially used by the FASB in Statement 33.[10]

(2) <u>Replacement cost of equivalent service potential.</u> This cost represents the cash or other consideration needed to acquire the equivalent service potential. This approach is particularly appealing in those situations where, due to technological changes, the assets currently used are no longer the most efficient available. Although Edwards and Bell have presented a comprehensive and rigorous analysis defending their version of a replacement cost accounting system, which essentially envisages physical replacement of existing assets, the concept of replacement of equivalent productive capacity appears to be more realistic in view of its assumptions regarding technological change. To elaborate:[11]

> A firm that wishes to maintain its physical operating capability is not interested in replacing resources in kind, but rather in replacing equivalent productive capacity. As improvements in technology are achieved, the firm will probably replace its present assets with technologically superior assets, and it is the replacement cost of the equivalent production capacity from the improved assets that is the relevant measure.

It is interesting to note that Paton and Paton had expressed a similar view over thirty years ago:[12]

> It should be understood that the significant replacement cost is the cost of providing the existing capacity to produce in terms of the most up-to-date methods available. Thus it is largely a waste of time to estimate the cost of replacing an obsolete or semi-obsolete plant unit literally in kind; such an estimate will never afford a basis for a sound appraisal of the property, nor furnish a useful measure of current operating cost. The fact of interest is what it would cost to replace the capacity represented in the existing asset with a machine of modern design. To put the point in another way, cost of replacing in kind as a significant basis on which to measure the economic importance of property in use only in the case of standard, up-to-date facilities.

This interpretation of current replacement cost was used by the SEC in its <u>Accounting Series Release No. 190</u> on replacement-cost disclosure.[13]

CURRENT COST VERSUS CURRENT REPLACEMENT COST

Although the terms "current cost" and "current replacement cost" are often used interchangeably, in particular instances their meanings could be significantly different. When an asset is to be replaced by an identical asset, its current cost and replacement cost are equal. For example, the current cost and replacement cost of inventories are the same to a firm, unless the possibility of a change in product line is considered. However, with respect to long-term assets, the two amounts could be significantly different from each other. Let us assume that a firm is currently using an old Model XYZ copying machine, which has the capacity to copy 50 pages per minute at a cost of 1.5 cents per page. If this machine were to be replaced today, let's assume that it would be replaced by the technologically superior new Model RST, having a capacity of 100 pages per minute and an operating cost of 1 cent per page. Given this situation, the current cost and the replacement cost of the copying machine could be quite different.

In the foregoing example, the current cost of the presently owned copying machine (Model XYZ) is the current purchase price of a used XYZ copying machine of the same age and in the same condition, whereas the replacement cost of the copying machine would be the current purchase price of the presently available copying machine—in our example, the current purchase price of the new Model RST copying machine.

In the event a used asset identical to the one presently owned cannot be obtained, the current cost can be estimated by adjusting the current replacement cost for differences in the production capacity and differences in operating costs. In the above example, the current cost of the copying machine is less than the current replacement cost because: (a) the production capacity of the presently owned machine is less than the production capacity of the new model that would replace it and (b) the presently owned old model has a higher operating cost and quite possibly a lower quality of output.

Appendix B to FASB Statement No. 33 (FAS 33) indicates the differences between "current replacement cost" and "current cost":[14]

> Current replacement cost is the amount of cash (or its equivalent) that would have to be paid to acquire the best asset currently available to undertake the function of the asset owned (less depreciation or amortization if appropriate.
> Current cost is equal to the current replacement cost of the asset owned, adjusted for the value of any operating advantages or disadvantages of the asset owned.

In regard to the difference between "current cost" and "current replacement cost," Appendix B to FAS 33 states:[15]

> Current cost differs from current replacement cost in that current cost measurement focuses on the cost of the service potential embodied in the asset owned by the enterprise whereas current replacement cost may be a measurement of a different asset, available for use in place of the asset owned.

In the absence of technological change, the "current cost" of an asset can be represented by its "current reproduction cost." Appendix C to FAS 33 defines "current reproduction cost" as "the amount of cash (or its equivalent) that would have to be paid to acquire an identical asset currently."[16]

According to the Canadian Institute of Chartered Accountants "current reproduction cost" is defined as:[17]

> the current buying price of a used asset of the same age in the same location and in the same condition as that owned, or the buying price of a new asset that has the same service potential as the existing asset had when it was new, adjusted for depreciation.

Assuming that an identical asset is readily available in the market, the reproduction cost could be the best measure of an asset's current cost. Also assuming the same asset is currently being produced, and that no technologically superior similar assets are available, then the current cost can also be determined from the reproduction cost of a new asset after adjusting for depreciation. In other words, for example, a company presently owns a model XYZ copying machine. This would mean that one can determine the current cost of the presently owned machine from the cost of manufacturing a new model XYZ machine and adjusting the cost for the depreciation of the presently owned machine.

It should be noted, however, that under certain circumstances the reproduction cost of an asset may not be a relevant measure of the current cost. In light of technological changes, reproducing a 1945 model car would be too costly. Thus, in order to determine the current cost of such a car, one would rely on the current replacement cost of a vehicle that would provide comparable service and adjust that cost for differences in age and differences in quality of service in addition to any operating cost savings associated with the new automobile.

Given that we have the reproduction cost of an identical asset, which is either readily available in the market in the same condition as the one owned or that can easily be reproduced new, then the current cost of a presently owned asset can be determined from its reproduction cost. However, in these instances where due to technological changes the same asset is no longer manufactured and no identical asset exists in the market, then the current cost of the asset owned is determined from current replacement cost—"the amount . . . that would have to be paid to acquire currently the best asset available to undertake the function of the asset owned . . . adjusted for the value of any operating advantages or disadvantages of the asset owned."[18]

As the foregoing discussion shows, there is a considerable difference in the meaning and interpretation of current cost and current replacement cost. One of the major differences between the current-cost data required by FAS 33 and the SEC's Replacement Disclosure Rule is related to the fact that FAS 33 "emphasizes measurement of the <u>assets owned</u> by the enterprise, whereas [SEC's] ASR 190 focuses attention on the assets that would <u>replace those owned</u> if replacement were to occur currently."[19] It is probably true that the need to draw a clearer distinction between current cost and current replacement cost was an outcome of the problems that had been raised in implementation of the SEC's Replacement Cost Disclosure Rule.[20] According to the definition given by the SEC:[21]

> Replacement cost is the lowest amount that would have to be paid in the normal course of business to obtain a new asset of equivalent operating or productive capacity.

A study of the replacement-cost disclosures pursuant to the SEC rule indicated there was a considerable disparity in the methods used to arrive at the replacement cost data.[22] One problem frequently cited that has reportedly led to such divergent approaches was the interpretation of the concept of the "current replacement cost of productive capacity." Several interpretations were used. Some construed the term "replacement cost of productive capacity" to mean "the most reasonable cost in dollars . . . required to replace existing facilities with facilities of equal capacity consistent with the type and style of production facilities the company is currently acquiring or consistent with the type and style it would acquire in the normal course of business."[23] Others interpreted replacement cost to be "the lowest cost required to replace existing productive capacity."[24] And still others viewed the term in reference to the replacement cost of all productive capacity at the balance sheet date. These interpretations—especially the last one—were a source of confusion, responsible for generating considerable criticism against the SEC's new rule.[25] Since it is inconceivable that a firm would replace all of its productive capacity at one time, the resulting data were regarded as hypothetical and, therefore, less meaningful, as the following note accompanying such replacement cost disclosures indicates:[26]

> Although the replacement cost data herein disclosed has, in the Corporation's view, been estimated in a reasonable manner, it is the opinion of management that these data are of no value because of the subjectivity necessarily involved in making these estimates, and because the concept is based on an unrealistic premise, i.e., the total replacement of all productive capacity at one time. [Emphasis added]

The validity and relevance of the disclosed data were also questioned because, in implementing the rule, most firms did not take into account the expected cost savings of replacing existing plant facilities with more efficient productive assets. Most companies indicated that they were unable to quantify such cost savings, and, therefore, refrained from attempting to provide estimates of such amounts.[27] Moreover, the preparers expressed serious reservations in their disclosures concerning the uncertainty and subjectivity of the data reported.[28] This problem was manifest by the time FAS 33 was issued, and thus the emphasis in FAS 33 has been on requiring current costs rather than current replacement costs. The same trend is now visible in Canada, the United Kingdom, and Australia.

BALANCE SHEET UNDER THE CURRENT-COST ACCOUNTING MODEL

Assets. In light of the foregoing discussion pertaining to the "current-cost" concept, the following approach is used as the basis for asset valuation, under the CCA model:

1. As a general rule, assets should be valued at the current cost of obtaining the same or equivalent services of the assets owned.
2. In those instances where there is an established market for assets of like kind and condition, the purchase price of such assets should be used to reflect the current cost of the assets owned: Such prices may be readily available for inventories, land, buildings, and certain types of equipment.
3. Where there is no established market for assets of like kind and condition, current costs may be estimated by reference to the purchase price of assets, which provide equivalent service capacity. The purchase price of such replacement assets should

be adjusted for differences in operating characteristics such as as cost, capacity, and quality.

4. In other cases, adjustment of historical cost by the use of specific price indexes may provide acceptable approximations of current cost.

Liabilities. There are at least two views with regard to the valuation of liabilities in the CCA model. One view is that liabilities should be valued at "an amount equal to the proceeds that would be received at the present time if a debt with equivalent payment requirements were incurred."[29] The other view calls for the reporting of liabilities based on their contractual amounts since liabilities represent fixed monetary claims to the resources of the entity. That assets should be valued at their current costs, in contrast to liabilities, which ought to be reflected at their original contractual amounts, should not be considered as an inconsistency in the application of the CCA model. Instead, it should be noted that the model is consistent because it deals only with the valuation of the assets of the entity. To the extent that common stock is not valued at the current market price of the stock, the same treatment is applied to debt, by ignoring its market price.

Income Measurement

Given that income is the amount that the corporation can distribute to the stockholders without encroaching upon its capital, the key factor in the income measurement process becomes the definition of capital that the corporation needs to maintain. Income under the CCA model, therefore, depends on whether one is concerned with maintaining intact (a) the financial capital or (b) the physical productive capital of the firm.

Income under Financial Capital Maintenance

According to the financial capital maintenance concept, income is defined as the amount that can be distributed while maintaining intact the firm's beginning-of-the-year money (financial) capital. Under the CCA model, the financial capital at any given time can be measured by valuing the assets of the firm at the current cost at that time. One can, therefore, determine the income for the period by comparing the beginning and ending financial capital of the firm, assuming there were no withdrawals or additional capital investments by the stockholders during the period.[30] Exhibit 7.1 provides comparative balance sheets of ABC Company on the current cost basis as of December 31, 19X1

EXHIBIT 7.1

ABC Company, Inc., Balance Sheets as of December 31, 19X1
and December 31, 19X2 (Measured in nominal dollars)
(Current-cost basis)

	December 31	
	19X1	19X2
Assets		
Cash	$12,000	$34,400
Inventory	33,600	33,840
Equipment (net)	17,600	15,000
Total assets	$63,200	$83,240
Liabilities and Stockholders' Equity		
Liabilities:		
Accounts payable	$ 7,200	$ 6,000
Stockholders' equity:		
Capital stock	40,000	40,000
Retained earnings	16,000	37,240
Total liabilities and stockholders' equity	$63,200	$83,240

(a detailed explanation of which is presented later). From these balance sheets, one can note that the financial capital of ABC Company, i.e., total assets minus total liabilities on the current-cost basis is equal to ($63,200 - $7,200) = $56,000, and ($83,240 - $6,000) = $77,240, on December 31, 19X1, and December 31, 19X2, respectively. Assuming that there were no additional investments or distributions to owners (dividends) during the year, a comparison of the financial capital of ABC Company at the two different dates indicates that ABC Company earned an income of $21,240 ($77,240 - $56,000). Assuming the firm has adequate cash resources, ABC Company can afford to distribute $21,240 as dividends to the owners at the end of the year and still be able to maintain its starting financial capital of $56,000 ($77,240 - 21,240).

The balance sheet approach discussed above provides an aggregate measure of income for the period by comparing financial capital of the firm on the CCA basis at the beginning and the end of the year. The same result should also be obtained from the CCA income statement. Exhibit 7.2, presents a CCA income statement for ABC Company

EXHIBIT 7.2

ABC Company, Inc., Income Statement for the Year Ended
December 31, 19X2
(Current-cost basis)

Sales		$82,800
Cost of goods sold		59,040
Gross margin		23,760
Depreciation expense	$ 4,700	
Other expense	10,000	14,700
Current-cost operating income		9,060
Add: realized holding gain on inventory	20,160	
realized holding gain (cost saving)		
on equipment depreciation	700	
Total realized holding gain		20,860
Current-cost operating income plus		
realized holding gain		29,920
Unrealized holding gain:		
at 12/31/X2	7,320	
at 1/1/X2	16,000	
Decrease in unrealized holding gain		(8,680)
Current cost based net income		$21,240

for the year ending December 31, 1982. The income statement shows
that the current income for the year is $21,240, which equals the
amount found using the balance sheet approach presented above. The
income statement, however, presents a detailed breakdown of the
components of the income for the year in terms of: (1) the current
cost operating income, (2) the realized holding gains or losses on
inventory sold and long-term assets consumed during the year, and
(3) the change in the unrealized holding gains or losses during the
year.

The CCA income statement reflects both the realized and unrealized holding gains (i.e., cost savings) and losses separately. This
breakdown is intended to illuminate the results of the firm's operating
and holding activities. (This intention is evaluated later in the chapter).
A realized holding gain (loss) results from having purchased a resource
at one price, which differs from its current cost on the day the resource is sold or used. Realized holding gains reflect the spread between the acquisition cost of the asset and its current cost at the time
of sale or during the period of its utilization. Unrealized holding gains
(losses) reflect the difference between the acquisition cost of an asset

and its current cost at the end of the year. It should be noted that CCA net operating income plus the realized holding gains (losses) comprise the net income under conventional, historical-cost accounting.

The addition of the change in unrealized holding gains (losses) during the year to the CCA net operating income plus the realized holding gains (losses) equals the CCA net income. It is important to point out that the change in unrealized holding gains (losses), not simply the unrealized holding gains in the ending inventory and undepreciated equipment, belongs in the CCA income statement. The change in the unrealized holding gains represents the unrealized holding gain in the ending inventory and fixed assets (i.e., the net undepreciated balance) at the end of the year minus the unrealized holding gains in these items at the beginning of the year. If an asset is consumed or sold during the period, the realized holding gain on the asset would be the difference between its CCA at the time of consumption or sale and its original acquisition cost. However, if any part of this difference were recognized in a previous period as an unrealized holding gain, the total realized holding gain would serve to double-count the holding gain. Therefore, it is the change in the unrealized holding gain rather than the end-of-year unrealized holding gain that should appear in the CCA income statement. [31]

The foregoing income measurement process is consistent with the Hicksian approach, in the sense that the reported income can be distributed to owners while maintaining intact the financial capital of the firm. However, such reported income also includes unrealized holding gains, as shown in the CCA income statement (Exhibit 7.2), which represents a violation of the "realization" principle underlying the conventional accounting model. A strict adherence to the "realization" principle under the CCA model would provide an income measure identical to the income obtained from the historical cost (conventional) accounting income statement. The reader can compare the historical cost income of $29,920, shown in Exhibit 6.2 (Chapter 6), and the sum of the current cost operating income ($9,060) and realized holding gains ($20,860), $29,920, shown on the CCA Income Statement given in Exhibit 7.2. (More information and the computational basis supporting these figures is presented later.) The advantages of the CCA income statement relative to its historical cost counterpart are that it provides (1) a breakdown of the historical cost income into current-cost operating income and realized holding gains and (2) information on the holding of productive assets such as inventories and equipment.

Measurement-Unit Problem under the CCA Model

The foregoing discussion has implicitly assumed that the measurement unit used, the dollar, is a stable unit of measurement. Such

EXHIBIT 7.3

ABC Company, Inc., Balance Sheets as of December 31, 19X1 and 19X2
(Current-cost/constant-dollar basis)

	CC/CD amount expressed in 12/31/X1 dollars			December 31, 19X1 CC/CD amount expressed in 12/31/X2 dollars	December 31, 19X2
Assets					
Cash	$12,000	x 170/140	=	$14,571.43	$34,400
Inventory	33,600	x 170/140	=	40,800.00	33,840
Equipment (net)	17,600	x 170/140	=	21,371.43	15,000
Total assets	$63,200			$76,742.86	$83,240
Liabilities and Stockholders' Equity					
Liabilities:					
Accounts payable	$ 7,200.00	x 170/140	=	$ 8,742.86	$ 6,000.00
Stockholders' equity					
Capital stock[1]	46,666.67	x 170/140	=	56,666.67	56,666.67
Retained earnings	9,333.33			11,333.33[2]	20,573.33[3]
Total liabilities and stockholders' equity	$63,200.00			$76,742.86	$83,240.00

1. See Note 7-3-A in this chapter, p. 164.
2. See Note 7-3-B in this chapter, p. 165.
3. See Note 7-3-C in this chapter, p. 165.

an assumption is realistic in a stable monetary environment. However, even in an economy characterized by a relatively stable general price level, the cumulative general price-level changes over several years could be significant, making a comparison of dollars from different time periods misleading. Therefore, the Hicksian approach to income measurement, which involves a comparison of capital at two points in time will only be able to give us a meaningful measure of income if we were to use a constant measurement unit. This would require the restatement of dollars of different times into dollars representing equivalent purchasing power. Such dollars are referred to as "constant dollars." Dollars of different purchasing powers are restated into constant dollars using general price-level indexes. In the United States, the Consumer Price Index for All Urban Consumers (CPI-U) is currently used for purposes of preparing constant dollar financial statements. The procedure involved in converting CCA financial statements into constant dollars is demonstrated later in this chapter.

It should be noted, however, that under the CCA model, assuming that all nonmonetary assets and liabilities are stated in terms of the end-of-year current cost, the balance sheet reflects all resources and obligations of a firm in terms of dollars as of the balance sheet date. Thus, unlike the conventional balance sheet that aggregates heterogeneous dollars, i.e., dollars of different times having different purchasing powers, the CCA balance sheet consists of homogeneous dollars. Thus, no restatement into end-of-year common dollars is required in preparing a current cost balance sheet at the end of a given year. However, for purposes of comparability, previous balance sheets (i.e., at the end of preceding years) should be restated into constant dollars at the end of the current year or at the end of a base year (see Exhibit 7.3).

In preparing a CCA income statement, the dollars representing revenues, cost of sales, depreciation, and other expenses are not homogeneous, unless zero or insignificant inflation is assumed. If the dollars do not represent the same unit of measurement, one cannot theoretically perform any meaningful mathematical manipulation. Accordingly, the preparation of a current-cost/constant-dollar income statement is also illustrated in this chapter (see Exhibit 7.4), using the ABC Company example.

CURRENT-COST/CONSTANT-DOLLAR ACCOUNTING MODEL

The current-cost/constant-dollar (CC/CD) model is designed to resolve the differences of using nominal dollars in financial reporting. In this regard, it overcomes the two related deficiencies of the conventional accounting model, by (a) using current costs in lieu of his-

EXHIBIT 7.4

ABC Company, Inc., Income Statement for the Year Ended
December 31, 19X2 (Current-cost/constant-dollars)
(In December 31, 19X2 dollars)

Sales		$90,812.90
Cost of goods sold		64,686.55
Gross margin		26,126.35
Depreciation expense	$ 5,154.84	
Other expenses	10,967.74	16,122.58
Income from operations		10,003.77
Realized holding gains		
from inventory	15,902.03	
from depreciated		
equipment (loss)	(511.83)	
Purchasing-power loss		
on holding net mone-		
tary assets	(3,312.44)	12,077.76
Net income		22,081.53
Unrealized holding gain		
(loss) at 12/31/X2	(536.77)	
unrealized holding gains		
at 1/1/X2	12,304.76	
Decrease in unrealized		
holding gain		(12,841.53)
Net current-cost/constant-		$ 9,240.00
dollar income		

torical costs in the income statement and the balance sheet and (b)
using constant dollars in lieu of nominal dollars in financial reporting.

The application of constant-dollar reporting in a current-cost
model generates purchasing-power gains or losses from holding monetary items. Monetary items are cash and claims receivable or payable
stated in a fixed number of dollars. The amount of monetary items
held does not change regardless of changes in price. Because of this,
monetary items produce purchasing-power gains and losses as the
general price level changes. For example, suppose one were holding
$100 cash during a year in which a 10 percent annual rate of inflation
occurred. Such an individual would experience a purchasing-power
loss because the number of dollars held is fixed, and because of inflation the purchasing power of each dollar would be less. The individual
in question would be able to buy fewer goods and services at the end of

the year than at the beginning of the year. The same result would occur with any monetary asset held during an inflationary period. By contrast, holding monetary obligations during an inflationary period entails purchasing-power gains, because one would be able to settle obligations using cheaper dollars. (In situations where we have longer term interest bearing obligations, the computation of purchasing-power gains is not simplistic. This topic is discussed in Chapter 9). Thus, in measuring income under the CC/CD model, using the financial capital maintenance approach, the purchasing-power gains (and losses) on holding monetary items should be considered a component of income. The computation of purchasing-power gains and losses for the ABC Company is shown in Exhibit 6.5 (Chapter 6).

CCA Income under the Physical Capital Maintenance Approach

It should be emphasized that asset valuation, e.g., using the CCA model, and capital maintenance are two separate issues. The CCA model is neutral with respect to capital maintenance, and, therefore, the model does not necessarily conform to either financial or physical capital maintenance. The treatment of holding gains under the CCA model, which is discussed below, determines which capital maintenance approach is used—financial or physical.

The CCA income measurement process under the financial capital maintenance concept has been criticized for including both realized and unrealized holding gains as components of income. It is argued that such an income measure, if distributed as dividends, would impair the firm's ability to maintain its current level of operations. During periods of increasing prices, the firm's original financial capital would not be sufficient to support the same level of operating capacity. Accordingly, other proponents of the CCA model would favor the measurement of income under the physical capital maintenance approach.

Under the physical capital maintenance concept, income is defined as the amount that can be distributed as dividends to owners while maintaining intact the productive capacity of the firm. In order to maintain the existing level of operations, the firm should be able to replace the merchandise it sells and the plant and equipment it consumes in its operations at the prevailing current prices of these resources. By matching against current revenues the current cost of inventories sold and fixed assets consumed, a measure of income can be derived that may be distributed as dividends while serving to maintain the firm's normal operating level. This income measure is aptly referred to as "distributable" income.

Under physical capital maintenance, holding gains resulting from

increases or decreases in the current cost of productive capacity of
the firm are treated as capital maintenance adjustments, which cannot
be used for dividends without impairing the operating capacity of the
firm. Thus, the appropriate approach is to exclude both realized and
unrealized holding gains and losses from the income and reflect such
items as direct adjustments to stockholders' equity, indicating the
amount that needs to be retained in order to maintain the existing productive capacity. Since holding losses serve to reduce income, they
do not have to be reflected as capital maintenance adjustments. In
other words, the holding losses may appear in the income statement.

There is a difference of opinion among proponents of the physical
capital maintenance concept regarding the need for backlog depreciation, which arises when the current cost increases steadily. Backlog
depreciation represents the difference between the accumulated depreciation that would have been recorded based on the latest current cost
and the accumulated depreciation actually recorded. Those who favor
the disclosure of backlog depreciation argue that the firm would not
be able to replace its current production capacity through depreciation
charges unless amounts for backlog depreciation were reflected. This
position, however, is opposed by others, who contend that if a firm
had a regular asset replacement pattern, backlog depreciation would
be unnecessary. A discussion on this issue is provided in Chapter 4.

For a more comprehensive measure of distributable income,
some proponents of the physical capital maintenance approach have
argued for the inclusion of a monetary working capital adjustment
(MWCA) in the income statement. This argument is based on the
premise that firms have to hold a larger amount of monetary working
capital in order to sustain normal levels of operations during a period
of increasing prices. Thus, in order for a firm to maintain both its
physical and monetary working capital, a provision ought to be made
to reflect the cost of maintaining the increased amount of monetary
capital needs. This topic is discussed in Chapter 9.

Arguments against the Physical Capital Maintenance Approach

The CCA model under the physical capital maintenance approach
implicitly assumes that the firm is committed to staying in a particular
line of business. This assumption, in particular, has drawn strong
criticism against this version of the CCA model. One of the most vocal
and articulate opponents of this model is Chambers, who argues that:
"There is . . . in principle, no case for contending that the particular
assets must be replaced or that particular productive capacities must
be maintained by particular companies; or even for contending that the
ability to replace particular assets be maintained."[32] Among the key

assumptions underlying the model are that the firm will not change in any way, that all assets will be replaced, and that the firm will remain concerned about maintaining its productive capacity. The need for making such an assumption and the underlying wisdom behind this assumption have been seriously questioned:[33]

> There is no dependable relationship between physical capacities and financial costs or consequences. If there were, no trader would become bankrupt, no company would fail—and prices would remain the same as long as the physical capacities of goods remained the same. . . . In an endeavor to maintain earning capacity many companies drop whole segments of their business and switch to new operations; sell properties and rent or lease space and plant to release funds for increases in working capital. The replacement of existing assets has nothing to do with these changes.

A similar view is expressed by May, Mueller, and Williams:[34]

> In extreme cases the increasing replacement costs of productive resources may mean that the enterprise will in the future actually change its line of business and will therefore cease to have need for the type of service provided by the assets now owned. In these cases the replacement cost of such assets may be no more useful in arriving at relevant measures of enterprise performance and disposable wealth than are long outdated original values.

Another argument against the physical capital maintenance approach is that it denies owners the opportunity to make their own investment decisions by limiting distributable income to the amount that can be distributed after maintaining the same level of operating capacity.[35]

The CCA model, using physical maintenance, is also criticized for implicitly assuming that all the additional investment required due to the increasing current cost of maintaining existing productive capacity should be financed internally. To the extent that some portion of the productive capacity of the firm is debt-financed, a portion of the increase in the cost of maintaining a given level of productive capacity can theoretically be financed through debt.

When the current cost of the firm's assets increases, the debt-equity ratio of the firm decreases, which may make additional borrowing possible in order to finance a portion of the additional funds needed to maintain physical capital within a given debt-capital structure. In this regard, the CCA operating income tends to understate the potentially distributable income. To correct this deficiency, a gearing or financing adjustment is advocated. This adjustment is designed to reflect the benefit accruing to owners as a result of financing a portion of the assets of the firm through debt in a period of increasing prices. Such benefits, as measured by the gearing adjustment, can be distributed to owners if additional borrowing were arranged to maintain the original debt/equity ratio. However, to the extent that the firm is not always able to secure additional borrowings, the idea of treating the gearing adjustment as distributable income is questionable. An examination of the gearing adjustment is presented in Chapter 9.

EVALUATION OF THE
CURRENT-COST ACCOUNTING MODEL

The CCA balance sheet represents a substantial improvement over the historical-cost balance sheet on at least two counts. As discussed earlier, one of the major problems with the historical-cost model is adherence to the historical-cost principle despite changing prices. The longer the asset is kept, the more pronounced the price adjustment tends to be. Under such circumstances, the traditional balance sheet shows the amount the firm had to pay originally in order to purchase the assets or their equivalent service potential as of the balance sheet date, as well as the claims of the equityholders on the resources of the firm as of that date.

Theoretically, for a firm to be willing to replace its assets or their equivalent productive capacity, the discounted present value of the expected net cash inflows from the use of such assets must equal or exceed their current cost. An extension of this argument is that those assets whose replacement cost exceeds the discounted present value or their net realizable value should not be reported at their replacement cost, but rather at their present value or net realizable value, whichever is higher. (See Chapter 3 for an examination of these cases.) Revsine, however, argues in favor of consistent valuation of all assets at their replacement cost regardless of whether the replacement cost exceeds the present value of such assets, since such reporting would "alert the statement reader that in the long-run it is uneconomical to replace those assets."[36]

The relevance of the CCA balance sheet has been challenged by Chambers and Sterling. The fundamental argument of these authors is that valuation of assets at current cost does not reflect the financial position of the firm at the balance sheet date. In their view, the balance sheet should reflect the "current cash equivalent" or the net realizable value of the assets. In other words, they prefer the current exit-value model over the current-cost model. An analysis of the current exit-value model is presented in the next chapter.

The second advantage of the CCA balance sheet over the conventional balance sheet is the fact that the CCA balance sheet is measured in terms of a homogeneous unit of measurement, i.e., the dollar as of the balance sheet date assuming that all nonmonetary assets and liabilities are stated in terms of their end-of-year current costs as opposed to the historical-cost balance sheet, which reflects assets acquired at different dates measured at their historical-dollar amounts.

In order to evaluate the income figure reported under the CCA model, one has to specifically identify the type of income measure. As previously discussed, the following income statement format can be presented under the financial-capital-maintenance approach to the CCA model:

1. Current-cost operating income
2. Current-cost operating income plus realized holding gains, the total of which equals the conventional income figure
3. Net current-cost income, which includes the current-cost operating income plus realized holding gains and changes in the unrealized holding gains during the year.
4. Net current-cost/constant-dollar income, which includes the constant-dollar adjusted current-cost operating income, realized holding gains, and changes in the unrealized holding gains during the year as well as the general purchasing-power gains and losses on monetary items.

The CCA current-operating income is derived by matching against current revenues the current cost of inputs used in generating the revenues. This income measure is referred to as "distributable" income in the sense that it represents what can be distributed as dividends while maintaining the physical capital of the firm. To the extent that the productive capacity is maintained, the "distributable" income is also viewed as "sustainable" income, indicating the normal operating income that the firm can sustain in the future assuming operations are continued under existing conditions. In other words, at least theoretically, the current-operating income of one year can be viewed as a suitable indicator of the operating profit of succeeding years.[37] A countervailing view is that since CCA fails to reflect changes in technology, the CCA operating income can be used to forecast earnings of the firm assuming that no changes in technology will occur from year to year.[38]

The CCA operating income can be viewed as a potentially distributable income, which investors can expect to receive. In this regard, Revsine and Weygandt have argued that the current operating income "not only can be used to predict cash operating flows of the firm, but can also be used to predict dividends of the owners, thereby meeting the objective of providing information useful for predicting, comparing and evaluating potential cash flows."[39]

In measuring the distributable income of a firm, a more complete CCA model would also include a monetary working capital adjustment, which represents the additional financing needed to maintain an increased level of monetary working capital due to increased input prices during periods of increasing prices. Some proponents of physical capital maintenance have pointed out the need for a monetary working capital adjustment in order to ensure the maintenance of both the monetary and physical operating capability of the firm.

There is a considerable difference of opinion with regard to the relevance of realized and unrealized holding gains. On the one hand, it is argued that to the extent that holding gains cannot be distributed without impairing the operating capability of the firm, their inclusion in income is potentially misleading. From the investor's viewpoint, holding gains are related to past events and to the extent that such gains are not repetitive, their relevance in investment decision making is questionable.

From the financial capital maintenance viewpoint, holding gains represent an increase in the financial capital of the enterprise and are, therefore, considered income of the period. However, the problem with financial capital maintenance is that the inclusion of realized holding gains and the change in unrealized holding gains in reported income could serve to impair the maintenance of the existing level of operations if such income were distributed to owners. In this regard, the purpose of including holding gains is not clear.

Revsine, however, has presented an argument defending the relevance of holding gains under certain restrictive conditions.[40] Arguing that holding gains, which he refers to as "realizable cost savings," are relevant data in assessing future cash flow potential of a firm. Revsine asserts that increases in the value of assets are a reflection of the expected increased cash flows from using the asset. This argument is based on the assumption that the current cost of an asset represents the discounted value of its expected cash flows. In this regard, holding gains are viewed as "lead indicators" of expected increases in cash flows. The income figure, which includes holding gains, can, therefore, serve as a lead indicator of future distributable operating flows. As Revsine observes: "Since future distributable operating flows are a prime determinant of future dividends, the ability of replacement-cost [income] to act as a lead indicator for operating flows would make this concept highly relevant to the information needs of long-term investors."[41] However, the foregoing argument is only true if there is a parallel movement between expected future flows and the change in the current cost of the asset. This condition is not always possible, even under perfectly competitive market conditions, as Revsine readily admits. Accordingly, he concedes that the replacement-cost net income (which includes holding gains) is only a surrogate for economic income under very restrictive conditions. As such, its relevance as a "lead indicator" is questionable. [42]

According to Edwards and Bell, one of the advantages of replacement-cost accounting is that it partitions the income of a given period into: (a) current operating profit and (b) holding gains and losses. Edwards and Bell contend that such a breakdown of the periodic income is useful for assessing the performance of managers by making a distinction between results of operating and holding activities. This argument, however, has been disputed by Drake and Dopuch, [43] and Prakash and Sunder, [44] who contend that such a separation of income into operating and holding activities is impossible to achieve. Since managers can decide to purchase and hold inventory whose price is expected to rise, any holding gains that arise under such circumstances may reflect upon managerial prudence. Hence, to consider such holding gains simply a result of holding activity, which implicitly assumes events beyond the control of management, could be fallacious. In fact, treating additional costs related to holding inventory as part of operating expenses, while excluding the holding gains, could provide a misleading measure of managerial performance. Such a measure of performance tends to penalize prudent managers.

Reliability. Current replacement cost is supposedly a market (entry) price. In this regard, this cost can be viewed as a verifiable figure to the extent that the replacement cost does not depend upon a subjective estimate by management. On the other hand, when verifiable replacement costs are not available, the replacement cost data have to be subjectively estimated. Moreover, the process of measuring current-cost data by computing an equivalent-service potential as well as the process of measuring current-cost depreciation involves considerable subjectivity. In this regard, the verifiability of current-cost data could be seriously questioned—a factor that poses serious concerns about the reliability of the current-cost data. It should be noted, however, that in assessing the reliability one has to recognize the trade-off between relevance and reliability. To the extent that one can contribute to the relevance of the information with a reasonable loss in the reliability of the data, the trade-off should be considered acceptable.

Comparability. In dealing with the comparability issue of current-cost accounting, two factors are important to remember. First, a cross-sectional comparison among firms would be considerably enhanced since the balance sheets of various firms would reflect a common attribute—the current cost of the assets. However, to the extent that subjective estimation is involved in the measurement of current costs for those situations where verifiable market data are not available directly, then there is some loss of comparability of the conventional accounting figures. The second aspect in assessing the comparability of current-cost data is related to the fact the CCA model reflects a homogeneous unit-of-measurement (unlike the situation in the conventional, historical-cost balance sheets, which reflects the summation of dollars having different purchasing powers).

With regard to the interperiod comparability of the current-cost data, it should be obvious that unless one assumes a stable monetary situation over extended periods, which is unrealistic, current-cost data should be restated in terms of constant dollars to make the data comparable over time. This is a strong justification for the adoption of the current-cost/constant-dollar accounting model.

An illustrative example of the application of the CCA model using nominal dollars and constant dollars follows.

APPLICATION OF THE CURRENT-COST ACCOUNTING MODEL

The following is an illustration of the application of the CCA model in preparing CCA financial statements for the ABC Company, Inc. Exhibit 6.1, in Chapter 6, presents comparative historical-cost balance sheets for the ABC Company. ABC Company's historical-cost income statement for the year ending December 31, 19X2, is also presented in Exhibit 6.2 in Chapter 6. The reader should review the basic information and explanatory notes presented in Notes 6-A, 6-1, and 6-2, in order to follow the mechanics in the application of the CCA model. We demonstrate the application of CCA under both nominal and constant dollars. Application of current cost/constant-dollar income statement as per FAS 33 is demonstrated in Exhibits 7.5 and 7.6. Exhibit 7.7 illustrates reconciliation of current-cost/constant-dollar and historical-cost income statements.

Exhibit 7.1 presents comparative current-cost balance sheets, as of December 31, 19X1, and December 31, 19X2, measured in nominal dollars. Note 7.1 provides relevant current-cost information and supporting computations for the current-cost balance sheets presented in Exhibit 7.1.

Note 7-1: Current-Cost Information and Supporting Computations for the Current-Cost Balance Sheets Presented in Exhibit 7.1.

7-1-A. Inventory
        (a) The current cost of the 4,800 units ending inventory on

EXHIBIT 7.5

ABC Company, Inc., Income Statement for the Year Ended
December 31, 19X2 (Current-cost/constant-dollar)
(In December 31, 19X2 dollars) (Application of current-cost/
constant dollar income statement as per FAS 33)

Sales		$90,812.90
Cost of goods sold		64,686.55
Gross margin		26,126.35
Depreciation expense	$ 5,154.84	
Other expenses	10,967.74	16,122.58
Current-cost income from operations		10,003.77
Purchasing-power gain (loss) on net monetary items		(3,312.44)
Total change in current cost of nonmonetary items	12,180.00	
Change in current cost of nonmone-tary items due to inflation	9,633.33	
Changes in current cost of nonmone-tary items net of inflation		2,546.67
Net current-cost/constant-dollar income		$ 9,240.00

December 31, 19X1, was $7 per unit, as of December
31, 19X1; thus, the 12/31/X1 inventory balance is
4,800 x $7 = $33,600.
(b) The current cost of the 3,600 units inventory on December 31, 19X2, was $9.40 per unit, or a total of 3,600 x
$9.40 = $33,840.

7-1-B. The current cost of a new equipment, similar to that owned
by ABC Company, was $22,000 on December 31, 19X1, and
$25,000 on December 31, 19X2. The increase in the replace-
ment cost of the equipment has occurred uniformly throughout the year.
    Thus, the current cost of the ABC Company equipment
on December 31, 19X1 is computed by deducting 1/5, representing the depreciation for one year, from the current cost
of the new equipment, or 4/5 x $22,000 = $17,600. The net
current cost of the equipment on December 31, 19X2 is
3/5 of $25,000, or $15,000.

7-1-C. The retained earnings figure on the current-cost balance
sheets, as shown in Exhibit 7.1, represents the balancing

EXHIBIT 7.6

Computation of the Price Change Effects of Nonmonetary Items for ABC Company, Inc.,
for the Year Ended December 31, 19X2

	Current cost at date of transaction or balance sheet	Conversion factor	Current cost stated in 12/31/X2 dollars
Inventory, 12/31/X2: 4,000 units $7.00	$33,600	170/140	$40,800.00
Purchase 6,000 units 8.00	49,200	170/140	53,961.24
Deduct: cost of goods sold	(59,040)²		(64,686.55)
Inventory, 12/31/X2	23,760		$30,074.74
Inventory, 12/31/X2 at current cost of 12/31/X2	33,840		33,840.00
Total increase in current cost due to increase in current cost of inventory	10,080		$ 3,765.26
Changes in current cost due to general inflation ($30,074.74 − $23,760)		$6,314.74	
Changes in current cost net of inflation ($33,840 − $30,074.74)			
Equipment			
Net CC balance 12/31/X1	17,600	170/140	21,373.43
Deduct: 19X2 CC depreciation	4,700	170/155	5,154.84
Ending balance at CC	12,900		16,218.59
Net CC balance at 12/31/X2	15,000		15,000.00
Total increase in CC	$ 2,100		$(1,218.59)
Change in CC due to general inflation ($16,218.59 − $12,900)		$3,318.59	
Change in CC of equipment net of general inflation			

Summary of Price Effects on Nonmonetary Items of ABC Company for 19X2

	Change in current cost	Change in CC due to general inflation	Change in CC net of general inflation
Inventory	$10,080	$6,314.74	$ 3,765.26
Equipment	2,100	3,318.59	(1,218.59)
Total	$12,180	$9,633.33	$ 2,546.67

1. See Note 7-2-B in this chapter.
2. See Note 7-4-B in this chapter.

EXHIBIT 7.7

ABC Company, Inc., Reconciliation of Current-Cost/Constant-Dollar and Historical Cost Income Statements for the Year Ended December 31, 19X2 (In end-of-year dollars)

	HC/CD	CC adjustment realized holding gains	CC/CD
Revenue	$90,812.90	$ -0-	$90,812.90
Cost of goods sold	48,784.52	15,902.03	64,686.55
Depreciation expense	5,666.67	(323.81)	5,342.86
Other expenses	10,967.74	-0-	10,967.74
Total expenses	$65,418.93	$15,578.22	$80,997.15
Current operating income	25,393.97		9,815.75
Purchasing power loss	(3,312.44)		(3,312.44)
	22,081.53		6,503.31
Realized holding gain	-0-	15,578.22	15,578.22
Net historical-cost income	$22,081.53		$22,081.53
Unrealized holding gains at 12/31/X2 Inventory[1]		1,463.23	
Equipment[1]		(2,000.00)	
Total at 12/31/X2 in 12/X2 dollars		(536.77)	
Unrealized holding gains, CC/CD basis, at 12/31/X1 Inventory[2]		13,600.00	
Equipment[2]		(1,295.24)	
Total at 12/31/X1 in 12/X2 dollars		$12,304.76	
Total decrease in unrealized holding gains in constant dollars			(12,841.53)
Net income on current-cost/constant-dollar basis			$ 9,240.00

1. See Note 7-4-G in this chapter.
2. See Note 7-4-F in this chapter.

residual amount after all other nonmonetary items in the
balance sheet have been reported at current cost. This balance can be checked by preparing an analysis of the impact
of restating the nonmonetary items on the current cost basis
plus any reported current cost income for the period.

For ABC Company, the retained earnings balance on
December 31, 19X1, is composed of the unrealized holding
gain on December 31, 19X1, inventory and the undepreciated
equipment balance, which resulted from the increase in the
current cost of these items relative to the original cost of
acquisition.

Thus, the December 31, 19X1, retained earnings balance is computed as follows:

(a) Unrealized holding gain
on inventory, $\qquad$ 4,800($7-4) = $14,400
(b) Unrealized holding gain on undepreciated equipment: 12/31/X1,
Net CC balance—12/31/X1
Net HC balance $\qquad$ ($17,600 - $16,000) = $\underline{1,600}$
$\overline{\$16,000}$

Similarly, the December 31, 19X2, retained earnings
balance can be verified as follows:

Retained earnings balance, 12/31/X1 $16,000
Add: CC net income for 19X2 (see Exhibit 7.2) $\underline{21,240}$
Retained earnings balance, 12/31/X2 $\overline{\$37,240}$

It can also be shown, from Exhibit 7.2, that the
December 31, 19X2, retained earnings balance is composed
of the following:

Realized income in 19X2:
Current operating income $ 9,060
19X2 realized holding gain $\underline{20,860}$
19X2 Total Realized Income $29,920
Unrealized holding gain, 12/31/X2 (Note 7-2-G) $\underline{7,320}$
Retained earnings balance, 12/31/X2 $\overline{\$37,240}$

Note 7-2: Supporting Computations for the ABC Company
Current-Cost Income Statement Presented in Exhibit 7.2.

7-2-A.   Under the current-cost model, the sales revenue is equal to
the historical-cost sales revenue reported for the period,
thus, $82,800.

7-2-B.   Cost of goods sold—current-cost basis:
Given that the current cost of inventory was $7 on 12/31/X1,

and \$9.40 on 12/31/X2, and that the increase occurred uniformly throughout the year at the rate of \$0.20 per month, the average current cost of inventory sold during the year is $1/2 (7 + 9.40) = \$8.20$. Recall that sales occurred uniformly throughout the year. Thus, the current cost of goods sold at the time they were actually sold was \$8.20 per unit. Hence, the total current cost of goods sold in 19X2 is equal to: 7,200 units sold x \$8.20 = \$59,040.

7-2-C. Depreciation expense—current-cost basis:
The current cost of the ABC Company equipment increased from \$22,000 to \$25,000 during the year. This provides an average current cost of the equipment for 19X2 of \$23,500. Since the equipment is expected to last five years and is not expected to have any salvage value, it is assumed that 1/5 of the equipment is depreciated in 19X2. Thus, depreciation for 19X2 is equal to \$4,700 (1/5 of \$23,500).

7-2-D. Realized holding gain on inventory:
A realized holding gain is measured by the difference between the current cost of the inventory at the time of sale and the acquisition price of the inventory.

The total goods sold is composed of two batches, that is, 4,800 units from the beginning inventory, with an original cost of \$4, and 2,400 units from the June 30, 19X2, purchases at an acquisition cost of \$8.20 per unit.

Given that the 7,200 units are sold uniformly throughout the year, the monthly sales is 600 units. Hence, the first batch of 4,800 units from the beginning inventory was sold from January 1 through August 31, 19X2, whereas the remaining batch—2,400 units—was sold from September 1 through December 31, 19X2.

The current cost of January 1, 19X2, is assumed to be \$7. Given that the current cost increased uniformly at \$0.20 per month, the current cost on August 31, 19X2, is equal to \$8.60 (i.e., \$7 + [\$0.20 x 8]). Thus, the average current cost in the first eight months is equal to \$7.80 $(1/2 [7 + 8.60])$; whereas, the average current cost at time of sale for the 2,400 units sold, is \$9, that is, 1/2 (\$8.60, September 1, + \$9.40, December 31).

Thus, the realized holding gain on inventory sold in 19X2 is equal to:

$$
\begin{array}{rl}
4,800 \ (\$7.80 - 4) = & \$18,240 \\
2,400 \ (\$9 - 8.20) = & \underline{1,920} \\
\text{Total realized holding gain, 19X2} & \underline{\$20,160}
\end{array}
$$

7-2-E. Realized holding gain (cost savings) on equipment depreciated in 19X2, on a current cost basis:

Depreciation on CC basis (see Note 7-2-C.)	$ 4,700
Depreciation on HC basis (1/5 x $20,000)	4,000
Realized holding gain on depreciated equipment in 19X2	$ 700

7-2-F. Unrealized holding gains, January 1, 19X2:
On beginning inventory: 4,800 units, current cost on 1/1/X2, $7 and original acquisition cost, $4, thus

4,800 x ($7 – 4)	$14,400
On equipment: Net CC book value at 1/1/X2,	$17,600
and net HC book value, at 1/1/X2	16,000
Unrealized holding gain on undepreciated equipment	1,600
Total unrealized holding gain on 1/1/X2	$16,000

7-2-G. Unrealized holding gain, December 31, 19X2:
On ending inventory:

3,600 units x ($9.40 – 8.20)	$ 4,320
On equipment: 3/5 x ($25,000 – 20,000)	3,000
Total unrealized holding gain, at 12/31/X2	$ 7,320

Note 7-3: Supporting Computations to the Current-Cost/Constant-Dollar Balance Sheets Presented in Exhibit 7.3.

7-3-A. The December 31, 19X1, balance sheet expressed in December 31, 19X2, dollars is obtained from the current-cost balance sheet shown in Exhibit 7.1. The only amounts that are different are the common stock, which was originally issued for $40,000, on 1/1/X1, is now restated in terms of 12/31/X1 dollars by multiplying the $40,000 by a restatement factor of 140/120, that is, the December 19X1 index divided by the January 19X1 index. Recall that the common stock was issued when the CPI-U was 120.

The retained earnings balance of $9,333.33 is obtained as a residual figure, but can also be verified as follows:

Unrealized holdings gains, at 12/31/X1, expressed in 12/31/X1 dollars:

On inventory, 4,800 units: ($7 – [$4 x 140/120]) =	$11,200.00
(note that the inventory was bought on 1/1/X1, when the CPI-U was 120, and the CPI-U on 12/31/X1 is 140)	

On equipment:

($17,600 − [$16 x 140/120]) =	(1,066.67)
Total CD unrealized holding gain on 12/31/X1	$10,133.33
Purchasing power loss on net monetary items	800.00
Retained earnings balance, at 12/31/X1 in 12/31/X1 dollars	$ 9,333.33

In preparing comparative CC/CD balance sheets on 12/31/X2, all items in the 12/31/X1 CC/CD balance sheet are restated by multiplying by a conversion factor of 170/140, that is, the 12/X2 index over the 12/X1 index.

7-3-B. Common stock, restated in terms of 12/31/X1 dollars = 40,000 x 140/120 = $46,666.67. Common stock, restated in terms of 12/31X1 dollars = 40,000 x 170/120 = $56,666.67. The retained earnings balance as of 12/31/X1, expressed in terms of 12/31/X2 dollars is obtained by multiplying the 12/31/X1 balance by 170/140, i.e., the 12/31/X2 CPI-U over the 12/31/X1 CPI-U, thus, $9,333.33 x 170/140 = $11,333.33.

7-3-C. The retained earnings balance of December 31, 19X2, can be obtained as a balancing item and can then be verified as follows:

Retained earnings balance, 12/31/X1, in 12/X2 dollars	$11,333.33
Add: Net CC/CD income of 19X2 (see Exhibit 6.4)	9,240.00
CC/CD retained earnings balance of 12/31/X2	$20,573.33

Note 7-4: Supporting Computations and Explanatory Notes of the Current-Cost/Constant-Dollar Income Statement Presented in Exhibit 7.4.

7-4-A. Sales: Since the sales revenue is generated uniformly, the historical-cost reported sales revenue figure of $82,800 is essentially measured in average 19X2 dollars. To restate sales figure into constant dollars as of 12/31/X2 requires multiplication by a translation factor of 170/155, that is, the 12/X2 index divided by the average index for 19X2. Note that the CPI-U was 140 on January 19X2, and has steadily increased to 170 by December 31, 19X2, resulting in an average index of 155 for 19X2.

7-4-B. Cost of goods sold: Considering that ABC Company uses FIFO, the cost of goods sold is composed of the 4,800 units from the beginning inventory and 2,400 units from the June 30, 19X2, purchases. Given that sales occurred uniformly, we can assume that the 7,200 units sold during the year were sold at the rate of 600 units per month. At this rate, the units in the beginning inventory were sold from January 1 through the end of August. The 2,400 units from the June 30 purchases were sold from September 1 through December 31.

The average current cost from January 1 through August 31 is determined by taking the average of the current costs as of January 31 and August 31. Recall that the current cost of inventory increased steadily at the rate of $0.20 per month, resulting in the August 31 current cost price of $8.60 (i.e., [$7 + 0.20 x 8]). Thus, the average current cost for the first eight months is $7.80 (i.e., 1/2 [7 + 8.60]). Also recall that the CPI-U has increased steadily from 140 in January to 170 in December 19X2—a 30 point increase, or an increase of 2.5 points per month. Accordingly, the index on August 31 is 160; therefore, the average price index during the first eight months was 150. This index is used to restate the average current-cost price to December 19X2 dollars. The average current cost for the last four months was $9, 1/2 [8.60 + 9.40]), and the average price index was 165, (1/2 [160 + 170]).

Therefore, the current cost of goods sold, stated in terms of December 19X2 dollars is equal to:

4,800 units @ $7.80 x 170/150	= $42,432.00
2,400 units @ $9.00 x 170/165	= 22,254.55
Total current cost of goods sold in 12/X2 dollars	$64,686.55

Note that, although the average cost for the year is $8.20, a short-cut approach of computing the current cost of goods sold by multiplying the units sold by the average current cost and then restating the resulting figure by the average index for the year gives a slightly different result: (7,200 units @ $8.20) x 170/155 = $64,753.55. The average current cost depreciation is $4,700 (see Note 7-2-C.) expressed in average 19X2 dollars. In terms of December 19X2 dollars, the depreciation for 19X2 is $4,700 x 170/155 = $5,145.84. (Or 1/5 [1/2 ($25,000 + 22,000)] x 170/155).

7-4-C. Other expenses: Incurred uniformly. Thus, to state in December 19X2 dollars: $10,000 x 170/155 = $10,967.74.

7-4-D.   Realized holding gains from inventory in 19X2, expressed in constant dollars:

In computing the realized holding gains in terms of constant dollars as of December 31, 19X2, two factors should be considered. First, the original cost of the inventory sold should be applied to the units sold, at the time such units are sold and then be restated in terms of December 31 dollars.

Recall that the goods sold are composed of two batches: 4,800 units from the beginning inventory, originally purchased in January 19X1, at a cost of $4 per unit; and 2,400 units from the June 30 purchases, at a cost of $8.20 per unit.

The first batch, 4,800 units, was sold from January 1 to August 31. Thus, the average current cost of these units was $7.80 (i.e., 1/2 of $7.00, January 1, 19X2, + 1/2 [$8.60, August 31, 19X2]). The average current cost, at time of sale of the next 2,400 units is $9, i.e., 1/2 ($8.60 September 1, + 9.40 December 31).

The general price index rose steadily from 140 in January to 170 in December 19X2. Accordingly, the CPI-U in August is 160 (140 + [2.5 x 8]). This means that the average index for the first eight months is 150, and the average index for the last four months can similarly be shown to be 165.

Therefore, the realized holding gain on the beginning inventory measured at time of sale:

4,800 units ($7.80 - [4 x 150/120])	= $13,440
The realized holding gain on the beginning inventory measured in December 31, 19X2, dollars: $13,440 x 170/150	= $15,232.00
The realized holding gain from 19X2 purchases measured at time of sale: 2,400 units ($9 - [8.20 x 165/155])	= $ 650.32
Realized holding gain from 19X2 purchases measured in terms of December 31, 19X2 dollars:	$ 670.03

Thus, the total constant-dollar realized holding gain from inventory in 19X2: $15,902.03

7-4-E.   Realized holding gain (loss) on depreciated equipment in constant dollars for 19X2: Current-cost depreciation in December 31, 19X2, dollars (see Note 7-4-B). $ 5,154.84

Historical-cost depreciation in December 31, 19X2, dollars $4,000 x 170/120   =   5,666.67
                                                                                       $ (511.83)

7-4-F. Unrealized holding gain at 1/1/X2, in terms of constant dollars as of 12/31/X2:

On beginning inventory:

(4,800 [$7 − 4 x 140/120]) x 170/140   = $13,600.00

On undepreciated equipment:

4/5 ($22,000 − [20,000 x 140/120]) x
170/140   <u>1,295.24</u>
                                              $12,304.76

7-4-G. Unrealized holding gain (loss) at 12/31/X2:

On ending inventory:

3,600 units (9.40 − (8.20 x 170/155))   = $ 1,463.23

On undepreciated equipment:

3/5 ($25,000 − [20,000 x 170/120])   = <u>(2,000.00)</u>
                                              $ (536.77)

NOTES

1. The term "current-cost accounting" has been used in recently issued standards dealing with reporting the effects of changing prices in the United States (FAS 33), Canada (1982), United Kingdom (SSAP 16), as well as the most recent proposed standard in Australia.

2. Schmidt and Limperg had different interpretations of the replacement price of an asset. While this point is briefly discussed below, a more detailed discussion is presented in Chapter 2.

3. See F. Schmidt, "The Basis of Depreciation Charges," Harvard Business Review, (April 1930): 257-64. For a detailed analysis of Schmidt's contributions to replacement-cost accounting, see R. Mattessich, "On the Evolution of Inflation Accounting—With a Comparison of Seven Major Models," working paper (Vancouver, Canada: University of British Columbia, 1981).

4. See Chapter 2 for further discussion and references on Limperg.

5. The recent Canadian pronouncement is identified as Section 4510, "Reporting the Effects of Changing Prices." This was issued in October 1982 by the Canadian Institute of Chartered Accountants.

6. R. G. May, G. G. Mueller, T. H. Williams, A New Introduction to Financial Accounting, 2nd. ed. (Englewood Cliffs, N.J.: Prentice-Hall, 1980), p. 544.

7. E. O. Edwards, P. W. Bell, The Theory and Measurement of Business Income (Berkeley, Calif.: University of California Press, 1961), p. 186.

8. Ibid.

9. Ibid.

10. FASB Statement No. 33, "Financial Reporting and Changing Prices, 1979, par. 17. For inventories, property, plant, and equipment, this statement calls for disclosure of the current cost or lower recoverable value (if current cost falls in between net realizable value and present value, current cost is used; should current cost exceed both net realizable value and present value, then the higher of net realizable value and present value would be used). For a discussion of the provisions of this statement, see Chapter 3.

11. May, Mueller, and Williams, A New Introduction to Financial Accounting, op. cit., p. 552.

12. W. A. Paton and W. A. Paton, Jr., Asset Accounting (New York: Macmillan, 1952), p. 325.

13. Securities and Exchange Commission, Accounting Series Release No. 190, "Notice of Adoption of Amendments to Regulation X-S Requiring Disclosure of Certain Replacement Cost Data," Washington, D.C.: U.S. Government Printing Office, March 23, 1976.

14. Financial Accounting Standards Board, Statement of Financial Accounting Standards No. 33. "Financial Reporting and Changing Prices," (Stamford, Conn.: September 1979), Appendix B, pars. 99 (c) and 99 (f).

15. Ibid., par. 99 (f).

16. Ibid., par. 99 (b).

17. Canadian Institute of Chartered Accountants, Re-Exposure Draft, "Reporting the Effects of Changing Prices," (Toronto, Ontario: CICA, December 1981), p. 12.

18. Appendix B to FAS 33, par. 99 (c) and (f).

19. See FAS 33, par. 17.

20. See A. Debessay, An Empirical Investigation of the Impact of Replacement Cost Disclosures on Capital Market Equilibrium: A Step Towards the Resolution of the Inflation Accounting Controversy, unpublished dissertation (Syracuse, N.Y.: Syracuse University, May 1979), pp. 72-5.

21. See Ernst and Ernst, "SEC Replacement Cost-Requirements and Implementation Guidance," Financial Reporting Developments, (Ernst and Ernst, 1977), p. 2.

22. See Debessay, An Empirical Investigation.

23. E. Barbatelli, "Implementing ASR 190," Management Accounting, (December 1977): 27.

24. Ibid.,

25. See E. J. Bailey, "The SEC and Replacement Cost: An Urgent Need to Find a Better Answer," Management Accounting, (December 1977): 19-22.

26. 1976 Annual Report, General Motors.

27. See Arthur Young, Disclosing Replacement-Cost Data (New York: Arthur Young and Company, 1977), p. 17. It is reported that few of the companies surveyed quantified potential cost savings, which is attributable not only to the sheer practical difficulties involved in so doing but also to the SEC's insistence that registrants be satisfied that reported savings are both "assured" and "reasonably quantifiable."

28. See Debessay, An Empirical Investigation. Several other "empirical studies" have also shown similar results.

29. May, Mueller, and Williams, A New Introduction to Financial Accounting, p. 551. This view is essentially based on Edwards and Bell's position with respect to the valuation of liabilities. See Edwards and Bell, The Theory and Management of Business Income, p. 239.

30. "Under this definition, reinvestment in the same or similar assets is not a necessary condition for income recognition (in contrast to physical capital maintenance), but is viewed as a separate financial management decision unrelated to earnings measurement. Management could choose to invest available funds in some other form. There is

no principle of financial management or of financial accounting which requires reinvestment of earnings in the same or similar assets." See R. A. Samuelson, "Should Replacement-Cost Changes Be Included in Income?" The Accounting Review, (April 1980): 254-68.

31. It should be noted that CCA income under the financial capital maintenance approach equals Edwards and Bell's "business income." Their format for computing business income, which follows, is, however, somewhat different from the income-statement approach presented in the body of the chapter:

(1) CCA operating income + (2) Realized and accrued holding gains (losses) during the year + (3) Unrealized holding gains (losses) accruing during the year = Business Income.

The differences between the two formats are as follows: Edwards and Bell reflect in their income statement only realized holding gains (losses) that have accrued in the current year, not realized holding gains (losses) that accrued in previous years. Consequently, in their approach, only the unrealized holding gains (losses) at the end of the year are added to the CCA operating income along with the realized accrued holding gains (losses) during the year. Under both formats, nevertheless, there is no double-counting. Since Edwards and Bell's framework includes only those realized holding gains (losses) accruing in the current year, the addition of CCA operating income and the realized holding gains (losses) in their income statement does not equal conventional, historical-cost income. The conventional historical-cost income is the sum of the CCA operating income and all the realized holding gains (losses) in the current period—whether accrued in this period or in preceding years. See Edwards and Bell, The Theory and Measurement of Business Income.

For a detailed analysis of Edwards and Bell's model, see their book (note 7).

32. R. J. Chambers, Accounting for Inflation: Methods and Problems, (Sydney, Australia: University of Sydney, August 1975), p. 81.

33. Ibid., p. 83.

34. May, Mueller and Williams, A New Introduction to Financial Accounting, p. 552.

35. Ibid., pp. 549-50.

36. L. Revsine, Replacement Cost Accounting, (Englewood Cliffs, N.J.: Prentice-Hall, 1973), p. 69.

37. This view has been advocated by several authors on the subject. Revsine (1973), and Revsine and Weygant (1974) have presented arguments that current-cost operating income is a suitable surrogate of a firm's expected future operating income. See also E. S. Hendrik-

sen, Accounting Theory, 4th edition, (Homewood, Ill.: Richard D. Irwin, 1982), p. 229.

38. See K. Lemke, "The Achilles Heel of Sandilands," The CA Magazine, September 1976.

39. L. Revsine and J. J. Weygandt, "Accounting for Inflation: The Controversy," The Journal of Accountancy, (October 1974): p. 75.

40. See Revsine, Replacement Cost Accounting, pp. 93 ff.

41. Ibid., p. 92.

42. Ibid., pp. 114-17.

43. D. F. Drake and N. Dopuch, "On the Case for Dichotomizing Income," Journal of Accounting Research, (Autumn 1965): 192-205.

44. P. Prakash and S. Sunder, "The Case Against Separation of Current Operating Profit and Holding Gains," The Accounting Review, (January 1979): 1-22.

8

THE CURRENT EXIT-VALUE MODEL

INTRODUCTION

As reflected in our discussion on the evolution of inflation accounting in Chapter 2, the idea of using current exit values as a basis for asset valuation has a long history. MacNeal, in his book <u>Truth in Accounting</u> (1939), made a strong appeal for exit values. [1] At present, Chambers and Sterling are among the best known proponents of this model. [2]

A current exit-value price is defined as the amount that could be obtained currently by selling an asset under conditions of nondistress, orderly liquidation. Chambers refers to this concept as the "current cash equivalent" of an asset defined as "the best possible approximation to the net selling prices in the ordinary course of business of those assets in their then condition as of the date of the balance sheet." [3] The current exit price of an asset is also referred to as the current net realizable value of an asset. This should not be confused with the <u>expected</u> net realizable value under conditions of present, as opposed to future, liquidation. In short, the current exit-value model advocates the use of current money equivalents or net resale prices as the basis for asset valuation. In contrast to the historical-cost and current replacement-cost models, exit valuation is based on selling prices, not acquisition prices.

BALANCE SHEET UNDER THE
CURRENT EXIT-VALUE MODEL

<u>Assets.</u> Using current exit valuation, the balance sheet reports the wealth of the firm by valuing its assets at their current net realiz-

able value or their current cash equivalent, i.e., at the best approximate net resale prices at the balance sheet date.

Liabilities. There are two schools of thought regarding the valuation of liabilities under current exit valuation. One school of thought advocates the valuation of liabilities at an amount that would be required to settle the obligation at the balance sheet date.[4] Proponents of this approach argue that in those cases where the firm has the option of redeeming a liability before the maturity date at an amount different from the face value of the obligation, the liability should be reported at its current cash equivalent. It is argued that this approach achieves internal consistency in the model since the same treatment is accorded both assets and liabilities. On the other hand, Chambers does not favor reporting liabilities at amounts other than the contractual obligations. Chambers argues: "Whether prices or price-levels subsequently go up or down, the money amount of a debt or claim is fixed in the ordinary course of events," and thus should be reported as such.[5] He insists that the balance sheet should indicate the "legal-financial interests" of the creditor at the balance sheet date.[6]

Income Measurement

There are two approaches to measuring income under each accounting model: the balance sheet and income statement approaches.

The Balance Sheet Approach. According to the balance-sheet approach, exit-value income for a given period is equal to:

Exit value (i.e., cash equivalent) of the net assets at the end of the period
Less: Exit value of net assets at the beginning of the period (assuming no additional investment or withdrawal by the owners during the period).

The above analysis is consistent with the Hicksian approach in measuring income, where income is defined as the increase in the wealth position of the firm due to its earning activities. By valuing all assets at their resale prices at the beginning and at the end of the period, the wealth position of the firm expressed in terms of the money equivalent of the net assets can be compared at two different points in time.

In a period of significant inflation, the dollars at the beginning and end of the period do not have the same general purchasing power, and, therefore, a direct comparison would not provide a suitable measure of income. Under exit-value/constant-dollar accounting, the beginning wealth position of the firm is adjusted to reflect dollars of equivalent purchasing power at the end of the period. The result is exit-value/constant-dollar income.

The Income Statement Approach. Another approach to income measurement under the exit-value and exit-value/constant-dollar models is to follow the conventional income statement approach, in which revenues and cost of goods sold as well as other operating expenses are accounted for at the amounts incurred. The formats for the exit-value and exit-value/constant-dollar income statements are provided below:

Exit-Value Income Statement

Sales
-Cost of goods sold
-Other expenses (except depreciation)
Subtotal
Add: Holding gains and losses (latest exit value
                                  -preceding exit value):
Inventories
+Equipment
+Land
Exit-value income

Exit-Value/Constant-Dollar Income Statement

Sales x appropriate conversion factor (to restate to end-
    of-year dollar)
-Cost of goods sold x appropriate conversion factor
-Other expenses x appropriate conversion factor
Subtotal 1
Add: Holding gains and losses (latest exit value minus
    preceding exit value restated for the end-of-year
    dollar using the appropriate conversion factor)
Inventories
+Equipment
+Land
Subtotal 2
+Purchasing-power gain or loss
Exit-value/constant-dollar income

GENERAL FEATURES OF THE
CURRENT EXIT-VALUE MODEL

Exit-value accounting has the following attributes:

1. It violates the realization principle. One of the distinguishing characteristics of exit-value accounting relative to alternative models is that it recognizes changes in the current cash equivalent value of an asset even though the asset has not been sold. In this regard, exit valuation is a departure from the conventional accounting model, in which income is reported only when it has been realized.

2. It disregards the going concern principle. The model values the assets of the firm at their current net resale value and as such does not rely on the going concern assumption. In conventional accounting, the firm is assumed to continue its normal operations in the absence of evidence to the contrary; no such assumption is necessary in exit-value accounting.

3. It avoids the allocation problem. One of the strong points of this model is that it avoids any arbitrary allocation of costs in measuring periodic depreciation under the other alternative models. Depreciation under this model, which constitutes an unrealized holding loss, is measured by taking the difference in the value of the fixed asset between the beginning and end of the period.

4. It possesses the additivity characteristic. The amounts shown on the balance sheet for assets can be properly added since they represent the same characteristic, i.e., money equivalents of the assets at the balance sheet date. Accordingly, all necessary mathematical calculations—such as computing ratios, percentages, additions, and subtractions—can be performed. This point is emphasized by Craswell, who claims: "A significant characteristic of exit-value accounting is the integrated measurement system whereby a single characteristic, the money equivalent of assets and liabilities is measured."[7] In stressing the importance of this characteristic he states: "[T]he measurement of a single property is an advantage for it means that the rules of arithmetic are complied with and the aggregate measure of assets obtained are capable of interpretation."[8]

EVALUATION OF EXIT-VALUE ACCOUNTING

In evaluating exit-value accounting, we apply the criteria for evaluating alternative accounting models that was discussed in Chapter 5. Recall that our evaluation process is based on two primary factors:

(1) assessing the extent to which a given model satisfies the objectives of financial reporting as set forth in <u>Statement of Financial Accounting Concepts No. 1</u> (SFAC 1), "Objectives of Financial Reporting by Business Enterprises" (1978), and (2) assessing the extent to which the desirable qualitative characteristics of accounting information identified in <u>Statement of Financial Accounting Concepts No. 2</u> (SFAC 2), "Qualitative Characteristics of Accounting Information" (1980), are reflected in the accounting data conveyed.

OBJECTIVES OF FINANCIAL REPORTING UNDER EXIT-VALUE ACCOUNTING

To assess the extent to which exit-value accounting satisfies the objectives of financial reporting, it is important to review its objectives. According to Chambers, the primary objective of financial reporting is to provide information that would enable interested parties to determine the "adaptive ability of the firm." Chambers argues that "[a]daptation is the dominant mode of economic behavior of persons and firms alike."[9] Exit-value accounting data provide a suitable measure of the firm's ability to adapt to changing economic conditions. Chambers maintains that it is only exit valuation that provides information about a firm's capacity "to go into a market with cash for the purpose of adapting oneself to contemporary conditions."[10] Following Chambers' thesis, a firm that holds assets having little resale value will have limited chances to take advantage of new business opportunities that might arise. In this sense, the current cash equivalent of the assets constitutes a measure of the flexibility of the firm.

Based on the foregoing rationale, Chambers' position is that the balance sheet "should represent the <u>wealth</u> at the command of a company and the respective legal-financial interests in that wealth at a stated date."[11] In Chambers' view, wealth should be defined as "the general purchasing power at a stated date."[12] In justifying his position, Chambers asserts:[13]

> Bankers, financiers, creditors, and analysts are interested in aggregate wealth, its composition and its growth; in the relationship of money available (or shortly to become available) and money shortly to be payable—the current ratio; in the relationship of the money amount of owners' equity in the net assets—the rate of return. None of these magnitudes or relationships is of any guidance or use unless the balance sheet does represent assets by their dated money amounts or dated money equivalents.

If one accepts Chambers' assumption, there should be little dispute about the relevance of accounting information generated by exit-value accounting. Neverthelsss, it is not necessary to completely accept Chambers' thesis to appreciate the relevance of the exit-value balance sheet for various purposes. In situations where there is doubt about the successful continuation of the firm's normal operations, exit values could be relevant to owners who wish to evaluate the wisdom of continuing normal operations versus the possibility of going into a new business venture.

The exit values of the assets can also be relevant to the firm's creditors. Although it can be argued that creditors are primarily interested in the continued successful existence of the firm, in order to maintain a long-term business relationship, exit-value data can provide relevant information that would enable creditors to assess the degree of protection they have in the event the firm cannot continue its present operations. Exit-value accounting is also considered useful in generating accounting information that is relevant in establishing a minimum value for firms that lack publicly traded stock—in takeover bids and purchase negotiations. [14]

To sum up, the data generated from exit-value accounting can be used as an indicator of:

1. The firm's wealth position as of the balance sheet date, as indicated by the cash equivalents the firm commands at the balance sheet date.
2. The firm's capacity to pay debts, dividends, interest, and the amount that could be distributed to owners if the firm were to undergo ordinary liquidation.
3. The net income calculated under this model can be viewed as a genuine income measured in the Hicksian sense, if one defines income as the amount that the firm can distribute to owners without encroaching the wealth position of the firm—wealth being defined as the general purchasing power of goods and services at the date of measurement.

RELEVANCE OF EXIT VALUATION
FOR POTENTIAL INVESTORS

In evaluating the relevance of exit valuation for investors, our approach is to examine the extent to which the model satisfies the information needs of investors as set forth in FASB Statement of Financial Accounting Concepts No. 1 (SFAC 1).

One of the primary objectives of financial reporting according to SFAC 1 is to provide information useful for assessing the amounts, timing, and the related uncertainty of prospective cash flows. Investors are presumably interested in the future performance of the firm—in terms of the firm's ability to generate favorable cash flows.

The FASB has not specified which types of accounting information (i.e., historical, historical-cost/constant-dollar, current cost, current-cost/constant-dollar, exit value, exit-value/constant-dollar) may be useful for potential investors. This issue is being studied as part of the FASB's Conceptual Framework Project. Nevertheless, SFAC 1 has called for information dealing with a firm's: (1) resources and financial obligations, (2) performance, and (3) sources and uses of cash, which are relevant for potential investors (par. 40).

The exit-value model does provide information about the firm's resources and obligations by valuing the resources of the firm at their current cash equivalent or current net realizable value, and the firm's obligations at their contractual amounts or their current cash equivalent. As previously stated, in the process of valuing a firm's resources at their current cash equivalent, certain assets that are expected to have favorable cash inflow prospects are valued at zero or at their scrap value if such assets do not currently have any significant resale value. One can contend, therefore, that the process of valuing assets at their resale value may not provide a suitable measure of a firm's resources from the point of view of investors, who are primarily concerned with the prospective cash flows based in the continuing operations of the firm.

Exit-value accounting also provides information about the performance of the firm. According to the exit-value model, income for any given period is measured by taking the difference between the aggregate exit prices of the net assets at the beginning and at the end of that period (assuming no dividends, withdrawals, or additional investments by owners).

One major problem with exit valuation is that it does not provide information about how the income for the period was earned and how much of the income stemmed from continuing operations. It is presumed, however, that investors need information about how past income was earned in order to forecast future earnings. In fact, the FASB has proposed that the earnings statement reflect disaggregated data.[15] The balance sheet approach to income measurement under this model provides an aggregate income measure, and to the extent that it does not provide a breakdown of the income components, its relevance for potential investors may be limited.

Chambers has shown that one can prepare a current exit-value income statement that provides some breakdown of the income figure. As L. A. Friedman has pointed out, however, such an income figure provides a mixture of book values and current exit values and does not provide a measure of income under normal operations.[16] To improve the relevance of the exit-value income statement, Friedman suggests the use of replacement cost within the context of an exit-value framework.

Viewed from the presumed information needs of potential investors, we find the current exit-value model deficient in providing a useful measure of a firm's resources and results from normal operations.

OTHER QUALITATIVE CHARACTERISTICS OF THE MODEL

The foregoing discussion has dealt with the relevance of exit-value data for various purposes. We now present a discussion of various other qualitative characteristics of the accounting data generated by exit-value accounting. In particular, our discussion deals with reliability and comparability of exit values.

Reliability

Generally, current exit values are actual current market values. Inasmuch as these values do not reflect cost allocations or future expectations, they are free from managerial bias, and, therefore, may be considered reliable. The exit value of an asset may be obtained through solicitation of special quotations. This approach, however, can conceivably introduce possibilities of manipulation. Chambers maintains that such isolated cases can easily be identified and checked for their reliability. According to Chambers, exit-value accounting is "the only system that gives up-to-date and realistic representations of financial position and results. It alone is free of the subjective choices of accounting methods and free of the subjective expectations of corporate officers."[17]

Although it may be true that the exit-value data is verifiable in particular markets (the more competitive, the better) and in this regard could be considered reliable, one can take issue with respect to the "representational faithfulness" of exit-value accounting. One of the desirable qualitative characteristics identified by the FASB in SFAC 2, "representational faithfulness," refers to whether the reported data represent the economic phenomenon in question.

According to exit valuation, assets that lack a ready outside market—such as work-in-process that cannot be sold before completion, certain specialized assets that lack a significant resale value, and intangible assets such as goodwill—are valued at zero or near-zero scrap value.[18] Although such assets may have a low resale value and hence a negligible exit value, it is obvious that such assets presumably have a relatively favorable economic value based on the expected future cash flows from using such assets. To the extent that exit valuation ignores expected future cash flows, its "representational faithfulness" and hence its reliability are questionable.

Chambers' view on this matter is that the valuation of specialized assets at zero is appropriate, and that such information is useful since it informs investors of the riskiness should the firm not be able to pursue its original intentions.[19] From this perspective, the "representational faithfulness" characteristic of the system is defended and hence its reliability also.

Comparability

Because the model essentially uses the same valuation approach in balance sheet valuation and in the income measurement from year to year consistently, the financial characteristics of a given firm over successive years can easily be compared directly in periods of monetary stability. In a period of fluctuating general price levels, however, one should convert prior-period financial statements to constant dollars. This can easily be done by restating prior statements into dollars having the same general purchasing power as the dollars of the most recent balance sheet date. From constant-dollar statements, an interperiod comparison can be made, including an analysis of trends over successive years.

Chambers is against the idea of completely restating exit-value financial statements to reflect constant dollars. In this regard, he contends that only his model avoids "retrospective corrections of or adjustments to previously reported figures."[20] Chambers considers the idea of speaking in terms of restated figures meaningless and confusing. In illustrating his point, he states:[21]

> If I had $700 in 1970 and $800 in 1972 . . . and if the general level of prices had risen by 50 percent in the interval, I do not say I had $1,050 of 1972 in 1970—there were no such things to have in 1970. . . . This is counter factual and . . . potentially misleading.

In spite of Chambers' position, however, complete restatement of financial statements to a common dollar in order to facilitate interperiod comparison is gaining support. The comparability of the current exit-value model, therefore, can be enhanced by using exit-value/constant-dollar financial statements.

Exit-value accounting also facilitates meaningful interfirm comparisons to the extent that all firms adopt the same rules in their valuation and income measurement approaches. That exit valuation does not permit a set of "generally acceptable" methods from which firms can choose and that exit valuation does not generate arbitrary cost allocations serve to make valid comparisons among firms possible.

SUMMARY AND CONCLUSION

The exit-value model reflects assets at their current cash equivalents or net realizable values, and liabilities at their contractual obligations as of the balance sheet date. Income can be measured by the difference between the aggregate exit values of the net assets at the beginning and at the end of the period (after making appropriate adjustments for any withdrawals or additional investments by owners). By valuing the resources of the firm at their current exit values, the objective underlying the model is to convey information regarding the "adaptive ability" of the firm.

Proponents of exit valuation argue that the net asset values generated by the model provide information about a firm's aggregate wealth position measured in terms of the purchasing power of the dollar at the end of the year. The income reflects an increase in the wealth position of the firm, indicating the amount that the firm can distribute to owners while remaining as well-off as it was at the beginning of the period.

The current exit-value balance sheet is regarded as relevant for creditors in assessing the degree of protection they have should the firm discontinue its current operations. Exit-value accounting also produces reliable information inasmuch as exit values are market selling prices. Exit valuation would also promote compatible accounting information if all firms were to follow the same approach in asset valuation and income measurement. Interperiod comparisons can be made by restating current exit-value financial statements in terms of constant dollars.

The major deficiency of the system is that it does not provide income from the continuing operations that can assist potential investors in predicting future cash flow prospects. It does not conform to the matching principle. Additionally, it does not adequately reflect the value, to the firm, of assets that lack a broad outside market.

ILLUSTRATION

To illustrate the application of exit-value accounting, we use the ABC Company example introduced in Chapter 6. The reader should refer to Chapter 6 for further explanatory information on the ABC Company, Inc. Exhibit 6.1 presents a comparative historical-cost balance sheet of the ABC Company, dated December 31, 19X2.

Assume that we have the following additional information that could serve as the basis for preparing comparative balance sheets as of December 31, 19X1, and December 19X2, according to exit-value accounting.

Additional Information on ABC Company

1. Assume that the current exit values of the inventory are $30,000 and $31,000 on December 31, 19X1, and December 31, 19X2, respectively.
2. Assume also that the exit values of the equipment owned by the ABC Company are $14,000 and $12,500 on December 31, 19X1, and December 31, 19X2, respectively. (These amounts represent cash that the ABC Company expects to collect, after deducting expenses related to the sale, if it were to sell the equipment it owned at the indicated balance sheet dates.)
3. Assume that the reported liabilities reflect the current cash equivalent of the obligations of the firm on the indicated balance sheet dates.

Based on the foregoing information, comparative balance sheets can be prepared, as shown in Exhibit 8.1.

Given the balance sheets displayed in Exhibit 8.1, the income for the year ending December 31, 19X2, can be computed by deducting the exit values of the net assets on December 31, 19X1, from the exit values of the net assets at December 31, 19X2. As shown in Exhibit 8.1, the exit value of the net assets of ABC Company on December 31, 19X1, equals $48,800, i.e., the total cash equivalent of the assets, $56,000, minus the current cash equivalent of the liabilities, $7,200. The exit value of the net assets of ABC Company on December 31, 19X2, is $71,900 (i.e., $77,900 minus $6,000).

Thus, the exit-value income for 19X2 is equal to:

Exit-value of the net assets at the end of the period	$71,900
Less: Exit value of the net assets at the beginning of the period	$48,800
Net income for 19X2	$23,100

For exit-value/constant-dollar accounting, in order to be able to directly compare wealth position of the firm at the beginning and end of the period, it is important to ensure that the beginning and the end wealth positions are measured in the same unit of measurement.

EXHIBIT 8.1

ABC Company, Inc., Balance Sheet as of December 31, 19X1
and December 31, 19X2 (Measured in nominal dollars)
(Current Exit-Price Basis)

	19X1	19X2
Assets		
Cash	$12,000	$34,400
Inventory	30,000	31,000
Equipment	14,000	12,500
Total Assets	$56,000	$77,900
Liabilities and Stockholders' Equity		
Liabilities:		
Accounts payable	7,200	6,000
Stockholders' equity		
Common stock	40,000	40,000
Retained earnings	8,800	31,900
Total liabilities and stockholders' equity	$56,000	$77,900
Proof:		
Retained earnings balance, 12/31/X1	$ 8,800	
Net income for 19X2	23,100	
Retained earnings balance, 12/31/X2	$31,900	

This can be readily performed by restating the beginning-of-the-period
exit value of net assets in terms of the end-of-the-year dollars. In
our illustrative example, this would mean restatement of the beginning
net assets to reflect December 31, 19X2, dollars. (See Exhibit 8.2.)

Recall that we have assumed that the general price index (CPI-U)
was 140 on December 31, 19X1, and 170 on December 31, 19X2. This
would mean that the December 31, 19X1, exit value of the net assets
of ABC Company would be restated to $59,257.14 (i.e., $48,800 x
170/140). Thus, to restate the beginning capital in terms of the end-
of-the-year dollar, we need to recognize a "capital maintenance adjustment," to use Chambers' terminology, of $10,457.14 (i.e.,
$59,257.14 - $48,800), based on a roll-forward of the beginning capital. The capital maintenance adjustment represents the amount that
should be added to the beginning capital, in order to convert the be-

EXHIBIT 8.2

ABC Company, Inc., Balance Sheet as of December 31, 19X1 and December 31, 19X2
(Exit-Value/Constant-Dollar Basis)
(In December 31, 19X2 dollars)

		19X1	19X2
Assets			
Cash	12,000 x 170/140	$14,571.43	$34,400.00
Inventory	30,000 x 170/140	36,428.57	31,000.00
Equipment	14,000 x 170/140	17,000.00	12,500.00
Total assets	56,000 x 170/140*	$68,000.00	$77,900.00
Liabilities and Stockholders' Equity			
Liabilities:			
Accounts Payable	7,200 x 170/140*	$ 8,742.86	$ 6,000.00
Stockholders' equity			
Common stock		56,666.67	56,666.67
Retained earnings		2,590.47	15,233.33
Total liabilities and stockholders' equity		$68,000.00	$77,900.00
Proof:			
Retained earnings balance, 12/31/X1		$ 2,590.47	
Net income for the year		12,642.86	
Retained earnings balance, 12/31/X2		$15,233.33	

*These figures have all been "rolled-forward" to reflect December 31, 19X2 dollars.

ginning capital in terms of dollars of equivalent purchasing power at the end of the period. In our illustration, for the ABC Company to remain as well-off at the end-of-the-period as it was at the beginning, the December 31, 19X2, capital should be restated to $59,257.14. This amount is equal to the beginning capital of $48,800 plus the capital maintenance adjustment of $10,457.14. Note that well-offness is defined here in terms of the general purchasing power of goods and services as measured by the consumer price index, CPI-U. Based on the foregoing discussion, the above stated balance sheet approach of measuring income can be restated as follows:

1. Exit value of the net assets at the end of the period, December 31, 19X2, $71,900.
2. Less: Exit value of net assets at the beginning of the period, December 31, 19X1, $48,800.
3. Less: Capital maintenance adjustment for the period, $48,800 x (170/140) - $48,800 = $10,457.14.
4. Exit-value/constant-dollar net income = $12,642.86.

Considering periods of significant inflation, dollars from such periods are not comparable. Accordingly, in order to facilitate interperiod comparison, we can prepare comparative balance sheets expressed in constant dollars. This can be done by restating the December 31, 19X1, balance sheet in terms of the December 31, 19X2, dollars. Given a price index of 140 on December 31, 19X1, and 170 on December 31, 19X2, the conversion into constant dollars is performed by multiplying each item (except the stockholders' equity) in the December 31, 19X1, balance sheet by a conversion factor of 170/140, i.e., the December 31, 19X2, index divided by the December 31, 19X1, index. Because the common stock was issued in January 1, 19X1, (for $40,000), when the general price index was 120, it is restated into December 31, 19X2, dollars by multiplying it by a conversion factor of 170/120, thus $40,000 x 170/120 = $56,666.67. The December 31, 19X1, retained earnings balance is arrived at as a balancing account.

From the constant-dollar comparative current exit-value balance sheets, one can easily compute the income for the period by comparing the exit value of net assets at the end of the period, December 31, 19X2, (total assets - liabilities), i.e., $77,900 - 6,000 = $71,900, with the exit value of the net assets at the beginning of the period December 31, 19X1, expressed in December 31, 19X2, dollars, $68,000 - 8742.86 = $59,257.14.

Net income = ($71,900 - $59,257.14) = $12,642.86

Given that there is no capital investment or withdrawal by owners, the $12,642.86, which is the difference between the beginning wealth position of the firm expressed in end-of-the-year dollars and the end-of-the-year wealth position, represents a real increase in the wealth position of the firm. This is an amount that the firm can distribute to owners in the form of dividends and still remain as well off, in terms of its command of general purchasing power, at the end of the year as it was at the beginning of the year.

The current exit-value model income statement, however, requires <u>unrealized holding gains or losses</u> in order to reflect the difference between the latest exit values at the end of the year and the exit values at the beginning of the year. In the event that such adjustments are made during the course of the fiscal year, the holding gain or loss will reflect these changes. Such holding gains or losses will apply to inventories, land, and buildings, as well as for machinery and equipment, which in a normal situation would indicate the amount of depreciation for the period.

We will illustrate the application of the exit-value model income statement, using the financial statements of the ABC Company. Recall the following given information, which is pertinent in preparing the income statement:

1. Sales revenue generated during the year is $82,800.
2. The exit value of the beginning inventory is $30,000. The historical-cost book value of the ending inventory is $29,520, while the exit value of the ending inventory on December 31, 19X2, is $31,000. This represents a holding gain on inventory of $1,480 (i.e., $31,000 – $29,520).
3. The total operating expense for the year is $10,000.
4. The exit value of the equipment is $14,000 on December 31, 19X1, and $12,500 on December 31, 19X2. This indicates a holding loss of $1500 ($14,000 – $12,500), representing the depreciation of the equipment for the year.
5. Given a beginning owners' equity of $48,800 on December 31, 19X1, (see Exhibit 8.1) and a price index of 140 on December 31, 19X1, and 170 on December 31, 19X2, the capital maintenance adjustment for the year would be $10,457.14 (i.e., 48,800 x 170/140) – $48,800.

Based on the foregoing data, the income statement for the year ending December 31, 19X2, on the exit-value basis can be presented as shown in Exhibit 8.3.

If we assume a period of significant inflation, the income statement presented in Exhibit 8.3 would require restatement in terms of constant dollars. During an inflationary period, the dollars of different time periods have different purchasing powers and as such cannot meaningfully be combined. To overcome this problem, the revenues,

EXHIBIT 8.3

ABC Company, Inc., Income Statement for the Year Ended
December 31, 19X2 (in nominal dollars)
(Current Exit-Value Basis)

Sales revenues		$82,800
Cost of goods sold		
Beginning inventory	$30,000	
Purchases during the year	49,200	
Goods available for sale	79,200	
Less: ending inventory, book value	29,500	49,680
Gross margin		$33,120
Less: operating expenses		10,000
		$23,120
Less: unrealized holding loss on		
equipment (i.e., depreciation)		1,500
		$21,620
Add: unrealized holding loss on inventory		1,480
Net income		$23,100

the cost of goods sold, the other expenses for the period, and the
holding gains or losses should be stated in terms of the end-of-year
dollars. For the purpose of preparing the exit-value/constant-dollar
income statement for the ABC Company, the following additional information should be recalled:

(a) The sales revenue for the period was generated uniformly
throughout the year; likewise the operating expenses were also incurred uniformly. To restate these amounts into end-of-year dollars,
we should use a conversion factor of 170/155, i.e., the end-of-year
index divided by the average-for-the-year index.

(b) In computing the cost of goods sold for the year, the beginning
inventory of $30,000 represents the exit value of the inventory on De-
cember 31, 19X1. This amount is restated to December 31, 19X2,
dollars by multiplying the amount by a conversion factor of 170/140,
i.e., the end-of-year index number over the beginning-of-year index
number. The purchases of $49,200 were made when the index was 155
and thus should be multiplied by 170/155. Since ABC Company is using
FIFO, the ending inventory is from the latest purchases of the year,
which should, therefore, be multiplied by 170/155.

(c) Computation of unrealized holding loss on equipment: Recall
the exit value of the equipment was $14,000 at 12/30/X1. In terms of
12/31/X2 dollars, this would be $17,000 (i.e., $14,000 x 170/140).

Since the exit value of the equipment on December 31, 19X2, is $12,500, the holding loss on the equipment, which represents the depreciation for the year, is equal to $4,500 ($17,000 - $12,500).

(d) <u>Holding gain or loss on inventory</u>: The restated book value of the inventory is $32,376.77 ($29,520 x 170/155), whereas the exit-value equivalent of the ending inventory at 12/31/X2 is given as $31,000. This situation, therefore, involves a holding loss on inventory of $1,376.77 ($31,000 - $32,376.77).

(e) <u>Purchasing-power gain or loss on holding monetary items</u> during the year is shown in Exhibit 6.5, in Chapter 6.

Based on the foregoing discussion, the income statement for ABC Company on the exit-value/constant-dollar basis can be prepared, as shown in Exhibit 8.4. The reader should note that the income for the period is the same as the amount reported, using the other approaches. The only advantage gained in Exhibit 8.4 is that all amounts are stated in the same measurement unit.

EXHIBIT 8.4

ABC Company, Inc., Income Statement for the Year Ended December 31, 19X2
(Exit-value/constant-dollar basis)
(In December 31, 19X2 dollars)

Sales	$82,800 × 170/155		$90,812.90
Cost of goods sold			
Beginning inventory	30,000 × 170/140	$36,428.57	
Purchases	49,200 × 170/155	53,961.29	
Goods available for sale		90,389.86	
Less: ending inventory (HC/CD)	29,520 × 170/155	32,376.77	58,013.09
Gross margin			32,799.81
Operating expenses	10,000 × 170/155		10,967.74
			21,832.07
Less: Unrealized holding loss on equipment (i.e., depreciation)		4,500.00	
Unrealized holding loss on inventory		1,376.77	
Purchasing power loss on holding net monetary items during the period (see Exhibit 6.5)		3,312.44	9,189.20
Net income			$12,642.86

NOTES

1. K. MacNeal, Truth in Accounting (Philadelphia, Pa.: University of Pennsyvalnia Press, 1939).

2. R. J. Chambers, Accounting, Evaluation and Economic Behavior (Englewood Cliffs, N.J.: Prentice-Hall, 1966). R. R. Sterling, Theory of the Measurement of Enterprise Income, (Lawrence, Kans.: University Press of Kansas, 1979).

3. R. J. Chambers, Securities and Obscurities, A Case for Reform of the Law of Company Accounts, (Melbourne, Australia: Gower Press, 1973), p. 219.

4. R. G. May, G. G. Mueller, T. H. Williams, A New Introduction to Financial Accounting, 2nd ed., (Englewood Cliffs, N.J.:, Prentice-Hall, 1980), pp. 602-3.

5. R. J. Chambers, "Continuously Contemporary Accounting" in Readings in Inflation Accounting, eds., P. T. Wanless and D. A. R. Forrester, (New York: John Wiley and Sons, 1979), p. 264.

6. Ibid.

7. A. Craswell, A Manual on Continuously Contemporary Accounting, (Hamilton, New Zealand: University of Waikato, 1977).

8. A. Craswell, "CCA Adds Up to Nothing," Current Cost Accounting: Identifying the Issues, eds., G. W. Dean and M. C. Wells, (Lancaster, England: University of Lancaster International Centre for Research in Accounting, 1977), p. 108.

9. Chambers, Accounting, Evaluation, and Economic Behavior, p. 200.

10. Ibid., p. 92.

11. R. J. Chambers, "Fair Financial Reporting—In Law and Practice," The Emanuel Saxe Distinguished Lectures in Accounting (1976-1977), New York: Bernard M. Baruch College, 1977, p. 9.

12. Ibid.

13. Ibid.

14. May, Mueller, and Williams, A New Introduction to Financial Accounting, p. 606.

15. See SFAC 1, par. 44.

16. L. A. Friedman, "An Exit-Price Income Statement," The Accounting Review, (January 1978): 18-30.

17. Chambers, Emanuel Saxe Distinguished Lectures in Accounting, p. 14.

18. User-value refers to the net present value of the expected cash flows from using the asset in question. Certain specialized assets may not have any current resale value, yet the net present value from using such assets could be quite substantial. Such user-value, however, is not considered under the current exit-value model, though it is considered in the deprival value model.

19. See note 16.

20. R. J. Chambers, Inflation Accounting: Methods and Problems, (Sydney, Australia: University of Sydney, 1975), p. 99.

21. R. J. Chambers, "NOD, COG, and PuPu: How Inflation Teases!" The Journal of Accountancy, (September 1975): 58.

9

ACCOUNTING FOR MONETARY ITEMS
UNDER CONDITIONS OF CHANGING PRICES:
AN INTERNATIONAL PERSPECTIVE

INTRODUCTION

Accounting for monetary items under conditions of changing prices is a perplexing reporting issue, judging from recently published accounting standards and proposed standards. In the United States, the Financial Accounting Standards Board (FASB) has acknowledged that it dealt inconclusively with, and deferred action on, particular accounting problems dealing with monetary items, when it issued Statement of Financial Accounting Standards No. 33 (FAS 33), "Financial Reporting and Changing Prices."[1]

The treatment of monetary items has also been a troublesome issue in England, as evidenced by the number of revisions that were made in proposed standards on accounting for current costs. Even the latest British standard, Statement of Standard Accounting Practice No. 16 on Current Cost Accounting (SSAP 16) still falls short of providing a comprehensive solution to the accounting problems arising from inflation, since SSAP 16 does not deal with the valuation of debt nor with the effects of inflation on holding debt.[2]

The Canadian accounting profession has also found the treatment of monetary items to be one of the controversial features of its 1979 Exposure Draft and its 1981 Re-exposure Draft.[3] The latest Canadian pronouncement on "Reporting the Effects of Changing Prices," issued in October 1982, is in many respects parallel to FAS 33 in the United States and possesses similar deficiencies in its treatment of monetary items.

The Australian Accounting Standards Committee (AASC) also failed to deal with the problem of monetary items in its Statement of Provisional Accounting Standards (DPS 1.1), entitled "Current Cost

Accounting," issued in October 1976, and in its amendment of August 1978.[4] Because of significant differences in opinion among the ranks of the Australian accounting bodies regarding the treatment of monetary items, the AASC decided that this "matter requires considerable further research . . . before any decision can be made as to the most appropriate accounting treatment."[5] Based on a study commissioned by the Australian Accounting Research Foundation (AARF), an Exposure Draft, "The Recognition of Gains and Losses on Holding Monetary Resources in the Context of Current Cost Accounting," was issued in July 1978 and revised in August 1979.[6] At present, there is a proposed standard on current-cost accounting in Australia that appears to take a more comprehensive approach to accounting for monetary items.[7] However, even this latest Australian proposed standard appears to have loose ends with respect to accounting for long-term liabilities; that subject will be reviewed later in this chapter.

Considering the controversial nature of the currently-proposed approaches to accounting for monetary items, the accounting profession is beset with a significant reporting problem that needs to be resolved. This challenge assumes particular importance in light of the findings by Modigliani and Cohn, who suggest that despite the claims about the efficiency of capital markets, "investors have systematically undervalued equity values for at least a decade, and are still undervaluing them by as much as 50 percent."[8] In discussing their startling observation, Modigliani and Cohn contend that "in the presence of significant inflation, adjusted accounting profits are a seriously misleading measure of true returns to the stockholders of a levered firm."[9] As Modigliani and Cohn have pointed out, this situation arises because of the failure to properly account "for the gain to shareholders accruing from depreciation in the real value of nominal corporate liabilities."[10]

The purpose of this chapter is to illuminate the perplexing problems of accounting for monetary items. To this end, a discussion of the conceptual issues underlying the treatment of monetary items is presented. An attempt is also made in this chapter to analyze and evaluate the American, British, Canadian, and Australian approaches to the treatment of monetary items.

The chapter is organized as follows: The first section provides a discussion of the conceptual issues associated with accounting for monetary items. The second section discusses the treatment of monetary items in the recent pronouncements issued in the United States, the United Kingdom, Canada, and Australia. The third section provides a comparative analysis of these pronouncements.

APPRAISAL OF THE CONCEPTUAL ISSUES
IN THE TREATMENT OF MONETARY ITEMS

The Impact of Inflation on Holding Monetary Assets. To understand the impact of inflation on holding monetary assets, it is important to recognize that "a monetary asset is money or a claim to receive a sum of money, the amount of which is fixed or determinable
without reference to future prices of specific goods or services" (FAS
33, par. 47). The economic significance of holding a given quantity of
money depends on the amount of goods and services one can buy with
the amount of money one holds, which is a function of the purchasing
power of the monetary unit.

Holding monetary assets—such as cash, accounts receivable,
notes receivable, and other forms of contractual claims to a fixed
amount of cash—during a period of increasing prices involves a loss
of purchasing power, since a given sum of money can buy fewer goods
and services. For example, assume that a firm holds $10,000 in cash
and claims to cash during a period in which a general price-level increase of 10 percent occurs. In view of the increase in prices, the
firm can buy fewer goods and services at the end of the period, compared to what it could have bought with the same sum of money at the
beginning of the period. In other words, the firm has suffered a loss
of purchasing power. In light of the 10 percent increase in prices, the
firm needs to hold $11,000 (i.e., $10,000 x 1.10) to be able to maintain the same purchasing power that it had at the beginning of the period. The fact that the company still holds $10,000 at the end of the
period, therefore, implies that the firm has suffered a $1,000 loss
of purchasing power.

There are two suggested approaches for computing the purchasing power loss on holding monetary assets during a period of increasing prices. One approach is to compute the purchasing power loss by
reference to the general purchasing power of the monetary assets as
a "pool of specific purchasing power," and measure the loss by reference to the changes in the prices of relevant inputs that the firm normally acquires in the conduct of its normal operations. (Accounting
for purchasing-power losses on holding monetary assets is discussed
later in the chapter in the subsection on the monetary working-capital
adjustment.)

The Impact of Inflation on Holding Monetary Liabilities. A monetary liability is defined as "an obligation to pay a sum of money, the
amount of which is fixed or determinable without reference to future
prices of specific goods or services" (FAS 33, par. 47). From the
debtor's viewpoint, the economic significance of a monetary liability
depends on the general purchasing power that the debtor has to sacrifice in settling the obligation. Holding monetary liabilities during a

period of inflation entails a purchasing-power gain since the debtor can pay the creditor with a fixed amount of dollars that has lower current purchasing power than at the time when the debt was originally contracted.

To understand the nature of purchasing-power gains on holding long-term liabilities during inflationary periods, it is necessary to consider the structure of interest rates. According to Irving Fisher, nominal interest rates are composed of two elements: (1) the real interest rate, which consists of a "pure" rate for risk-free debt instruments and a "risk" premium and (2) an "inflationary factor," the additional premium demanded by lenders to offset the expected loss of purchasing power while the debt is outstanding, due to anticipated deterioration of the general purchasing power of the monetary unit.[11]

This can be expressed as follows:

$$\gamma = R + \alpha$$

where γ is the nominal interest rate, R is the real rate, and α is the rate of inflation per year expected to prevail over the life of the debt.[12] The above formulation, which is known as the Fisher effect, simply states that the nominal rate of interest embodies an inflation premium sufficient to compensate lenders for the expected loss of purchasing power associated with the receipt of future dollars. Put another way, lenders demand a nominal rate of interest high enough to enable them to earn an expected real rate of interest. Thus, when inflation is correctly anticipated, lenders would be able to earn their expected real rate of interest since the nominal rate would fully compensate them for the loss of purchasing power from holding fixed monetary claims. Similarly, although debtors will pay higher nominal interest, they are fully compensated for the higher interest charges they have to pay through the benefits they receive in the form of purchasing-power gains from holding a fixed monetary obligation in an inflationary period. Consequently, as long as inflation is correctly anticipated, neither borrowers nor lenders gain or lose because of inflation. Lenders end up receiving the real rate of interest they expected, and borrowers pay the real interest rate they expected to pay when they received the funds.

The foregoing discussion can be illustrated by: Case 1. Suppose that the real rate of interest that lenders expect from XYZ Company is 10 percent (taking into account the risk classification of the firm). Let us assume now that XYZ Company issues $10,000 in bonds maturing after three years. Assume further that an inflation rate of 8 percent per year is expected furing the life of the bond issue. Under this situation, the Fisher effect suggests that the lender will demand a nominal interest rate of 18 percent ($\gamma = R + \alpha = 10\% + 8\%$). The 8 percent inflation factor is meant to offset the expected loss of purchasing power due to inflation. Thus, with a coupon rate of 18 percent the bond is expected to be issued at par.

If we now assume that the actual inflation rate for the first year turns out to be the same as expected—i.e., inflation was correctly anticipated—and if we assume that the long-run anticipated inflation still remains 8 percent, then at the end of the first year neither the borrower nor the lender gains or loses from the realized 8 percent inflation for the year, as the following computations of the real rate of interest on the bond demonstrate:

Nominal interest expense on the loan	
($10,000 x 18% nominal interest rate)	$1,800
Less: Purchasing power gain on loan	
(10,000 x 8% inflation)	800
Real interest expense on loan	$1,000
Therefore, the real interest rate equals $\dfrac{\$\,1,000}{10,000} =$	10%

The Impact of Unanticipated Inflation on Holding Debt. The foregoing discussion assumed a case in which inflation for the year was correctly anticipated and the expected long-run inflation rate was unchanged. Let us now consider two other cases involving unanticipated inflation using the bond issue of XYZ, as presented above.

Case 2. Assume that actual inflation in year 1 is 10 percent, indicating a 2 percent unanticipated increase in inflation. Let us assume that this was a temporary phenomenon and that the long-run anticipated inflation still remains unchanged at 8 percent.

This case illustrates a situation where debtors enjoy real purchasing-power gains at the expense of creditors, resulting in a lower real interest rate on the bond issue relative to the expected real interest on the loan. This is illustrated as follows:

Nominal interest expense on the loan	
($10,000 x 18% nominal interest rate)	$1,800
Less: Purchasing power gain on loan	
($10,000 x 10% inflation)	1,000
Real interest expense on loan	$ 800
Therefore, the real interest rate equals $\dfrac{\$\quad 800}{10,000} =$	8%

As a result of a one-period realized, unanticipated increase in inflation, the borrower (XYZ Company) gained at the expense of the lender, who now earns a real return of 8 percent on the investment instead of the expected 10 percent real return on the loan. In this sense, there is a transfer of real wealth from creditors to debtors. Of course, the impact of an unanticipated <u>decrease</u> in inflation would be the opposite—benefiting lenders at the expense of borrowers. Since we have assumed that the long-run inflation rate is unchanged, there will be no change in the nominal interest rate, and accordingly no expected change in the market value of the outstanding debt.

Case 3. Consider the possibility where the inflation rate for the first year was 10 percent as stated above <u>and</u> that the expected long-run inflation rate has now increased to 10 percent instead of the 8 percent that was anticipated at the time the bond was initially issued.

Because of the anticipated increase in the inflation rate, the nominal interest rate on newly issued debt instruments for XYZ Company will increase to 20 percent relative to the 18 percent on the outstanding bonds. Such an increase in the nominal interest rate results in a decrease in the market value of the outstanding debt.[13] Hence, firms that have debt outstanding at a time when there is an increase in the expected long-run inflation rate experience gains because of the decrease in the market value of their debt, which would enable them to retire, at least theoretically, the outstanding debt at a lower cash outlay than before. In this particular case, where we assumed an actual inflation rate greater than anticipated and an increase in the future, anticipated inflation, the debtor (XYZ Company) is benefiting on two counts: (1) the purchasing power gain from unanticipated inflation during the year and (2) the holding gain from the decline in the market value of the outstanding debt due to the increase in the long-run anticipated inflation rate, which resulted in the increased nominal interest rate on newly issued debt instruments. Similarly, a decrease in the expected long-term inflation rate would result in decreasing interest rates, which, in turn, would lead to an increase in the market value of outstanding debt, resulting in a loss to debtholders (since a larger cash outlay would be required to retire the obligation before the maturity date).

In the event of a decrease in the market value of debt, it is important to note that the purchasing-power gain should be computed based on the market value of the debt and not on the face value of the debt instrument. Theoretically, the market value of the debt represents the cash outlay required to settle an existing obligation, and hence the purchasing power gain should be related to the amount needed to repay the loan.

The foregoing discussion can be summed up as follows: (1) When inflation is correctly anticipated, there is no real gain or loss from holding debt. The purchasing-power gain on the debt should be viewed as an offset against the nominal interest charges on the loan, in order to provide an expected real interest rate commensurate with the risk classification of the debt. What determines the real purchasing-power gain or loss on holding debt is the presence of unanticipated inflation; and (2) Changes in anticipated long-run inflation subsequent to the issuance of debt engender changes in the market value of the debt. Any subsequent computation of the purchasing-power gain or loss should be based on the market value of the debt, not its face value.

ACCOUNTING FOR GAINS AND LOSSES ON MONETARY ITEMS UNDER A CURRENT-COST MODEL

The foregoing discussion has indicated that holding monetary assets during an inflationary period entails a purchasing-power loss, and holding monetary liabilities results in a purchasing-power gain. It has also been pointed out that due to the Fisher effect no real economic gains arise from holding debt so long as inflation is perfectly anticipated. Real economic gains occur as a result of unanticipated changes in the inflation rate. When changes occur with respect to the long-term anticipated inflation, a change in the market price of outstanding debt also occurs, (e.g., the market value of outstanding debt). Changes in the market value of outstanding debt instruments are related to changes in nominal interest rates on new loans in response to changes in the anticipated long-term inflation rate. The next question is how to report such gains and losses on monetary items in the current-cost model. The answer depends on whether one upholds the entity theory or the proprietary theory of the firm. To facilitate a better understanding of the issues involved, the distinction between the entity and proprietary theories is explained first. Then a discussion is provided on how gains and losses from holding debt are accounted for consistent with each of these theories.

The Entity Theory. Under the entity theory, the firm constitutes an entity separate and apart from its stockholders and creditors, with assets financed by two forms of equityholders—stockholders and creditors. According to the entity theory, income belongs to the firm until it is distributed in the form of dividends. Additionally, income taxes and interest costs are viewed as distributions of profit. [14]

The Proprietary Theory. The proprietary theory focuses on the firm from the viewpoint of the stockholders. According to this theory, the stockholders' interests are paramount. The assets of the firm are assumed to be owned by the stockholders or proprietors, and likewise the liabilities are viewed as their debts. In this theory, income is viewed as an increase in the wealth of the proprietors, whereas income taxes and interest costs are generally considered expenses. [15]

Purchasing-Power Gains and Losses
on Holding Monetary Items

In dealing with the treatment of purchasing-power gains and losses on holding monetary items, a distinction should be made between purchasing-power gains and losses on holding monetary working-capital items, which is handled through the "monetary working-capital adjustment," and purchasing-power gains or losses on long-term debt. A discussion of the monetary working-capital adjustment is first presented, to be followed by the treatment of purchasing power gains and losses on long-term liabilities.

Monetary Working-Capital Adjustment

Firms maintain a given net monetary working capital position (short-term monetary assets less short-term monetary liabilities) in order to enable them to maintain their normal operating capacity. The net working capital position, which under normal circumstances is expected to be a monetary asset position, can be viewed as a pool of specific purchasing power maintained for an acquisition of specific inputs normally required by the firm in the conduct of its normal operations. Thus, the loss of purchasing power on holding a net monetary asset position should be computed by reference to the increase in the prices of the relevant inputs. The purchasing-power loss on holding working-capital assets should then be considered in measuring the current cost profit of the enterprise. The rationale for this approach is provided by Australia's 1982 Proposed Standard as follows: "To the extent that an entity's resources are held in the form of monetary assets, losses are incurred when relevant prices rise and need to be recorded because the operating capability of those resources has been impaired."[16] This argument is consistent with the operating capital maintenance concept, which considers both monetary and physical assets.

Under the financial capital-maintenance approach, there would be no need to report the purchasing-power gains and losses on monetary working-capital items. Instead, a combination of purchasing-power gains and losses on all monetary items would be reported in measuring the income for a given period. Recall that the objective of the financial capital-maintenance approach to income measurement is to arrive at the maximum amount that the firm can distribute without eroding the beginning-of-the-period net financial capital of the firm (see Chapter 4).

Purchasing-Power Gains and Losses
on Long-Term Liabilities

Ideally, the purchasing power gains and losses on holding long-term liabilities should be reported as two separate elements: (1) purchasing power gains from anticipated inflation, which should be reported as an offset against the nominal interest charges on the loan and (2) the purchasing-power gains or losses from unanticipated changes in the inflation rate, which should be reported as gains and losses for a given period. Such reporting requires a knowledge of the anticipated inflation rate impounded in establishing the nominal interest rate on the debt. However, in most instances, it is not possible to clearly identify the anticipated inflation rate at the time the debt was issued. Because of the inability to make a distinction between the purchasing-power gain from anticipated inflation and the purchasing power gains or losses from unanticipated inflation, the alternative approach is to treat the total realized purchasing-power gain on the outstanding loan as an offset to the nominal interest cost for the period. It is important to note, however, the purchasing-power gain from inflation should be computed based on the market value of debt at the beginning of the period, and not merely on the face value of the outstanding debt. This approach is applicable both under the entity approach as well as the proprietary approach. The only difference between these two approaches reflects how interest costs are perceived and how interest costs are reported in the income statement. As noted earlier, the entity approach views interest as a distribution of an enterprise income, similar to dividends and tax payments, whereas the proprietary approach views interest cost as an expense that should be considered in measuring the net income attributable to the owners of the firm.

ACCOUNTING FOR HOLDING GAINS AND LOSSES ON LONG-TERM DEBT

Accounting for holding gains and losses on long-term liabilities under a current-cost model depends on the entity theory or the proprietary theory. The entity theory is based on the equation:

Assets = Equities (Liabilities + Stockholders' Equity)

The current-cost model would value the assets of the entity at their current cost as of the balance sheet date. The right-hand side of the equation represents the claims of the two types of equityholders: the creditors and stockholders. To the extent that creditors have fixed monetary claims against the assets of the entity, one can argue that the liabilities should be reported at their original contractual obligations regardless of what happens to the market price of the debt from unanticipated inflation or other factors. This approach implies that holding gains or losses on monetary liabilities resulting from changes in market values of the debt should not be reported. This position is reinforced by the argument that the entity does not benefit from declines in the value of debt as a result of changes in anticipated inflation that led to increased nominal interest rates. As long as the firm is to maintain its normal productive capacity, even if it were in a position to retire an outstanding debt whose market value has fallen, the firm would need to issue new debt in order to raise the cash consumed in retiring an existing loan. The new loan, however, will have to be issued at a higher nominal interest rate. Accordingly, the total cash outflow regarding the debt would leave the position of the firm unchanged.[17] In this regard, from the viewpoint of the entity, the holding gains on outstanding loans should not be reported as gains at all. This means that long-term liabilities should simply be reported at their face value regardless of changes in the market value of the debt. By contrast, the proprietary theory would recognize holding gains on debt as a component of income resulting from decline in the market value of the debt outstanding. To understand the rationale for this approach, consider the following equation, which applies to the proprietary theory:

$$\text{Assets} - \text{Liabilities} = \text{Owners' Equity}$$

In this framework, an increase in owners' equity, which could arise from an increase in assets and/or decrease in liabilities, constitutes income to the owners that could be properly distributed while maintaining the financial capital (the amount of cash investment) of the proprietors. To be internally consistent, the proprietary theory applied to the current-cost model should value both assets and liabilities, the left-hand side of the above equation, at their current costs and recognize holding gains on debt, just as the model reflects gains from holding assets as components of the "comprehensive income"[18] to the proprietors.[19] It can, therefore, be stated that application of proprietary theory to the current-cost model recognizes holding gains from debt when there is unanticipated inflation reflected in market price changes.

Gearing or Financing Adjustment

Thus far, the focus of our discussion has been on the impact of anticipated and unanticipated inflation on debt. However, there is another aspect of debt financing that needs to be recognized under the physical capital-maintenance approach to the current-cost model. This approach measures the current-cost operating income using current-cost data. Holding gains on nonmonetary assets of the firm are not treated as income, whether realized or not. Instead, holding gains, i.e., increases in the value of the nonmonetary assets, are viewed as capital-maintenance adjustments. As long as the firm continues its normal operations, it needs to maintain its physical productive resources intact. Hence, increases in the value of nonmonetary assets cannot be treated as gains that can be distributed without eroding the physical productive capacity of the firm.

However, to the extent that a portion of a firm's physical assets are financed by debt, and given that long-term liabilities are fixed monetary obligations, there is a benefit that accrues to shareholders from debt financing when the prices of such assets are increasing. Thus, when there is debt in the capital structure of a firm, the present shareholders do not have to bear the total increased current-cost adjustment applied in measuring the current-cost income of the firm. A portion of the realized holding gain should be recognized as income to the shareholders.

The gearing or financing adjustment pertains to the treatment of the gains that accrue to shareholders from debt financing. The gearing adjustment is designed to show the benefit to common stockholders from debt financing in a period of increasing prices. This adjustment provides a method of arriving at a measure of income attributable to shareholders. The current-cost income, which is based on a physical capital-maintenance concept, represents a measure of the maximum amount that the entity can distribute as a dividend while maintaining the entity's productive capacity. However, the "income attributable to shareholders" is based on the proprietary theory, representing an income measure under financial capital maintenance. In this regard, the gearing or financing adjustment can be viewed as a "concept that attempts to reconcile between the entity (physical capital) and proprietary (financial capital) views of income."[20] It is important to note, however, that the benefit accruing to the shareholders as represented by the gearing adjustment does not reflect income that can be distributed to the firm's shareholders without eroding the operating capability of the enterprise, unless borrowing is increased.

When the current cost of the firm's assets increase, the debt/equity ratio of the firm decreases. This suggests that when additional funds are needed to maintain physical capital at higher prices, part of the increase can be provided for by additional borrowing. Thus, assuming that the firm can arrange additional financing through debt in order to maintain its original debt/equity ratio, the income attributable to shareholders, which reflects the gearing adjustment, can be distributed without impairing the operating capability of the firm. This argument, however, is based on two crucial assumptions: (1) that the initial debt/equity ratio represents the optimal capital structure the firm intends to maintain and (2) that additional financing is available. To the extent that such assumptions are not valid, the amount represented by the gearing adjustment cannot be distributed without eroding the operating capability of the firm.

Modigliani and Cohn have argued that under normal circumstances the leverage policy of the firm is unaffected by inflation. This means that firms would increase their debt holding in nominal terms at the rate of inflation such that the amount of debt in their capital structure would remain constant in real terms.[21] Under this assumption, the gearing or financing adjustment can be viewed as distributable income. Funds obtained from the increase in debt needed to maintain a given debt/equity ratio can be distributed without eroding the normal operating capacity of the firm.

Thus far, we have discussed various conceptual issues involved in the treatment of monetary items. The next section discusses the treatment of monetary items in the United States, the United Kingdom, Canada, and Australia.

United States

In the United States, large firms are required to report purchasing-power gains or losses on net monetary items in accordance with FAS 33. It is clearly specified that the general purchasing-power gain or loss on net monetary items "shall not be included in income from continuing operations."[22]

One of the stated objectives of FAS 33 is to provide an improved basis for the "assessment of the erosion of general purchasing power."[23] The required information pertaining to the purchasing-power gain or loss on holding net monetary items is related to this objective. The computation of the general purchasing power gain or loss is straightforward. As stated in FAS 33 (par. 50):

> The purchasing power gain or loss on net monetary items shall be equal to the net gain or loss found by restating in constant dollars the opening and closing balances of, and transactions in, monetary assets and liabilities.

As reflected in the background discussion accompanying FAS 33, the board contemplated treating the general purchasing-power gain or loss on holding monetary items as a component of income or as a reduction in the interest expense incorporated into the computation of income. However, "in view of some comments on the Exposure Draft, expressing doubt about the usefulness of the item, the Board concluded that it would be preferable for it to be displayed separately, pending further experience with its use in practice."[24]

Kaplan has pointed out that the computation of purchasing-power gains on debt during inflationary periods based on the book value of the outstanding debt instead of the market value tends to exaggerate the purchasing-power gains accruing to highly leveraged companies.[25] Consequently, the disclosure of purchasing-power gains and losses on holding monetary items as presently required by FAS 33 can be misleading.

Under FAS 33, the valuation of debt is the same under the conventional historical-cost model, the historical-cost/constant-dollar model, and the current-cost model. Debt is reported at the face value of the debt instrument plus or minus the unamortized premium or discount.

FAS 33 neither requires a separate monetary working-capital adjustment nor a gearing adjustment. The FASB, however, has recognized these omissions as stated in Appendix C (pp. 58-59) of FAS 33:

[A]n enterprise may need to increase its net working capital to maintain operating capability and that factor is ignored in the measurement of current cost income. Moreover, an enterprise may be able to obtain some of the capital required to maintain operating capability by borrowing or by raising new equity capital from external sources: That possibility also is ignored in the measurement of current cost income.

As a result, the treatment of monetary items in FAS 33 leaves a great deal to be desired.[26]

United Kingdom

In the United Kingdom, the latest pronouncement dealing with accounting for the effects of changing prices is Statement of Standard Accounting Practice No. 16 (SSAP 16), "Current Cost Accounting" (1980). According to SSAP 16, most large firms in the United Kingdom are required to produce a current-cost accounting (CCA) balance sheet and a CCA income statement either as the main or supplementary statements to the conventional financial statements.

In dealing with the treatment of monetary items, SSAP 16 requires a monetary working-capital adjustment to arrive at the entity's "CCA income from operations" and a gearing adjustment to measure "income attributable to shareholders." The monetary working-capital adjustment required by SSAP 16 is based on the physical capital-maintenance concept of income. According to this concept, income is the amount that can be distributed after the firm has provided for maintenance of its existing operating capability. During a period of increasing prices, a firm may be required to hold a larger amount of monetary working capital to sustain its normal level of operations. Some proponents of the physical capital-maintenance concept would then argue that a monetary working-capital adjustment (MWCA) ought to be made to arrive at a distributable income measure in order to maintain both the monetary and physical operating capability of the firm.

Referring to the MWCA, SSAP 16 states: "This adjustment should represent the amount of additional (or reduced) finance needed for monetary working capital as a result of changes in the input prices of goods and services used and financed by the business" (par. 11). The rationale for the MWCA is that a firm may not be able to sustain its normal operations unless it provides for the increased monetary working capital required by the increased input prices.

Although it is probably true[27] that firms need to increase the absolute amount of their net monetary working capital during a period of increasing prices, the relevant data for determining distributable income should not be the required increase in net monetary working-capital assets, but the opportunity cost of maintaining the required additional monetary working capital as measured by the loss of purchasing power from holding monetary assets. In this respect, the MWCA required by SSAP 16 can be regarded as conceptually deficient.

SSAP 16 requires a gearing adjustment. The net effect of the gearing adjustment in a period of increasing prices is to increase the reported CCA operating income. The gearing adjustment recognizes the benefits to the shareholders from increases in the current cost of the operating assets, which are financed by debt. In effect, the gearing adjustment is a reduction of the CCA adjustments for depreciation, cost of goods sold, and the MWCA to the extent that these items are financed through debt. The gearing adjustment, according to SSAP 16 is calculated by:

1. Expressing net borrowing as a proportion of the net operating assets using average figures for the year from the current-cost balance sheet
2. Multiplying the total of the charges or credits made to allow for the impact of the price changes on the net operating assets of the business by the proportion determined at (a).

The integration of the monetary working-capital and the gearing adjustments in the CCA statement as required by SSAP 16 is shown in Exhibit 9.1.

EXHIBIT 9.1

XYZ Company, Current-Cost Income Statement for the Year
Ended December 31, 19X2
(In pounds sterling)

Historical-cost profit before interest and taxes		10,200
Less: current cost operating adjustment—		
Cost of sales	760	
Monetary working-capital (MWC) ad-		
justment: loss on holding net MWC assets	450	
Depreciation	1,200	2,410
Current-cost operating profit		7,790
Interest on borrowings		1,800
		5,970
Taxation		2,000
Current-cost profit after interest and taxation		3,970
Add: gearing adjustment (gain)		560
Current-cost profit attributable to shareholders		4,530

Source: Adapted from Statement of Standard Accounting Practice No. 16, "Current Cost Accounting," London: ASC, 1980, Appendix.

Canada

In December 1979, the Accounting Research Committee of the Canadian Institute of Chartered Accountants (CICA) issued an Exposure Draft, "Current Cost Accounting." In substance, this Exposure Draft is similar to the United Kingdom's SSAP 16. The Exposure Draft calls for a "net productive monetary items adjustment" and a "financing adjustment," which are essentially comparable to SSAP 16's monetary working-capital and gearing adjustments, respectively. In response to the comments received on the Exposure Draft, a Re-exposure Draft, "Reporting the Effects of Changing Prices," was issued in December 1981. The major change contained in the Re-exposure Draft pertains to the treatment of monetary items. The provision for a separate "net productive monetary adjustment" has been eliminated, while the "financing adjustment" is to be computed on all the net monetary items.

Subsequent to an extensive discussion of its Re-exposure Draft, the Canadian Institute of Chartered Accountants in October 1982 issued an accounting standard Section 4510, "Reporting the Effects of Price Changes." According to this latest Canadian Accounting standard, large firms are required to provide certain supplementary information. With respect to the impact of inflation on monetary items, the Canadian standard, similar to FAS 33, requires separate suplementary disclosure of the general purchasing-power gain or loss that results from holding net monetary items during the reporting period. However, the computation of the gain or loss on purchasing power is based on the book value of the monetary items, which is also the case with the FAS 33 requirement, instead of the market value of the outstanding debt. Consequently, as pointed out earlier, the disclosed gain or loss on general purchasing power is misleading. Furthermore, there is no provision in this standard to disclose any holding gain or loss resulting from changes in the market value of outstanding long-term liabilities in response to unanticipated changes in the long-term inflation rates.

The Canadian standard does not require disclosure of income attributable to common shareholders on a current-cost basis. However, in order to enable interested users to compute the income attributable to shareholders under both an operating capability concept of capital and a financial concept of capital measured in constant dollars, the standard requires the disclosure of supplementary information regarding the financing or gearing adjustment based on current-cost adjustments made to income for the period (par. 4510.20). The financing adjustment represents the portion of the current-cost adjustment financed by debt.

The latest Canadian standard does not provide any provision for a monetary working-capital adjustment. However, all monetary items are taken into account in computing purchasing-power gains or losses on monetary items. Exhibit 9.2 (Appendix D in the Canadian standard) provides an example of the Canadian Income Statement on a current-cost basis together with the additional supplementary information that is required to be disclosed.

Australia

Although a standard dealing with the treatment of monetary items has yet to be issued, the Australian accounting profession has been active in its attempt to meet the challenges of accounting under inflationary conditions. A Statement of Provisional Accounting Standards (DPS 1.1), entitled "Current Cost Accounting," was issued in October 1976 and later amended and reissued in August 1978. These statements, however, have not been concerned with the problem of monetary items, dealing instead with the cost of sales and depreciation adjustments. Because there were considerable differences in opinion within the Australian accounting profession at the time DPS1.1 was issued, with respect to the treatment of monetary items, it was decided to defer action pending further study of the subject. An Exposure Draft, entitled "The Recognition of Gains and Losses on Holding Monetary Resources

EXHIBIT 9.2

Statement of Income on a Current-Cost Basis and Other
Supplementary Information for the Year Ended December 31, 1980
(In thousands of dollars)

As reported in the historical-cost statements 1980		Current-Cost Basis	
		1980	1979
$169,000	Sales	$169,000	$150,700
116,000	Cost of goods sold	121,190	115,500
8,000	Depreciation	13,750	12,900
20,900	Selling, general, and administrative expenses	20,900	16,390
1,000	Amortization of deferred charges	1,000	1,320
3,900	Interest	3,900	3,080
(800)	Gain on sale of property, plant, and equipment	—	—
149,000		160,740	149,190
20,000	Income before income taxes	8,260	1,510
6,000	Income taxes—current	6,000	6,600
2,000	—deferred	2,000	—
8,000		8,000	6,600
$ 12,000	Income (loss) on a current cost basis	$ 260	$ (5,090)

Other supplementary information	1980	1979
Increase in the current-cost amounts of inventory and property, plant, and equipment	$ 14,740	$ 15,500
Effect of general inflation	9,471	10,260
Excess of increase in current cost over the effect of general inflation	$ 5,269	$ 5,240
Gain in general purchasing power from having net monetary liabilities	$ 2,275	$ 2,750
Financing adjustment	$ 3,685	$ 4,184

The financing adjustment amounts to $2,935 (1979, $3,600), based on the
current-cost adjustments made to income during the reporting period.

The 1979 comparative amounts have been restated in (approximately)
1980 average dollars.

Source: Section 4510, "Reporting the Effects of Price Changes," Canadian Institute of Chartered Accountants, 1982, Appendix B, p. 3. Reprinted with permission from CICA Handbook, published by the Canadian Institute of Chartered Accountants, Toronto, Canada,

in the Context of Current Cost Accounting," was issued by the Australian Accounting Research Foundation in July 1978 and later revised in August 1979. The framework of this Revised Exposure Draft was in substance similar to Britain's SSAP 16, although the presentation of the gearing and monetary working-capital adjustments was somewhat different.[28]

The Current Cost Accounting Standards Committee of the Australian Accounting Research Foundation has very recently prepared an integrated statement on CCA.[29] Issued as a "Proposed Standard" with its "Guidance Notes" in February 1982, the new standard has yet to be approved by the Australian Society of Accountants and the Institute of Chartered Accountants in Australia, under whose names accounting standards are published.

In the proposed standard, the CCA income of the entity reflects MWCA, showing gains or losses on the net monetary working-capital balance. There is a significant difference, however, regarding the accounting treatment of long-term monetary liabilities. The recent Australian proposed standard does not include any provision for a gearing adjustment; nor does it show the "CCA income attributable to common shareholders" in the body of the CCA profit and loss statement, in contrast to SSAP 16 and the 1979 Australian Revised Exposure Draft. However, paragraph 19 of the proposed standard states:

> There should also be disclosed, as a note to the CCA
> profit and loss statement, CCA entity net profit and
> gain/loss on loan capital . . . and then total.

The proposed standard does not provide an explanation (1) for eliminating the gearing adjustment from the body of the income statement nor (2) for downplaying the significance of the "CCA income attributable to Common Shareholders," by disclosing such information in a footnote for the interest of "readers who wish to see a proprietary result."

Exhibit 9.3 shows the structure of the CCA income statement in accordance with the 1982 Australian proposed standard. The explanatory note to the income statement provides information with respect to the gains or losses on long-term monetary liabilities. Thus, in an indirect way, readers who are interested in the purchasing-power gains on holding long-term debt in an inflationary period have access to such information. In this regard, there is a similarity between the latest proposed standard in Australia, FAS 33 in the United States, and the Re-exposure Draft in Canada. Both the American and Canadian pronouncements require separate disclosure of the purchasing power gains and losses on holding monetary items. Of course, it should be emphasized that both the United States and Canadian documents do not call for an MWCA.

EXHIBIT 9.3

CCA Profit and Loss Statement

The following assumes all relevant prices have risen:

1. Historical-cost operating profit before income tax and interest	$XX	$XX
2. Less: CCA adjustments		
a. cost of goods sold	XX	XX
b. depreciation	XX	XX
c. losses (gains) on holding monetary items (excluding loan capital) (i)	XX	XX
d. other (refer note . . .)	XX	XX
	XX	XX
3. CCA operating profit before interest and income tax	XX	XX
4. Income tax expenses thereon (ii)	XX	XX
5. CCA operating profit before interest	XX	XX
6. Less: interest (net of income tax)	XX	XX
7. CCA operating profit	XX	XX
8. Add: extraordinary items (net of income tax) (iii)	XX	XX
9. CCA entity net profit	XX	XX
10. Less: minority interest therein (including $XX relating to extraordinary items)	XX	XX
11. CCA entity net profit attributable to members of the holding company	$XX	$XX

Notes:

(i) Losses (gains on holding monetary items (excluding loan capital)
have been determined as follows:

Losses (gains) on—		
Trade debtors	XX	XX
Other monetary assets	XX	XX
	XX	XX
Less: gains (losses) on		
Trade creditors	XX	XX
Other monetary liabilities	XX	XX
Loan capital		
Losses (gains) on holding all monetary items	XX	XX
Less: transfer of gain on loan capital to gain on loan capital reserve	XX	XX
Losses (gains) on holding monetary items (excluding loan capital)	$XX	$XX

	19X1	19X0
(ii) Reconciliation of income tax expense with income tax expense shown in the conventional profit and loss statement is as follows:		
Tax expense reported in the conventional profit and loss statement	XX	XX
Plus: tax in relation to interest	XX	XX
Tax expense reported in the CCA profit and loss statement	$XX	$XX

(iii) Reconciliation of extraordinary items with extraordinary items shown in the conventional profit and loss statement is as follows:

Extraordinary items reported in the conventional profit and loss statement	XX	XX
Less/Add: CCA adjustments	XX	XX
Extraordinary items reported in the CCA profit and loss statement	$XX	$XX

	19X1	19X0
For readers who wish to see a proprietary result calculated, the following is given:		
CCA entity net profit attributable to members of the holding company	XX	XX
Add: Gain on loan capital	XX	XX
Less: Minority interest in gain on loan capital	XX XX	XX XX
	$XX	$XX

As gains on loan capital do not increase operating capability, and hence are not an element of the CCA net profit of the entity, any distributions made to shareholders from the gain on loan capital reserve constitute a reduction in the operating capability of the entity unless replaced by additional equity funds or loan capital.

Source: Proposed Statement of Accounting Standards on Current Cost Accounting, Appendix I, Australia, 1982.

SUMMARY

A study of the development of inflation accounting in the United States, the United Kingdom, Canada, and Australia indicates that accounting for monetary items is a complex problem. This chapter has attempted to highlight the issues involved in the treatment of monetary items in periods of changing prices.

The chapter has emphasized the need to recognize the purchasing-power gains and losses on holding monetary items during periods of changing prices. For those cases in which inflation is correctly anticipated, the purchasing-power gains from holding debt would be offset against the nominal interest charges. The Fisher effect suggests that there would be no real gain or loss from holding debt as long as inflation is correctly anticipated. Only when the actual inflation differs from the anticipated inflation would there be a real wealth transfer between debtors and creditors.

When there is a change in the anticipated long-term inflation rate subsequent to issuing debt, the nominal interest rate on a newly issued loan is expected to change. Such a change in interest rates affects the market value of existing debt. Whether any holding gains or losses on outstanding debt should be recognized as income depends on whether one upholds the entity or proprietary theory view of the firm. Under the entity theory, holding gains on outstanding debt are not recognized to the extent that the position of the firm remains unchanged inasmuch as any holding gain or loss represents a transfer of wealth between the equityholders. Under the proprietary theory, however, holding gains on debt would be recognized as unrealized income similar to unrealized holding gains on nonmonetary assets.

When the relevant specific prices rise, the service potential of the net monetary working-capital assets is impaired and should be considered in the measurement of CCA net profit. To the extent that an entity's resources are held in the form of monetary assets, purchasing-power losses are incurred when relevant prices rise, and such losses ought to be recognized. Likewise, in the event a firm holds a net monetary-liability position, then purchasing-power gains would be recognized.

Whereas FAS 33 and the recent Canadian standard do not consider MWCA in arriving at CCA profit, both pronouncements call for disclosure of purchasing-power gains and losses on holding monetary items in general. On the other hand, SSAP 16 requires an MWCA, which represents the amount of additional (or reduced) finance needed for monetary working capital as a result of changes in the input prices of goods and services used and financed by the business. The rationale for the British MWCA is that a firm may not be able to sustain its existing normal operations unless it provides for the increased monetary working capital needed as a result of the increase in input prices. However, this reasoning is faulty. Although it is probably true that firms are required to hold larger monetary working capital during a period of increasing prices either through supplier credits or short-term bank loans, the cost of maintaining larger working capital should be reflected in the interest charges for the period. Accordingly, the only factor that need be considered is the gains and losses on holding monetary working-capital items in order to measure CCA profit. Since the recent Australian proposed standard's MWCA reflects gains and losses on monetary working-capital items, it is superior to the SSAP 16's MWCA provision, which considers the cost of maintaining an increased amount of monetary working capital.

It should be pointed out that although the disclosure of purchasing-power gains and losses on holding monetary items is required by FAS 33 and the 1982 Canadian standard, as well as by the Australian proposed standard, the amount computed is based on the book value of the debt outstanding instead of the market value. Consequently, the disclosed amount tends to overstate the gains from holding debt during inflationary periods.

SSAP 16 and the Canadian standard require the disclosure of a gearing or financing adjustment. Such an adjustment is meant to show the benefit accruing to shareholders in a period of increasing asset prices from financing a portion of the firm's plant assets through debt. The Australian proposed standard does not call for a gearing adjustment in the body of the CCA profit and loss statement, but instead recommends a separate footnote disclosure to show the gearing adjustment and the income attributable to common shareholders, for the benefit of users who might be interested in such information.

Exhibit 9.4 presents a comparative summary of the different methods of dealing with monetary items in the American, British, Canadian, and Australian inflation-accounting pronouncements.

EXHIBIT 9.4

Comparative Analysis of the Treatment of Monetary Items

	United States	United Kingdom	Canada	Australia
Standard or exposure draft	Standard (FAS.33, Sept. 1979)	Standard (SSAP 16, March 1980)	Section 4510 (October 1982)	Proposed standard (Feb. 1982)
Price-change method adopted	CCA <u>and</u> general price level	CCA	CCA (+ some supplementary general price-level data	CCA
MWCA	No	Yes	No	Yes
Gearing or financing adjustment	No	Yes	Yes	Yes—but shown in a footnote rather than in the body of the CCA profit and loss statement
Gains/ losses on holding monetary items	Yes—but separately shown and not included in profit figure	No	Yes—to be disclosed in a footnote	Yes—but in an indirect manner, as part of the footnote explanation for MWCA

NOTES

1. See Financial Accounting Standards Board, Statement of Financial Accounting Standards No. 33, "Financial Reporting and Changing Prices," (Stamford, Conn.: FASB, September 1979), p. 28; and also par. 129, p. 63.

2. Accounting Standards Committee, Statement of Standard Accounting Practice No. 16, "Current Cost Accounting" [SSAP 16] (London: ASC, March 1980). See par. 33, which states: "SSAP 16 does not measure the effect of changes in the general value of money or translate the figures into currency of purchasing power at a specific rate. Because of this it is not a system of accounting for general inflation."

3. Accounting Research Committee, Exposure Draft: Current Cost Accounting (Toronto, Ontario: Canadian Institute of Chartered Accountants, December 1979). Accounting Research Committee, Re-exposure Draft: Reporting the Effects of Changing Prices (Toronto, Ontario: Canadian Institute of Chartered Accountants, December 1981). The Re-exposure Draft was approved with minor changes and issued as Section 4510, Reporting the Effects of Changing Prices in October 1982.

4. The Institute of Chartered Accountants in Australia and Australian Society of Accountants, Statement of Provisional Accounting Standards, "Current Cost Accounting," DPS 1.1, (October 1976, amended August 1978).

5. The Institute of Chartered Accountants in Australia and Australian Society of Accountants, Explanatory Statement: "The Basis of Current Cost Accounting," DPS 1.2 (October 1976, amended August 1978), see par. 12.24. In response to the call for further research on the treatment of monetary items, the Australian Accounting Research Foundation (AARF) commissioned a study on the treatment of purchasing-power gains and losses on monetary items in the CCA system. The study was conducted by M. S. Henderson and C. G. Peirson, CCA and Purchasing Power Gains and Losses on Monetary Items, Australian Accounting Research Foundation, August 1977.

6. Australian Accounting Research Foundation, Exposure Draft: "The Recognition of Gains and Losses in Holding Monetary Resources in the Context of Current Cost Accounting," July 1978, and reissued as a Revised Exposure Draft under the same title, in August 1979.

7. See R. S. Gynther, "Accounting for Inflation: Developments in Australia and Overseas," unpublished paper presented at the New South Wales Congress of the Australian Society of Accountants, February 10, 1982. See also R. S. Gynther, "Accounting for Monetary Items Under CCA: A Comment," Accounting and Business Research, (Spring 1983): 95-101.

8. F. Modigliani and R. Cohn, "Inflation, Rational Valuation and the Market," Financial Analysts Journal, (March–April 1979): 35.

9. Ibid., p. 30.

10. Ibid., p. 24.

11. I. Fisher, The Theory of Interest (New York: Macmillan, 1930).

12. More formally, the nominal rate γ is as follows:

$$(1 + \gamma) = (1 + R)(1 + \alpha)$$
$$\gamma = R + \alpha + R\alpha$$

However, in a situation where inflation is moderate, the cross product R is small and is usually ignored. J. Van Horne, Financial Management and Policy, 6th. ed. (Englewood Cliffs, N.J.: Prentice-Hall, 1983), p. 505.

13. R. S. Kaplan, "Purchasing Power Gains on Debt: The Effect of Expected and Unexpected Inflation," The Accounting Review, (April 1977): 369–78; L. Revsine, "Inflation Accounting for Debt," Financial Analysts Journal, (May–June 1981): 20–2; L. D. Brooks and D. Buckmaster, "Accounting for Interest and Long-Term Debt in an Inflationary Period," Management Accounting, (May 1982): 26–9.

14. For an expanded discussion of the entity theory, read E. S. Hendriksen, Accounting Theory, 4th. ed. (Homewood, Ill., Richard D. Irwin, 1982), pp. 455–57.

15. Ibid., pp. 453–55.

16. See par. 19 of the Guidance Notes to the Australian 1982 Proposed Statement of Accounting Standards on Current Cost Accounting.

17. See L. Revsine, "Inflation Accounting for Debt," Financial Analysts Journal, (May–June, 1981): 27. Revsine elaborates as follows: "Consider the case of bonds that have no call penalty and thus can be retired at market value. If unanticipated inflation causes the price of such bonds to fall, the firm could retire the bonds immediately by expending cash equal to the new, lower market price of the bonds. But if the expended cash must be replaced in order to finance future operations, new bonds must be issued at the new, higher interest rate. The total debt-associated cash flows to the entity after refunding will equal the debt-associated cash flows it would have received without refunding."

18. The term "comprehensive income" has been recently defined by the FASB in an exposure draft of a proposed statement of financial accounting concepts—"Reporting Income, Cash Flows, and Financial Position of Business Enterprises," November 1981. According to this exposure draft, comprehensive income is the increase in net assets from transactions and other events in the period (excluding investments

and distributions to owners). Comprehensive income is consistent with the concept of financial capital maintenance.

19. Revsine, in "Inflation Accounting for Debt," has made persuasive arguments in support of this view.

20. Ibid., p. 24.

21. Modigliani and Cohn, "Inflation, Rational Valuation and the Market."

22. FAS 33, par. 29 (b).

23. FAS 33, par. 94 (b); see also par. 3 (d).

24. FAS 33, par. 155.

25. Kaplan, "Purchasing Power Gains on Debt," p. 371.

26. For a critical analysis of FAS 33, see Chapter 3 of this book.

27. The amount of monetary working capital that a firm maintains is a function of several factors, such as the prudence of the financial management of the firm, the capital turnover, the credit and collection policy, and the availability of short-term financing and supplier credit. It is difficult to generalize how firms may adjust their monetary working-capital position in response to increasing input prices of the firm.

28. Unlike Britain's SSAP 16, where the CCA income for the entity is first presented, to which the gearing adjustment is added, Australia's 1978 Revised Exposure Draft first presents "Profit and Gearing Gains Attributable to Shareholders" from which the "gain on loan capital" is subtracted to arrive at the "Entity's Net Profit."

29. Australian Society of Accountants and the Institute of Chartered Accountants in Australia, Statement of Accounting Standards: Current Cost Accounting; and Guidance Notes in Statement of Accounting Standards Current Cost Accounting (February 1982).

10

THE OBJECTIVES AND REPORTING REQUIREMENTS OF RECENT INFLATION-ACCOUNTING PRONOUNCEMENTS: AN INTERNATIONAL PERSPECTIVE

INTRODUCTION

How best to overcome the deficiencies of the conventional accounting system in periods of prolonged inflation is still an unresolved, controversial subject. Accounting professionals in several countries are actively searching for satisfactory solutions to the financial reporting problems caused by general and specific price-level changes.

The United States is the first highly industrialized country in which a financial reporting standard on inflation accounting—Statement of Financial Accounting Standards No. 33 (FAS 33)—has been issued. [1] In the United Kingdom, Statement of Standard Accounting Practice No. 16 (SSAP 16)[2] on current-cost accounting was released in March 1980, effective for fiscal periods starting on or after January 1, 1980. Canada issued a standard on "Reporting the Effects of Changing Prices" in October 1982. [3] Australia has been very active in its search for a satisfactory approach to the inflation accounting problem. Currently, a proposed standard on current cost accounting has been issued. [4]

This chapter is intended to analyze and compare the objectives and required disclosures set forth in inflation-accounting standards currently in effect or proposed in the United States, the United Kingdom, Canada, and Australia. After discussing the stated objective and the nature of the required disclosure, we compare the stated objectives and reporting requirements set forth in these pronouncements and proposed standards.

U.S. STANDARD ON INFLATION ACCOUNTING

Background

As discussed in Chapter 2, the impact of changing prices on financial reporting has been of concern to the accounting policy-making bodies in the United States for many years.[5] It was not until the 1970s, however, that more serious attention was given to this subject. In 1969, the Accounting Principles Board (APB) issued APB Statement No. 3, Financial Statements Restated for General Price-Changes, which recommended supplementary disclosure of general price-level information. In general, very little importance was given to price-level information. As inflation became a significant problem, however, there was a flurry of interest on this subject, and the FASB responded accordingly.[6] In 1974, the FASB issued an Exposure Draft, Financial Reporting in Units of General Purchasing Power, which proposed mandatory supplementary disclosure of general price-level adjusted statements.

While the FASB's 1974 Exposure Draft was under study, the SEC, in 1976, surprised the accounting profession by issuing Accounting Series Release No. 190 (ASR 190), which required large firms to disclose particular replacement cost data.[7] This was one unusual instance in which the SEC usurped the role that it had delegated to the private sector and intervened in financial reporting to require mandatory disclosure of certain accounting information. By issuing ASR 190, the SEC played an important role in engendering significant changes in the direction, and in sharpening the focus, of accounting under inflationary conditions in the United States. Shortly after ASR 190 was issued, the FASB withdrew its 1974 Exposure Draft. Subsequent to considerable examination of this subject in relation to its Conceptual Framework Project, the FASB in 1979 issued Statement of Financial Accounting Standards No. 33 (FAS 33), "Financial Reporting and Changing Prices."

Objectives of FAS 33

To shed light on the objectives of FAS 33, it is essential to review the nature of the financial reporting environment in the United States and the circumstances that led to the issuance of FAS 33. One of the distinctive features of the financial reporting environment in the United States is that it has a dual regulatory structure, with the SEC and FASB being the primary regulators. The SEC was given statutory power by the Securities Acts of 1933 and 1934 to ensure the consistency of financial reporting with the public interest. In particular, the SEC

is empowered to establish the accounting standards for reports filed
with the commission. In setting standards for "full and fair disclosure," the SEC aims:

> to assure the public availability in an efficient and reason-
> able manner on a timely basis of reliable, firm-oriented
> information, material to informed investment, and cor-
> porate sufferage decision making. [8]

The SEC had usually relied on the accounting profession to establish
generally accepted accounting principles with respect to annual reports
and statements filed with it. [9] ASR 190, however effectively preempted
the FASB efforts in accounting for inflation. That the SEC imposed its
replacement-cost disclosure regulation while the FASB had been inviting comments on its exposure draft clearly suggests that the SEC
was dissatisfied with the FASB's approach. The SEC presumably believed that the public interest had not been adequately served with the
FASB's exposure draft.

In issuing FAS 33, the FASB appeared to share the concern of
the SEC about the deficiencies of conventional financial statements
stemming from inflation. The FASB indicated its concern about providing useful information to the various constituents of financial reporting, such as investors, creditors, and regulators:

> The Board believes that this Statement meets an urgent
> need for information about the effects of changing prices.
> If that information is not provided: Resources may be
> allocated inefficiently; investors' and creditors' under-
> standing of the past performance of an enterprise and
> their ability to assess future cash flows may be severely
> limited; and people in government who participate in de-
> cisions on economic policy may lack important information
> about the implications of the decisions. The requirements
> of the Statement are expected to promote a better under-
> standing by the general public of the problems caused by
> inflation. Statements by business managers about those
> problems are unlikely to have sufficient credibility until
> financial reports provide quantitative information about
> the effects of inflation. [FAS 33, p. ii].

By issuing FAS 33, which requires mandatory supplemental
information pertaining to the effects of changing prices on business
operations, the general objective of the FASB has been to improve the
relevant informational content of financial statements. In this endeavor,
the FASB had intended to achieve the objectives set forth in its State-

ment of Financial Accounting Concepts No. 1, "Objectives of Financial Reporting by Business Enterprises" (1978). The key objective in this document is stated as follows:

> Financial reporting should provide information that is useful to present and potential investors and creditors and other users in assessing the amounts, timing, and uncertainty of prospective cash receipts. Since investors' and creditors' cash flows are related to enterprise cash flows, financial reporting should provide information to help investors, creditors, and others assess the amounts, timing, and uncertainty of prospective net cash inflows to the related enterprise. (p. viii).

One distinctive feature of FAS 33 is that it spells out its objectives promulated in the FASB Concepts Statement No. 1. FAS 33 establishes four objectives to assist users of financial statements in evaluating the impact of changing prices on their investment, lending, and other decisions. Thus, FAS 33 intends to provide users with information presumably relevant for the assessment of:[10]

1. Future cash flows
2. Enterprise performance
3. Erosion of operating capability
4. Erosion of general purchasing power

With the foregoing objectives in mind, FAS 33 requires certain large firms[11] to provide supplementary financial data.

Disclosure Requirements

The following data are required to be disclosed in accordance with FAS 33:[12]

1. Income from continuing operations adjusted for the effects of general inflation
2. Income from continuing operations on a current-cost basis
3. Purchasing-power gains and losses on holding monetary items reported separately (i.e., not included in the income from continuing operations)
4. Holding gains on nonmonetary items net of inflation and reported separately as "increases or decreases" on nonmonetary items
5. Current costs on lower recoverable amount of inventory and property, plant, and equipment at the end of the current fiscal year.

In addition, disclosure is required of a five-year summary of specific relevant financial data expressed in constant dollars.

Comparison of Stated Objectives and Required Information

A closer examination of the specific provisions reveals that some of the provisions of FAS 33 are neither consistent with all the stated objectives nor conceptually defensible. One of these provisions is the disclosure of income from continuing operations on a historical-cost/constant-dollar (HC/CD) basis. In order to make this adjustment, a general price-level index is used, which is an average measure of the individual price changes taking place in the economy. Because individual prices in a given firm may not move at the same rate or even in the same direction as the general price level, the relevance of the restated figures is questionable. By the board's own admission, there was little support for the HC/CD data from users of financial statements.[13] The rationale for its inclusion appears to be the insistence of preparers and public accounting firms. For understandable reasons, many preparers of financial reports and public accounting firms favored HC/CD information due to "lower cost . . . , higher verifiability and representational faithfulness."[14] Such concerns have not been stated as objectives of the statement and, in this respect, it appears that there is an inconsistency between the stated objectives and this particular provision of the statement. In expressing a dissenting opinion, a member of the board asserted in connection with the apparent inconsistency of the board's position:

> A major criterion that the Board has established for choosing among alternative disclosures is usefulness of the information for predicting earnings and cash flows. The evidence presented to the Board on usefulness in this sense was sketchy, but virtually all of it favored the current cost approach. In fact usefulness for predicting earnings and cash flows has rarely been associated with the historical cost/constant dollar approach even by its supporters.[15]

Nevertheless, HC/CD data are intended to satisfy the objective set forth in FAS 33 regarding the assessment of the erosion of general purchasing power.

FAS 33 requires the disclosure of general purchasing-power gains from holding monetary liabilities and monetary assets, respectively, during a period of inflation. However, the purchasing-power gain or loss on net monetary items is not included in measuring the income of the period. As the background discussion in the statement indicates, there was a lack of consensus among the members of the board regarding the nature and treatment of purchasing-power gains and losses. As discussed in Chapter 9, properly computed purchasing-power gains on monetary liabilities in a period of inflation should be treated as an offset to interest charges for the period in order to reflect the real interest cost. In computing the purchasing-power gain, it is important to do the computation on the market value, not on the face value of the debt. One major weakness of FAS 33 is that the requirement for disclosure of the purchasing-power gain on monetary liabilities is based on the book value of the outstanding debt. When inflation is anticipated, the nominal interest rate on debt impounds a premium for the anticipated inflation, the so-called Fisher effect. Thus, unless the interest charges are partly offset by the gains that accrue from holding monetary liabilities, the reported income for the period would be understated. Viewed in this manner, FAS 33 is deficient both in terms of the method of computation and the manner of reporting the purchasing-power gains on debt.

Additionally, FAS 33 requires the disclosure of holding gains and losses from inventories, property, plant, and equipment less the general inflation component that produces an illusory, fictitious gain or loss. To the extent that a portion of these assets are financed through debt, part of the realized holding gain can be treated as income attributable to the present shareholders. In the United Kingdom, the gearing adjustment is used to recognize a portion of the realized holding gains in measuring the income attributable to present shareholders. FAS 33, however, does not have any provisions for a gearing or financing adjustment.

FAS 33 requires the reporting of income from continuing operations on a current-cost basis (or lower recoverable value). Although FAS 33 is deficient in its treatment of monetary items and does not provide a monetary working-capital adjustment, the current-cost income from continuing operations may be viewed as "distributable" or "sustainable," indicating the amount the firm can sustain in the future or distribute as dividends while maintaining its capital and continuing normal operations. Such data should be relevant for investment decision making to the extent that such income measures can help investors to predict cash flows.

FAS 33 also requires the presentation of comparative financial data stated in constant dollars for the five most recent years. This aspect of FAS 33 recognizes the measurement problem inherent in using the dollar as a unit of measure. In periods of general price-level changes, the dollar has a serious limitation as a unit of measure since it is unstable. Dollars of different time periods have varying degrees of purchasing power. Consequently, financial statements of different periods should be restated in terms of a common unit of measure to enable meaningful interperiod comparisons. In this regard, FAS 33 has attempted to be a comprehensive inflation-accounting pronouncement.

BRITISH STANDARD ON INFLATION ACCOUNTING

The evolution of the present current-cost accounting standard in the United Kingdom has also taken several twists and turns. A provisional Statement of Standard Accounting Practice (No. 7) favoring general price-level adjusted historical-cost accounting (otherwise known as CPP accounting) was issued in 1974.[16] This statement was similar to the FASB's 1974 Exposure Draft, which also advocated general price-level accounting. In 1975, a government-appointed committee on inflation accounting headed by F. E. P. Sandilands proposed a current-cost accounting system having no provisions for the impact of general inflation on monetary items.[17] Because of strong negative reaction to the Sandilands Report, a new Steering Group was formed. In 1976, the Steering Group prepared an Exposure Draft (ED 18),[18] which was essentially a proposal for a current-cost system with supplementary disclosure of adjustments for general inflation on the monetary holdings of a firm. ED 18 was strongly opposed, particularly by financial institutions, because of its inadequate treatment of monetary items, and was subsequently abandoned as a result. A more refined approach to the treatment of monetary items was proposed in 1977 by the Hyde Committee, known as the Hyde Guidelines,[19] which led to the issuance of ED 24.[20] Finally, ED 24 became the basis for the present British standard on inflation accounting: SSAP 16.[21]

Stated Objectives of SSAP 16

The basic objective of the U.K.'s Statement of Standard Accounting Practice No. 16, "Current Cost Accounting" [SSAP 16] is "to provide more useful information than that available from historical-cost accounts alone for the guidance of the management, shareholders, and others on such matters as:

(a) the financial viability of the business
(b) return on investment
(c) pricing policy, cost control, and distribution decisions
(d) "gearing" (SSAP 16, par. 5)

SSAP 16 applies to most listed companies and other large entities.

Disclosure Requirements

To achieve the foregoing objectives, SSAP 16 requires a two-stage current-cost income statement and current-cost balance sheet. The two-stage CCA income statement, illustrated in Exhibit 10.1, shows the current cost operating profit by deducting current-cost adjustments for the cost of sales, depreciation, and monetary working capital. The current-cost operating profit is based on the concept of physical capital maintenance, which emphasizes the operating capacity of the firm. By adding the "gearing adjustment" to the current-cost operating profit, the "current cost profit attributable to shareholders" is measured. The gearing adjustment is a measure of the benefit (or cost) accruing to the shareholders for having financed part of the operating assets through debt. Given that debt constitutes a fixed obligation, any increase (decrease) in the current cost of the assets financed by debt is viewed as a benefit (cost) to the shareholders. From another dimension, the gearing adjustment constitutes a reduction to the cur-

EXHIBIT 10.1

ABC Company, Inc., Current-Cost Profit and Loss Account for the Year Ended December 31, 19X1

Profit before interest and taxation on the historical-cost basis		XXX
Less: current-cost operating adjustment		
Cost of sales	XXX	
Monetary working capital	XXX	
Depreciation	XXX	XXX
Current-cost operating profit		
Add: gearing adjustment	XXX	
Less: interest expenses (net of interest receivable)	XXX	XXX
Current-cost profit before taxation		XXX
Less: taxation		XXX
Current cost profit attributable to shareholders		XXX

Source: Statement of Standard Accounting Practice No. 16, "Current Cost Accounting, London, 1980, Appendix.

rent-cost adjustments that were made to arrive at the current-cost operating profit of the enterprise.

SSAP 16 requires the presentation of a current-cost balance sheet, the assets of which are shown "at their value to the business based on current price levels."[22] The "value to the business" concept is equivalent to the lower of the current (replacement) cost or the recoverable amount of the asset, as in FAS 33.

Comparison of Stated Objectives and Required Information

The stated objectives and the required financial information in SSAP 16 appear to be consistent. By disclosing the current replacement cost or lower recoverable amount of a firm's assets, the balance sheet provides a more realistic assessment of the resources used by a firm and should enable users to compute return-on-investment ratios for comparative purposes.

The current-cost profit can be viewed as a reasonable measure of "distributable income" arising from the normal operations of the firm. This measure of income, which serves to maintain the firm's operating capability, is presumably relevant to investors for their assessment of future cash flows.

Consistent with the stated objectives of providing information pertaining to gearing, the current-cost profit and loss account shows the gearing adjustment in determining "the current cost income attributable to shareholders." The gearing adjustment represents the benefit accruing to common stockholders as a result of financing a portion of a firm's assets through debt during a period of increasing asset prices. The gearing adjustment does not, however, represent an amount that can be distributed as a dividend without impairing the operating capability of the firm unless additional borrowing is possible. However, firms are normally expected to maintain a given debt/equity ratio in real terms, which suggests that the nominal amount of debt should increase at the rate of inflation.

SSAP 16 requires a monetary working-capital adjustment to ensure the measurement of CCA profit consistent with the physical capital maintenance concept underlying SSAP 16. Among the current inflation-accounting pronouncements considered in this chapter, SSAP 16 is the only one that does not require the disclosure of purchasing-power gains or losses on holding monetary items. As discussed in Chapter 9, there is a strong argument that can be made in favor of including properly computed purchasing-power gains on holding monetary liabilities in an inflationary period. Because interest charges on long-term loans are normally expected to reflect the anticipated inflation rate (the Fisher-effect argument), failure to consider the purchasing-power gain from holding debt as an offset to interest charges would lead to understated income. In this regard, SSAP 16 is obviously deficient.

Another shortcoming of the U.K. standard is that it does not address the measurement-unit problem in financial reporting. Investors and other interested financial statement users presumably make comparative trend analyses. Such time-series analyses can only be facilitated by financial statements that are restated in a common unit of measurement, such as the "constant dollars" required by FAS 33. The need for a constant unit of measure is acknowledged in SSAP 16, although this standard does not call for such a measurement unit at this time in order to reduce the complexity of implementing the new CCA standard.[23]

Aside from the deficiency regarding the measurement-unit problem and the failure to properly account for purchasing-power gains on debt in an inflationary period, SSAP 16's CCA information set appears to be superior to FAS 33's current-cost information. Since FAS 33 does not require MWCA, its current-cost income cannot be considered a complete, comprehensive measure of "distributable income." Unlike FAS 33, SSAP 16 does not require price-level adjusted (HC/CD) data. Overall, SSAP 16 seems to have accomplished its objective of providing relevant information to users.

CANADIAN STANDARD ON INFLATION ACCOUNTING

The Canadian Institute of Chartered Accountants (CICA), which is the accounting standard-setting authority in Canada, took a significant step in issuing its 1979 Exposure Draft, proposing a current-cost accounting system for the reporting of the effects of changing prices by large, publicly held Canadian enterprises. Based on the comments received on the Exposure Draft, a Re-exposure Draft entitled, Reporting the Effects of Changing Prices was issued in December 1981, and the standard was subsequently released in October 1982. One of the prominent features of the standard, which also applies to the exposure drafts, is a detailed and clear exposition of the objectives underlying the proposed approach, with a considerable discussion on how the recommended data could satisfy the specified objectives.

Stated Objectives of the Canadian Inflation-Accounting Standard

The latest standard reaffirms the importance of the conventional account financial statements as "reliable and independently verifiable" measures of actual arm's-length transactions. At the same time, it acknowledges the limitations in the usefulness of conventional financial statements during periods of prolonged inflation. Thus, without suggesting changes per se in the conventional financial statements, the standard recommends supplementary data about the effects of changes in the prices of the specific goods and services purchased, produced, and used by an enterprise. It also recommends supplementary data about the effects of changes in the measurement unit resulting from changes in the general purchasing power of the monetary unit. Such supplementary data are expected to help users of financial statements achieve a better understanding of the effects of changing prices on business enterprises—in making investment, credit, and other economic decisions.

The standard identifies five objectives that can be achieved by reporting the required supplementary data. These objectives are concerned with assessment of:[24]

1. The maintenance of the operating capability of the enterprise
2. Operating capability financed by common shareholders
3. Enterprise performance
4. General purchasing power of capital
5. Future prospects

Disclosure Requirements

The Canadian standard requires the disclosure of certain supplementary information about the effects of changing prices together with the basic historical-cost financial statements. The required supplementary information deals with specific price changes as well as the impact of changes in the general purchasing power of the monetary unit.

The following balance sheet items are to be reported at end-of-the-year current-cost values, identifying any reduction from current cost to lower recoverable amount:

1. Inventory
2. Property, plant, and equipment
3. Net assets, after restating inventory, property, plant, and equipment on current-cost basis

This standard requires the disclosure of comparative data, showing the corresponding amounts for the preceding period restated in constant dollars. For the balance-sheet items stated above, the use of end-of-year constant dollars for the current year is recommended.

The standard also requires the disclosure of current-cost income for the period showing the cost of goods sold, and depreciation, depletion and amortization on current-cost basis. In addition, the following information is to be disclosed separately (i.e., without being included in the computation of income for the period):[25]

1. The changes in the current-cost values of inventory, plant, and equipment during the reporting period, together with information about any reduction from current cost to lower recoverable amount, if any.
2. The amount of changes in the current-cost amounts of inventory and property, plant, and equipment that is attributable to the effects of general inflation.
3. The amount of the gain or loss in general purchasing power that results from holding net monetary items during the reporting period. This amount is to be disclosed separately and not included in computing the income for the period.
4. The financing adjustment based on the current-cost adjustment to income for the period.

The foregoing information is to be shown on comparative basis with the corresponding data for the preceding year stated in constant dollars. For the income-statement items, the use of average constant dollars for the current year is recommended.

The income statement, which is illustrated in Exhibit 9.2, is primarily designed to show the current-cost income of the enterprise. However, since there is no provision for a monetary working-capital adjustment, such an income measure cannot be considered a comprehensive current-cost income measure of the enterprise. With the disclosed additional supplementary information, users may be able to compute the income attributable to shareholders under both an operating-capability concept-of-capital and a financial concept-of-capital.

Apart from the financing-adjustment disclosure, which is not required by FAS 33, and historical-cost/constant-dollar data, which are not required by the Canadian standard, the two pronouncements are quite similar.[26] Unlike the British standard and the Australian proposed standard, the Canadian and U.S. standards constitute an attempt to provide a comprehensive solution to the accounting problems resulting from general and specific price-level changes.

Comparison of Stated Objectives and Disclosure Requirements

Although one of the stated objectives of the standard is to provide information helpful for the maintenance of operating capability of the enterprise, the required information does not appear to provide a complete foundation for such an assessment. The same can also be said about FAS 33. The income measure that is consistent with the maintenance of operating capability of the enterprise is a current-cost income measure similar to that required by SSAP 16. The Canadian income statement includes no provision for a monetary working-capital adjustment. Such an income measure cannot, therefore, be considered a comprehensive current-cost income measure.

Consistent with their stated objective of providing information that is presumably helpful in assessing whether an enterprise has maintained the general purchasing power of its capital, both the Canadian standard and FAS 33 require information on the purchasing-power gains and losses from holding monetary items. (As previously observed, SSAP 16, on the other hand, does not require such information.) The relevance of the purchasing-power gains and losses, particularly the manner in which such data are computed both in the Canadian standard and in FAS 33, has been seriously questioned. (For further discussion on the computation and relevance of purchasing-power gains and losses, refer to Chapter 9.) In general, while there appears to be much consistency between the stated objectives and the required supplementary information. the Canadian standard shares some of the shortcomings of FAS 33, particularly with the treatment of monetary liabilities.

AUSTRALIAN PROPOSED STANDARD ON INFLATION ACCOUNTING

In Australia prior to the early 1970s, the accounting problems caused by inflation and their proposed solutions were considered primarily in academic circles. However, in view of the inflationary spiral in the last decade, there has been a heightened interest within the Australian business community in the effects of inflation on financial reporting. The Australian business community was, nevertheless, more concerned with the inclusion of holding gains in taxable income than it was with the financial reporting problem per se.[27] In response to the concern of the business community, the Australian government established a committee in 1974 to consider such tax issues.[28] Simultaneously, the Australian accounting authorities began to study the accounting problems caused by inflation. After promulgating several exposure drafts and statements of provisional accounting standards on accounting for the effects of inflation, the Australian accounting profession in 1982 issued a proposed Statement of Accounting Standards on Current Cost Accounting.[29] The proposed standard applies to large, publicly traded companies (with assets of $20 million or more) as well as large government and semigovernment business undertakings (with assets of $100 million or more).[30]

Objectives of the Proposed Standard

According to Australia's proposed Statement of Accounting Standards on Current Cost Accounting, "the objective of financial reporting is to satisfy needs of users for relevant information on the economic affairs of a business entity" (par. 2). This statement acknowledges the deficiencies of conventional accounting during periods of changing prices and suggests the recognition of the impact of the changes in the prices of specific goods or services currently needed by the firm.

The proposed statement asserts that "the objective of CCA is to ensure that, having regard to changes in specific prices, the results and resources of an entity are realistically measured so as to be of maximum value to users" (par. 4). More specifically, the proposal claims that the current-cost information will assist investors, managers, and other users in better assessing the economic performance of the entity (as measured by its profitability), the financial viability of the entity, and dividend policies. In addition, the CCA information is also supposed to "assist management in optimizing its use of resources, in cost control, in determination of pricing policies, and capital-raising decisions" (par. 7).

Disclosure Requirements

To meet the foregoing objectives, the proposed statement requires the computation of income and the presentation of the balance sheet on a current-cost basis. The Australian proposed standard is based on the concept of physical capital maintenance, which provides a measure of income that the enterprise can distribute as dividends while maintaining its operating capability.

The current-cost data are to be presented as supplemental information together with a statement of changes in shareholders' equity on a current-cost basis along with specific explanatory notes in addition to the conventional financial statements. This proposed statement does not, however, preclude the presentation of CCA financial statements as the principal financial statements; in this respect, the Australian and British pronouncements are alike. On the other hand, the current-cost data are expected to be disclosed only as supplementary information, according to FAS 33 and the Canadian standard.

One distinctive feature of the Australian CCA standard is that it does not show the CCA profit attributable to common shareholders in the CCA profit and loss statement proper. Recall that SSAP 16's CCA income statement shows both the current-cost income of the enterprise and the current-cost income attributable to common shareholders in the same statement. It is important to note, however, that the Australian proposal calls for additional disclosure as a note to the CCA profit and loss statement of information that may enable interested readers to determine the current-cost income attributable to common shareholders. This is done by adding the "gain on loan capital"[31] to the CCA net profit. Exhibit 9.3 illustrates the format of the supplementary CCA income statement as suggested by the 1982 proposed Australian CCA standard.

Comparison of Stated Objectives and Required Information

The objective of the Australian CCA standard is to provide useful information by realistically stating the value of the resources of the firm and the results of its operations. During periods of changing prices, the conventional balance sheet, which is based on the historical-cost principle, has serious limitations in conveying relevant measures of the assets of a firm and the income for the period. In this respect, the current-cost supplementary data should be beneficial to financial statement users. The Australian CCA profit is based on the concept of physical capital maintenance, which implies that the reported current-cost income is the amount the firm can distribute as dividends while maintaining its operating capacity. Such a measure of income is presumed to be relevant to users who are interested in making predictions about future cash flows of the firm. In this respect, the Australian proposal appears to require information consistent with its stated objectives. However, the Australian proposed standard also shares the same weakness as the other standards in its method of computation and treatment of purchasing power gains and losses from holding debt during inflation. Another weakness with the proposed Australian CCA system is that it does not deal with the measurement-unit problem. Although this problem is not particularly serious with the CCA model in dealing with a given time period, the need for a constant unit of measurement is evident for interperiod comparative analysis. Recall that SSAP 16 is characterized by the same shortcoming. On the other hand, both FAS 33 and the Canadian standard call for the use of constant dollars in presenting comparative financial data. To provide a comprehensive solution to the inflation accounting problem, it is necessary to address the measurement-unit problem.

SUMMARY

Among the inflation-accounting pronouncements covered in this study, FAS 33 and the Canadian standard go to great length to clarify their objectives and explain how the proposed required information satisfies these objectives. To a lesser degree, both the British SSAP 16 and the latest Australian proposed standard provide statements of objectives underlying their respective requirements.

In comparing the American, British, Canadian, and Australian price-level accounting standards and proposals, the following summary analysis can be made:

1. <u>Statement of Objectives</u>. FAS 33 and the Canadian standard have almost identical statements of objectives. [32] In fact, it appears that the Canadian standard has "borrowed" a great deal from FAS 33. On the other hand, there is considerable similarity between SSAP 16 and the 1982 Australian proposed standard.

Both the American and Canadian documents have specifically stated their intent to provide information useful for predicting cash flows. On the other hand, the British and Australian statements do not explicitly call for the revision of information that users may find relevant in assessing future cash flows. Nevertheless, both the British and Australian approaches assert the importance of providing useful information for managerial decision making. In the United States, and apparently also in Canada, the accounting standard-setting authorities are primarily concerned with establishing accounting standards for external reports. This might explain, therefore, why no reference is made in the statement of objectives of the American and Canadian documents to information for managerial decision-making purposes.

The American and Canadian standards call for information dealing with purchasing-power gains and losses on holding monetary items as separate supplementary disclosures. The British and Australian standards, on the other hand, do not require such information. It should be pointed out, however, that the Australian document does call for information on purchasing-power gains and losses from holding monetary items, as a footnote disclosure in connection with the computation of its monetary working-capital adjustments. In all cases, the computation and the treatment of gains and loss on holding debt during inflation are seriously deficient. This issue is discussed in Chapter 9.

The British SSAP 16 requires the disclosure of information with respect to "gearing" as one of its stated objectives. A similar provision is also required to meet one of the stated objectives of the Canadian standard, dealing with information to assess the "maintenance of operating capability <u>financed by common shareholders</u>." To accomplish this objective, the Canadian standard recommends a "financing adjustment," which is similar to the British "gearing adjustment." These adjustments are designed to reflect the benefit or cost to common stockholders from financing a portion of a firm's operating assets through debt in a period of changing prices. FAS 33 does not contain this objective; nor does FAS 33 require disclosure of a gearing or financing adjustment. Nevertheless, FAS 33 does assert the objective of providing information presumed to be useful in assessing the erosion of the firm's operating capabilities. In a marked departure from an earlier exposure draft, the recent Australian proposed standard does not show any gearing adjustment in the main body of the CCA income statement, which is primarily designed to report the CCA income of the enterprise. However, in what appears to be a compromise solution, the Australian pronouncement mandates the disclosure of "gains and losses on loan capital," which, in effect, is equivalent to a gearing or financing adjustment for the benefit of those readers who might be interested in the income attributable to common stockholders. While FAS 33 and the Canadian standard are neutral on the concept of capital maintenance, SSAP 16 and the Australian proposed standard seem to emphasize the concept of maintaining operating capability as a common objective.

   2. Disclosure Requirements. FAS 33 is the only one that requires the disclosure of supplementary historical-cost/constant-dollar (HC/CD) data in addition to current-cost information. In other respects, FAS 33 and the Canadian standard are alike. Both standards attempt to reflect the effect of specific price changes and the impact of general price-level changes on the general purchasing power of the monetary unit. On the other hand, there are striking similarities between SSAP 16 and the proposed Australian standard. All the pronouncements considered call for supplementary current-cost data or lower recoverable amounts. It should be pointed out, however, that none of the pronouncements examined in this chapter requires the current-cost measurement of liabilities. With the exception of SSAP 16, all the pronouncements require the disclosure of general purchasing-power gains or losses on holding monetary items.

   Unlike SSAP 16 and the Australian proposed standard, FAS 33 and the Canadian standard do not require a monetary working-capital adjustment in measuring the current-cost income of the entity. As stated earlier, SSAP 16 requires a gearing adjustment in the CCA profit and loss statement. There is no provision for gearing in FAS 33, while the Canadian standard and the Australian proposal call for a gearing or financing adjustment to be disclosed separately for the benefit of users who may be interested in computing income attributable to shareholders.

   FAS 33 requires income from continuing operations both on current cost and general price-level adjusted bases. The Canadian standard and the Australian proposed standard, on the other hand, require a current-cost income statement primarily designed to show the current-cost income of the enterprise. By contrast, the British SSAP 16 requires a two-stage current-cost income statement showing: (1) current-cost operating profit and (2) current-cost profit attributable to shareholders.

Both the British and Australian statements require a current-cost balance sheet, which can be presented either as a supplementary or primary statement, whereas the American and Canadian standards require only the disclosure of balance sheet items on a current-cost basis, with holding gains on monetary items reflected net of general inflation.

Only FAS 33 and the Canadian standard require the restatement of comparative financial data in terms of constant dollars. FAS 33 requires a five-year summary of selected financial information, whereas the Canadian approach seems to be limited only to two years of comparative data. There is no mandatory requirement for presenting comparative data stated in a common unit of measurement in the British and Australian CCA accounting pronouncements. The British Accounting Standards Committee is currently considering the measurement-unit problem. British enterprises are encouraged to give comparative figures adjusted to a common price basis.[33]

3. Comparison of Stated Objectives and Required Information. The required information generally appears to be consistent with the objectives set forth in the inflation accounting pronouncements and proposals covered in this study. The only exception, where we were unable to find a satisfactory link, was with regard to the historical-cost/constant-dollar data that are required by FAS 33. Restatement of historical-cost data using a general index results in uninterpretable data. In most other instances, although one might take issue with particular disclosure requirements there seems to be consistency between stated objectives and the required information. It should be pointed out that the failure to require a properly computed monetary working-capital adjustment in both FAS 33 and the Canadian standard results in an incomplete CCA income measure, one that is less than fully consistent with the maintenance of operating capability of the firm. It should be emphasized that both FAS 33 and the Canadian standard are neutral on the concept of capital maintenance. All the standards considered in this chapter are deficient in their treatment of the impact of changing prices on holding debt.

CONCLUSION

This chapter has analyzed and compared the objectives and reporting requirements underlying the price-level accounting methods that have been recently issued or proposed in the United States, the United Kingdom, Canada, and Australia. An understanding of the objectives set forth in these documents provides a framework for evaluating the internal consistency of a given pronouncement and enhances an understanding of the reporting differences that exist among the different countries.

This comparative analysis, which is summarized in Exhibit 10.2, reveals points of tangency among pronouncements and proposed standards. The stated objectives and reporting requirements enunciated in these statements are generally similar. As evidenced by all the similarities among the pronouncements, there has been a considerable international exchange of ideas on inflation accounting.

The price-level accounting standards that have been either adopted or proposed in the United States, the United Kingdom, Canada, and Australia apply, in all cases, to large publicly held companies. These countries have highly developed capital markets, although perhaps with varying degrees of efficiency. Based on these observations, it can be hypothesized that the financial-reporting environment among these countries is essentially similar, and consequently the objectives of financial statements and the nature of required information ought to be similar, as the study confirms to a large extent. [34]

In dealing with publicly held companies, the overriding concern for external reporting purposes should be to provide relevant information for investment decisions. Such information should assist prospective investors in the assessment of cash flow prospects. The American inflation-accounting pronouncement and the Canadian standard appear to be keenly aware of the need for providing investor-oriented information. On the other hand, the British and Australian documents do not explicitly emphasize the objective of providing information to assist investors in assessing the amount, timing, and uncertainty of future cash flows.

This study reveals instances where some of the required information was not strictly consistent with the stated objectives. The historical-cost/constant-dollar information in FAS 33 is a case in point. Such instances can be explained as the product of the politicization of the policy-making process. [35] Policy-making authorities have to settle for compromising solutions that will satisfy their different constituencies, [36] of the accounting policy-making bodies.

EXHIBIT 10.2

Summary of Disclosure Requirements in Selected Inflation-Accounting Pronouncements

Standard or proposal	Size test	Stated objectives	Required information	Stated or implied capital maintenance concepts
U.K.	All entities, except: (a) those that do not have share or debt instruments listed on the stock exchange and satisfy at least two of following criteria: (1) turnover of less than $5 million per year (2) historical-cost balance sheet total less than $2.5 million (3) less than 250 employees on average and other exclusions (see par. 46)	To provide more useful information than the historical-cost data for the benefit of managers, shareholders, and other such matters, as— (a) the financial viability of the business (b) return on investment (c) pricing policy, cost control, and distribution decisions (d) gearing	1. Two-stage current-cost income statement showing: (a) current cost operating profit arrived at by deducting: (1) current-cost depreciation (2) current cost of sales (3) monetary working-capital adjustment. (b) current-cost profit attributable to shareholders—by adding the gearing adjustment to the above. 2. Balance sheet—showing assets at their value to the business based on current price level	Physical capital maintenance concept (including a monetary working capital adjustment) reconciled with financial capital maintenance concept through the gearing adjustment
U.S.A. FAS 33, 1979	Gross inventory, property, plant, and equipment $125 million OR total assets net of accumulated depreciation $1 billion	To provide information useful for assessment of: 1. future cash flows 2. enterprise performance 3. erosion of operating capability 4. erosion of general purchasing power	1. Historical-cost/constant-dollar* income from continuing operations 2. Current-cost* income from continuing operations 3. Purchasing-power gains and losses 4. Increase in nonmonetary assets, net of inflation 5. Current cost* of inventory, property, plant, and equipment on the balance sheet. *or lower recoverable amount	No preference stated

Canada	Inventories, property, plant, and equipment (gross) $50 million, or total assets net of accumulated depreciation $350 million—all other enterprises encouraged	To provide useful information to assist users in their assessment of: (a) maintenance of operating capability of the enterprise (b) maintenance of operating capability financed by common shareholders (c) performance evaluation (d) maintenance of general purchasing power of capital (e) future prospects	1. Current-cost income deducting from sales: (a) cost of sales and depreciation, depletion, amortization—all on current-cost basis. 2. Other supplementary information: (a) changes in the inventory cost of inventory, property, plant, and equipment for the period (b) changes in the current cost of inventory, property, plant, and equipment attributable to inflation (c) purchasing-power gain or loss on holding monetary items (d) financing adjustment (e) end-of-period current cost or recoverable value of inventory and property, plant, and equipment (f) end-of-period net assets (shareholders' equity) on current-cost basis (g) comparative preceding years' data on constant dollars in preceding years dollars converted to end-of-reporting-period dollars	No preference stated (see par. A.8)

(continued)

Exhibit 10.2 (continued)

Standard of proposal	Size test	Stated objectives	Required information	Stated or implied capital maintenance concepts
Australia	(a) Publicly held companies with total assets (net of accumulated depreciation) exceeding $20 million (b) All government and semigovernment business undertakings with total assets of $100 million (other business enterprises also encouraged)	1. To provide users with realistic measures of a firm's results and resources 2. To provide information useful in better assessment of the economic performance of the entity 3. Financial viability assessment 4. To provide management with relevant information for managerial decision making	1. Supplementary CCA profit and loss statement 2. Current-cost balance sheet on current-cost or recoverable amount 3. Current-cost statement of changes in shareholders' equity 4. Explanatory notes, CCA income includes gains (losses) on holding monetary working capital items 5. An explanatory note that shows gain/loss on loan capital 6. Current-cost reserve and gain on loan capital reserve as separate items of shareholders' equity	Physical capital maintenance (including a monetary working-capital adjustment)

NOTES

1. Financial Accounting Standards Board, Statement of Financial Accounting Standards No. 33, "Financial Reporting and Changing Prices," (Stamford, Conn.: FASB, September 1979). It should be noted, however, that various forms of inflation accounting have been used in other countries (e.g., Brazil, Argentina) for many years, often as a response to extreme inflationary conditions.

2. Accounting Standards Committee, Statement of Standard Accounting Practice No. 16, "Current Cost Accounting," (London: ASC, March 1980).

3. Accounting Research Committee, Section 4510, CICA Handbook: "Reporting the Effects of Changing Prices, (Toronto, Ontario: Canadian Institute of Chartered Accountants, October 1982).

4. The Institute of Chartered Accountants in Australia, and Australian Society of Accountants, Proposed Statement of Accounting Standards: Current-Cost Accounting, February 1982.

5. In 1947, 1948, and 1953, the Committee of Accounting Procedure of the American Institute of Accountants, and in 1965 the American Principles Board in APB Opinion No. 6, considered the accounting problems related to the general increase in price levels. Primary concern, however, was with the general price-level changes since no special reference was given to the impact of specific price-level changes. For further discussion on the evolution of FAS 33, read Chapter 2 of this book.

6. The FASB placed the price-level accounting problem in its agenda in January 1974. In February 1974, the FASB issued a Discussion Memorandum: Reporting the Effects of General Price-Level Changes in Financial Statements, and held a public hearing in April 1974. In December 1974, an Exposure Draft titled Financial Reporting in Units of General Purchasing Power was issued.

7. Securities and Exchange Commission, Accounting Series Release No. 190 (Washington, D.C.: U.S. Government Printing Office, March 23, 1976). For general reaction to the SEC rule, see F. Andrews, "Replacement Cost Accounting Plan Adopted by SEC," The Wall Street Journal, March 25, 1976.

8. See W. H. Beaver, Financial Reporting: An Accounting Revolution (Englewood Cliffs, N.J.: Prentice-Hall, 1981), p. 14.

9. The SEC's Accounting Series Release No. 150 delegates this authority to the FASB.

10. FAS 33, pp. 1-2.

11. FAS 33 applies "to public enterprises that have either (1) inventories and property, plant, and equipment (before deducting accumulated depreciation) amounting to more than $125 million, or (2) total assets amounting to more than $1 billion (after deducting accumulated depreciation)." See par. 23.

12. See FAS 33, p. 11–13.

13. See FAS 33, p. 26.

14. See FAS 33, p. 56.

15. See FAS 33, p. 26.

16. Accounting Standards Steering Committee, Provisional Statement of Standard Accounting Practice No. 7: Accounting for Changes in the Purchasing Power of Money (London: ASC, May 1974).

17. Accounting Standards Committee, Inflation Accounting: Report of the Inflation Accounting Committee, (London: Her Majesty's Stationery Office, 1975).

18. Accounting Standards Committee, Proposed Standard of Accounting Practice, Ed. 18: Current Cost Accounting (London: ASC, November 1976).

19. Accounting Standards Committee, Inflation Accounting, An Interim Recommendation (London: ASC, 1977).

20. Accounting Standards Committee, Proposed Statement of Standard Accounting Practice, Ed. 24: Current Cost Accounting, (London: ASC, 1979).

21. Accounting Standards Committee, Statement of Standard Accounting Practice, No. 16, Current Cost Accounting, (SSAP 16) (London: ASC, March 1980).

22. See SSAP 16, par. 7; and for a definition of the "value of business," see par. 42 of SSAP 16. Also refer to FAS 33, par. 62–3, for further elaboration on this concept.

23. See par. 6 of the standard.

24. See note 3.

25. See pars. 18 and 24 of the standard.

26. There are minor differences in the computation of the Canadian "financing adjustment" and the British gearing adjustment. The Canadian financing adjustment is computed as follows:

$$\left(\frac{\text{Average net monetary liability for the year}}{\text{Average net monetary liability+Average Common Shareholders' Equity on Current-Cost Basis}}\right) \times \left(\text{Current-cost adjustments}\right)$$

The net monetary liability accounts for all liabilities, including current liabilities, whereas the current-cost adjustments reflect adjustments on current-cost basis for cost of sales, depreciation, and depletion. Unlike SSAP 16, no MWCA is included here.

The British gearing adjustment on the other hand is computed as follows:

$$\left(\frac{\text{Net borrowing}}{\text{Net operating assets on current cost basis}}\right) \times \left(\text{Current-cost adjustments}\right)$$

Net borrowing does not include monetary working-capital items, unlike the Canadian approach. The current-cost adjustment reflects the adjustment for cost of sales, depreciation, depletion, etc., and MWCA. In this regard, the Canadian and British financing and gearing adjustments are somewhat different.

27. See M. S. Henderson and C. G. Peirson, CCA and Purchasing Power and Losses on Monetary Items (Australian Accounting Research Foundation, August 1977), p. 5.

28. Committee of Inquiry into Inflation and Taxation (Mathews Committee) Report (Canberra: Australian Government Printing Service, 1975).

29. Australian Society of Accountants and The Institute of Chartered Accountants in Australia, Proposed Statement of Accounting Standards: Current Cost Accounting, February 1982.

30. Ibid., par. 8.

31. "Loan capital" according to the Australian document is defined as the amount borrowed for financing the operating capability of an entity. Loan capital includes the current position of long-term debt but excludes other current monetary liabilities.

32. There is, however, one notable exception between the stated objectives of the Canadian standard and FAS 33. Although both documents include the "maintenance of the operating capability of the enterprise" as a stated objective, the Canadian standard specifically contains an additional objective on the "maintenance of the operating capability of common shareholders." [Emphasis added]

33. See SSAP 16, par. 37.

34. For a discussion on the impact of the financial reporting environment upon accounting standards, read W. H. Beaver, Financial Reporting: An Accounting Revolution (Englewood Cliffs, N.J.: Prentice-Hall, 1981), chapters 1 and 7.

35. A discussion on the politicization of accounting policy making is given by C. Horngren, "The Marketing of Accounting Standards," The Journal of Accountancy, (October 1973): 61-6. See also D. Solomons, "The Politicization of Accounting," The Journal of Accountancy (November 1978): 65-72, and S. A. Zeff, "The Rise of Economic Consequences," The Journal of Accountancy (December 1978): 56-63.

36. For a discussion on the political compromise that seems to have influenced FAS 33, see R. Bloom and A. Debessay, "A Critique of FAS No. 33," Management Accounting (May 1981), pp. 48-53.

11

THE INFORMATIONAL CONTENT
OF INFLATION-ACCOUNTING DISCLOSURES

INTRODUCTION

In 1976, the Securities and Exchange Commission (SEC) issued Accounting Series Release No. 190 (ASR 190). This release required all corporations with inventories and gross plant and equipment aggregating more than $100 million and constituting more than 10 percent of their total assets to disclose the current replacement cost for inventories and productive capacity as well as the cost of sales and depreciation expense computed on the basis of replacement cost.

By issuing ASR 190, the SEC has played an important role in introducing current-value accounting in the United States. Earlier in 1974, the Financial Accounting Standards Board (FASB) had issued an exposure draft favoring general price-level adjusted, i.e., historical-cost/constant-dollar data as a supplement to the conventional accounting statements. While this exposure draft was being studied and debated, the SEC issued ASR 190, thereby forcing the FASB to shelve its exposure draft pending further study and deliberation. In 1979, the FASB published Statement of Financial Accounting Standards No. 33, "Financial Reporting and Changing Prices," hereafter called FAS 33, which is to some degree a hybrid of the 1974 exposure draft and ASR 190. In view of FAS 33, the SEC decided to rescind ASR 190.

The requirement to disclose inflation-accounting data constitutes a major policy change by the regulators of external accounting reports. The objective of ASR 190 was "to provide investors with meaningful additional information not otherwise available." By requiring these

---

Hans Heymann, Ph.D., Associate Professor of Business Administration, Illinois Institute of Technology, collaborated with the authors in the preparation of this chapter.

245

disclosures, it is recognized that conventional financial-accounting statements are not adequately conveying financial data.

This chapter considers the costs and benefits of inflation-accounting disclosures. Since there is no unified theory of what constitutes relevant disclosure, several different approaches exist, which can be partitioned into market and individual user frameworks. The market approach emphasizes the role of accounting data in promoting efficient capital markets,[1] whereas the individual user approach is concerned with different user groups and their specific needs for financial data. While specific users are not identified, specific tasks can be delineated.[2] We consider benefits as improvements in the evaluation of individual enterprise performance. The costs of the disclosure requirements are more readily identified and are treated on a social and a private basis. A discussion is included of recent capital-market studies on the informational content[3] of ASR 190 and FAS 33 on the prices of common stocks. Additional empirical evidence on the relevance of general price-level adjusted (constant-dollar) historical costs is furnished.

ANALYSIS OF THE COSTS AND BENEFITS OF CURRENT VALUE DISCLOSURES

A. Costs.

According to <u>FASB Statement of Financial Accounting Concepts No. 2</u>,[4] the costs of accounting data include the following:

To the Preparer

- collecting, processing, and storing the data
- circulating the data
- litigation associated with the data
- conveying information to competitors and trade unions

To the User

- analyzing and interpreting the data

To the Regulator

- developing and enforcing the standard as well as litigating the regulations

This list can be extended to include public accountants. The foregoing costs can be considered private costs, which are readily identifiable on an individual basis. In addition, there are social costs that relate to the potential misallocation of resources due to misleading or missing financial data. Since they are not directly observable, these costs are more difficult to assess. The cost of misallocations can only be identified in terms of the ideal, which itself is unknown.

Beaver[5] discusses various sources of social costs associated with the disclosure or nondisclosure of financial data. Monopolistic access to information may lead to abnormal returns to insiders and additional costs to the public required to attain such information through expensive channels. If the FASB is requiring firms to report data whose value is less than the cost of attaining it through other channels, this requirement would result in excessive costs borne by the public.

B. Benefits.

The reporting of current value data as required by the FASB is supposed to benefit users. FAS 33 suggests that these data will assist users in:

1. Forecasting cash flows
2. Evaluating enterprise performance
3. Assessing the erosion of operating capability
4. Appriasing the erosion of general purchasing power

Additionally, the data may be helpful to individual decision makers in terms of assisting them, along with the conventional accounting data set, in assessing the riskiness of their securities. The data should be of assistance to individual investors in selecting optimal portfolios. Also, the current-value data may be helpful in evaluating the performance of management, i.e., its financial and operational stewardship.[6] In view of these benefits, the data should have positive effects on capital formation, stock prices, and resource allocation in general.

Providing inflation-accounting data in financial statements is consistent with the "events" approach[7] to accounting, which calls for disclosure of a vast array of different kinds of accounting data in financial statements for the purpose of assisting users in making their own analysis. According to this view, financial statements ought to convey a variety of data to presumed users, who can pick and choose among the data elements furnished according to their needs. Included in this data set may well be inflation-accounting data, presumably relevant.

Current value disclosure in terms of current (replacement) cost may be a more suitable proxy for economic income, when compared to the conventional accounting data. Conventional accounting data are based on the historical-cost principle, which in times of prolonged

inflationary price changes, often result in an overstatement of reported earnings compared to economic income. Economic income is
defined as the operating earnings plus the change in asset values during a time period. Under current-cost reporting, the reported income
equals economic income in a perfectly competitive equilibrium market
system. During periods of adjustment to temporary disequilibrium
conditions, current-cost income may or may not approximate economic income. When asset market prices move in directions opposite
to expected cash flows, there tends to be a difference between current-
cost income and economic income, i.e., the assets are overvalued.
On the other hand, when asset values move together with expected
cash flows, current-cost income tends to approximate economic income quite well. [8]

Current-value data may have better predictive ability than other
accounting numbers. Predictive ability of accounting data constitutes
one criterion for evaluating the desirability of alternative accounting
policies. [9] In general, whether or not current-cost data are useful to
specific user groups, the data are conveyed for stewardship purposes,
i.e., to provide accountability to outside parties on the use of corporate resources. Stewardship, however, is not an end per se. In the
final analysis, data are desired to facilitate decision making or to
help individual users analyze the economic position and performance
of the firm.

A different approach to analyze the benefits of accounting data
is to assess their contribution to promote efficient capital markets.
In the semi-strong test of the efficient market hypothesis, it is postu-
lated that security prices act as if they fully reflect all publicly available information including that contained in the financial statements.
If the hypothesis is true, then security prices should react to new
information in an unbiased and rapid fashion. [10]

With respect to stock price reaction to ASR 190 data, Beaver
has established the following propositions: [11]

> If we adopt a naive notion of price formation . . . , we
> are asked to believe that the market has been fooled by
> the "illusory" profits reported under historical cost sys-
> tem. If so, then are we to expect a massive reduction in
> stock prices when the replacement cost data are reported?
> However, once we abandon a perception of a naive
> market relying only on reported numbers, there is no
> obvious reason to predict any systematic adjustment of
> stock prices across firms. In particular there is no rea-
> son to believe there will be downward revision in prices
> because the replacement cost data willingly lower earnings.
> This belief is due to (a) the extent to which changes

> in specific (commodity) prices [that] affect each industry
> is approximately known, and (b) the use of a broad set of
> information by the securities markets.

If current-cost data has new informational content, then security market prices should be affected by disclosure of such data. Changes in such prices due to this disclosure might be expected since the reporting of current-cost data may well constitute an expansion in the informational content of financial reports.

A question that has been raised is: If disclosure of current-value data in annual reports produces no significant impact on security prices, should companies be required to disclose this supplementary data? Perhaps FAS 33 should be revised to require more relevant, market-desired information. This argument is based on the observation that if the market does not react to these data, then it must be irrelevant. One view on this point could be that the market ignores the new data, because they are considered too uncertain or too subjective. Another possibility is that the market does not know what to do with these data. The market goes through a learning period to gain experience. It is more conceivable, however, that the observation that the market's failure to react to the reported current-cost data is a methodological problem of the efficient market test. One possibility is that the market has already reflected the reported information, and the disclosure requirement only verifies the information obtained from other sources. Another possibility is that the systematic change in information is reflected in the market index, and, therefore, does not enter the analysis. See the review of capital-market research studies, which follows.

The role of financial statements in creating an efficient capital market should be considered. However, the fact that markets are efficient does not provide a basis on which to decide which data ought to be reported. Capital markets have been found to efficiently reflect information, which, in turn, indicates that information is available to the market. The relevant questions are whether financial statements have a comparative cost advantage over other sources of information and whether the reporting of current-cost data has improved the efficiency of the market. The answers to these questions are difficult to obtain. There are additional questions related to the efficient market hypothesis and the role of accounting data: What kinds of data ought to be reported in financial statements and companion footnotes as opposed to other financial-reporting media, such as press releases and newspapers? Do financial statements have a comparative advantage over other media in conveying particular kinds of data? To what extent do financial statements serve to complement other media?

REVIEW OF CAPITAL-MARKET RESEARCH STUDIES

ASR 190

Various studies have been conducted on the reaction of stock prices and volume to the disclosure of current-cost data, several of which are summarized below. Gheyara and Boatsman (1981)[12] performed several tests to determine the informational content of ASR 190 replacement cost disclosures in 1976. The researchers examined distributions of rates of return on common stocks using time-series and cross-sectional data. There was no significant effect on stock prices. Nevertheless, even if there is no new informational content, it cannot be concluded that the SEC's decision to require current replacement cost data was ill-advised. ASR 190 "might have prompted others such as Value Line to produce the forecasts which preempted the disclosures by firms."[13] As Hendriksen observes:[14]

> If the securities markets do not react to financial accounting reports at the time they are published, it may still be possible that the reports are relevant. Financial reports may at least confirm information published by other sources and confirm or refute forecasts made on the basis of other information. This permits financial analysts and investors to evaluate the reliability of other sources and forecasts.

Saftner offers the following hypothesis to explain the market's apparent failure to react to the ASR 190 disclosures:

> It may be the case that the replacement cost disclosures had more information content for certain risk categories or industries than for the market as a whole. By looking at all risk categories and industries together, a significant reaction by the stock market to one category or industry might be hidden in the averaging process.[15]

Saftner studied stock market returns during one year to find reactions to the reporting of current replacement cost. The null hypothesis tested was that there is no reaction by the stock market to the replacement cost disclosures after controlling for the effect of conventional, historical-cost disclosures. Based on this analysis, it appears that supplementing financial statements with ASR 190 data yields more informational content than the conventional financial statements alone. The holding gain variables may add significant information to the historical-cost financial statements.[16]

Debessay (1979)[17] examined the effect of ASR 190 disclosures on various firms. He compared firms most likely and least likely to be affected by these disclosures on the basis of differences between historical cost and current replacement cost incomes. No significant effects on stock prices were found. This study, however, did not distinguish between expected and actual replacement cost income figures.

Beaver et al. (1980)[18] investigated the statistical dependency between changes in security prices and ASR 190 data at the time ASR 190 was proposed, at the time it was adopted, and at the time of initial filing by firms with the SEC. No significant dependencies were found. There was no evidence of new information provided to the market. However, as the researchers maintain: "The study is a showcase for the common problems found in empirical tests of information content. These issues include sample selection, timing of the effective knowledge of the information, and confounding effects of other events."

Ro (1980)[19] investigated both the compliance costs on common stock returns and the informational content of ASR 190 data for several dates involving ASR 190. As in the other studies, no significant impact of compliance costs on stock returns was found. Nor was there an appreciable informational content observed from the disclosed data.

Additionally, Ro (1982)[20] examined whether the ASR 190 disclosures had an impact on weekly transaction volumes of common stocks. No effect on the volume of shares traded for firms required to conform to ASR 190 was found. Accordingly, one may infer the lack of informational content from the ASR 190 disclosures.

Gaumnitz (1982)[21] hypothesized that the inability of empirical research to detect any significant informational content from current income disclosures reflects their lack of objectivity, not their inherent uselessness. Based on data from the closed-end investment company industry, using four statistical approaches to test the association between unrealized holding income and changes in common stock prices, the hypothesis was supported.

Freeman (1982)[22] has suggested that the lack of market reaction to ASR 190 disclosures is due to the phenomenon that stock prices for a particular firm reflect similar opportunities for firms in the same industry. In addition, industry price trends are easy to forecast since such trends are closely followed. In view of these premises, the market should become familiar with the information associated with current-cost data in advance of the disclosure of this information in annual reports. Freeman tested for lead/lag relationships among current-cost income, conventional income, and security returns. Preliminary evidence shows that industry trends in current-cost income after adjustment to constant dollars are anticipated by the market well before the release of the annual report. Freeman concludes that it would be desirable in future market reaction studies to differentiate between inter-industry and intra-industry differences in accounting numbers.

FASB Deliberations

Sepe (1982)[23] finds that stock prices were differentially affected by the FASB's 1974-76 deliberations on the inflation-accounting issue. The author demonstrates empirically that historical-cost/constant-dollar (HC/CD) or general price-level adjusted data appear to be relevant information for security market participants, or at least it became relevant once public disclosure of the information was proposed. Sepe used the same time periods that the FASB followed in considering its 1974 HC/CD proposal so that the results of this study would coincide with the FASB timetable with a view to making stronger conclusions about the market's reactions to the FASB's policy deliberations.

Finally, Beaver and Landsman (1982) provide preliminary findings on the association of security prices and price changes with earnings reflected in conformity with FAS 33.[24] The tentative findings are as follows:

(1) Taken at face value, the value of stockholders' equity implied by current cost and constant dollar accounting is considerably different from that implied by the market value of common equity. If one of the purposes of FAS 33 is to provide information regarding value in use, this disparity deserves further consideration. Alteration of methods used to assess current costs and greater use of the lower recoverable amount provisions of FAS 33 are two possible avenues to consider.

(2) From the perspective of statistically explaining cross-sectional differences in security returns, FAS 33 data appear to provide little or no incremental explanatory power. The one possible exception is a comprehensive measure of current cost savings that includes purchasing power gains, holding gains, net of the effects of inflation.

(3) From the perspective of explaining cross sectional differences in the level of market prices of common stock, historical cost earnings appears to provide greater explanatory power than any of the FAS 33 variables. This research is particularly tentative because of the behavior of the risk term, among other reasons.

The appendix to this chapter provides additional empirical evidence on the informational content of HC/CD data.

IMPLICATIONS AND CONCLUSION

Almost all the empirical studies on the market impact of ASR 190 using different research methods have failed to show any signifi-

cant informational content. The studies dealing with FAS 33 are preliminary in nature and thus inconclusive at this time. A market-learn-
ing phenomenon may exist with respect to the inflation-accounting
data, which the empirical studies fail to consider. Perhaps the market did not react to these new data as it attached little confidence to
their validity. Considering the disparaging remarks made by management on the usefulness of these required supplementary data, which
have appeared in numerous annual corporate reports, it would not be
surprising that the market failed to react to the disclosures.

The published studies do not deal with reactions by creditors,
governmental officials, and the public at large to current-cost disclosures. Almost none of the studies deals with the issue of possibly
different price reactions due to different risk categories.

It should also be noted that if inflation-accounting data were useful, such data might well have been predicted by the market before
the ASR 190 and FAS 33 requirements took effect. Accordingly, a
change in stock prices might not be expected upon disclosure of such
data in the financial statements.

This chapter has considered the costs and benefits of inflation-
accounting disclosures. While there is no theory of relevant disclosure,
alternative approaches can be used to evaluate this concept. The market approach emphasizes the perceived benefits of promoting an efficient capital market, while the individual user approach stresses the
different uses of financial statements.

Empirical research on the informational content of current-
value data may well have implications for establishing accounting
standards, as Whittington observes:[25]

> Empirical research which attempts the more ambitious
> task of assessing utility (such as recent studies of the
> impact of accounting information on share prices) is of
> too recent an origin to have had a significant impact on
> the debate on standards, particularly as its somewhat
> esoteric methodology introduces an additional time-lag
> before it is understood by accountants in practice. How-
> ever, research of this type is flourishing at present,
> and it would be a false "lesson of history" to assume
> that, because it had had no significant influence on the
> evolution of standards in the past, it will not have an
> influence in the future.

It will be interesting to see the results of current empirical research
on the impact of FAS 33 on the stock market.

Reporting of inflation-accounting data in financial statements
reflects a policy decision by the SEC (ASR 190) and FASB (Statement

33) that affects the overall level of disclosure. The purpose of such disclosure is to provide relevant and reliable information in a timely fashion to facilitate investment decision making. This policy decision ought to be based on the benefits and costs of this requirement as well as the information needs of the user audience. There is no indication, however, that either the SEC or FASB made such assessment with respect to ASR 190 and FAS 33, respectively. Accounting reports should not be expanded beyond the point that the incremental costs exceed the incremental benefits of so doing.

In conclusion, even before inflation-accounting data were reported in the footnotes to financial statements, it was determined that capital markets were efficient. In light of inflation-accounting disclosures in financial reports, the question is whether such disclosures serve to improve market efficiency. The problem here is the undefined concept of "improved efficiency." It is not clear whether the efficiency of the market can be enhanced. Additionally, our tools are too crude to use to test for greater efficiency if it, in fact, exists. Moreover, in considering the value of disclosing data in financial statements, the possible transfer of costs from individuals to firms providing the data should be assessed.

In view of the fact that an FASB data bank is now available on FAS 33 disclosures by all the firms required to report such data, [26] more empirical research studies on the informational content of this data can be anticipated.

APPENDIX: ADDITIONAL EMPIRICAL EVIDENCE
ON THE INFORMATIONAL CONTENT OF
HISTORICAL-COST/CONSTANT-DOLLAR DATA

Empirical evidence on the relevance of historical-cost/constant-dollar (HC/CD) data is mixed. Here is a sample of summaries of such studies. Petersen[1] attempted to study the impact of HC/CD statements on portfolio selection and concluded that such statements could affect investment decisions. Basu[2] investigated the association between HC/CD earnings and security prices and found no significant informational content in HC/CD data beyond that obtained from historical-cost data. Basu observes that "the intercorrelation levels are sufficiently high [between HC/CD and historical cost data] so as to suggest that the two alternative sets of numbers are, to a large extent, interchangeable." In another study, Baran, Lakonishok, and Ofer[3] investigated the extent to which HC/CD data conveyed information not included in historical-cost (conventional-accounting) data, through an examination of the association between the accounting beta and market beta (beta being the systematic risk, the degree to which the return on common stock reflects the variability of the market as a whole). Baran et al. report that their findings "appear to support the hypothesis that price-level adjusted [HC/CD] data contain information which is not included in the financial reports currently available." Contradictory results have been reported by Morris[4] who, from a study of stock market reactions to HC/CD data, concluded that there is very little indication that the market has responded to the restated figures.

There is no conceptual basis to support the relevance or informational content of HC/CD data, so it is difficult to interpret the foregoing findings. Nevertheless, most of these studies do provide some evidence to support the relevance of historical-cost/constant-dollar data.

NOTES

1. "Efficiency" is defined in this context as the efficient use of information. Beaver contends that: "there is no direct or simple relationship between the greater market efficiency and 'improved' allocation of resources. Since a distinction must be made between allocational and informational efficiency. They are distinct concepts and the relationship between them has not been rigorously derived." See W. H. Beaver, Financial Reporting: An Accounting Revolution, (Englewood Cliffs, N.J.: Prentice-Hall, 1981), p. 168.

2. Relevant disclosure must be considered in light of the particular user audience, the decision models employed by the users, and the data requirements for these models. However, the specific users of financial statements have not been identified, and the information needs of these users are not understood. Moreover, how users incorporate accounting data into their decision-making process, and which models are used in this process, remain unknown. Thus, it is not known what is relevant, and we can only make certain assumptions pertaining to relevance.

3. In regard to security prices, "information content means that a statistical dependency exists between the signals of an information system and stock prices." See W. H. Beaver, Financial Reporting: An Accounting Revolution, (Englewood Cliffs, N.J.: Prentice-Hall, 1981), p. 153, footnote 10. To elaborate on the definition of information content: "If . . . security prices do in fact adjust rapidly to new information as it becomes available, the changes in security prices will reflect the flow of information to the market. An observed revision of stock prices associated with the release of the income report would thus provide evidence that the information reflected in income numbers is useful." Also see R. Ball and P. Brown, "An Empirical Evaluation of Accounting Income Numbers," Journal of Accounting Research, (Autumn 1968): 159-178.

4. Financial Accounting Standards Board, Statement of Financial Accounting Concepts No. 2, "Qualitative Characteristics of Accounting Information," (Stamford, Conn.: FASB, May 1980).

5. W. H. Beaver, "What Should Be the FASB's Objectives?" The Journal of Accountancy, (August 1973): 49-56.

6. See L. Revsine, Replacement Cost Accounting, (Englewood Cliffs, N.J.: Prentice-Hall, 1973).

7. G. H. Sorter, "An 'Events' Approach to Basic Accounting Theory," The Accounting Review, (January 1969).

8. L. Revsine, "On the Correspondence Between Replacement Cost Income and Economics Income," The Accounting Review, (July 1970).

9. W. H. Beaver, J. Kennelly, and W. Voss, "Predictive

Ability as a Criterion for the Evaluation of Accounting Data," The Accounting Review, (October 1968).

10. This refers to a change in the traditional accounting data reported. An experimental test ought to be able to show a change in the security prices before and after the information is reported. The methodological problems of such tests have been referred to W. H. Beaver et al., in "The Information Content of SEC Accounting Series Release No. 190," Journal of Accounting and Economics, Vol. 2, (1980).

11. See W. H. Beaver, "The Implications of Security Price Research for Disclosure Policy and the Analyst Community," in Financial Information Requirements for Security Analysis, ed. A. R. Abdel-khalik and T. F. Keller, (Durham, N. C.: Duke University Press, 1976), pp. 65-82.

12. K. Gheyara and J. Boatsman, "Market Reaction to the 1976 Replacement Cost Disclosures," Journal of Accounting and Economics, (June 1980).

13. Ibid.

14. E. S. Hendriksen, Accounting Theory, 4th ed., (Homewood, Ill.: Richard D. Irwin, 1982), p. 90.

15. D. V. Saftner, Stock Market Reaction to Replacement Cost Disclosures Required by the Securities and Exchange Commission, unpublished manuscript, December 1979, p. 37.

16. Ibid.

17. A. Debessay, An Empirical Investigation of the Impact of Replacement Cost Disclosures on Capital Market Equilibrium: A Step Towards the Resolution of the Inflation Accounting Controversy, unpublished doctoral dissertation, (Syracuse, N. Y.: Syracuse University, January 1979).

18. Beaver, Christie, and Griffin, The Information Content.

19. B. T. Ro, "The Adjustment of Security Returns to the Disclosure of Replacement Cost Accounting Information," Journal of Accounting and Economics, Vol. 2, (1980).

20. B. T. Ro, "The Disclosure of Replacement Cost Accounting Data and Its Effect on Transaction Volumes," The Accounting Review, (January 1981).

21. B. R. Gaumnitz, Income Determination and Closed-End Investment Companies, unpublished doctoral dissertation, (Madison, Wis.: University of Wisconsin, 1982).

22. R. N. Freeman, "Alternative Measures of Profit Margin: An Empirical Study of the Potential Information Content of Current Cost Accounting," presented at the 1982 American Accounting Association Meeting, San Diego, Calif.

23. J. Sepe, "The Impact of the FASB's 1974 GPL Proposal on the Security Price Structure," The Accounting Review, (July 1982).

24. W. H. Beaver and W. Landsman, "The Incremental Informational Content of FAS 33 Disclosures," presented at the 1982 American Accounting Association Meeting, San Diego, Calif.

25. G. Whittington, "The Role of Research in Setting Accounting Standards: The Case of Inflation Accounting," in Accounting Standards Setting: An International Perspective, eds. M. Bromwich and A. Hopwood (London: Pitman, 1983), p. 128.

26. "The FASB Data Bank is stored on computer tape and contains information about changing prices and pensions disclosures for more than 1100 companies. It can be used easily with other financial information data banks containing historical cost data, such as Standard & Poor's Compustat Services (Compustat) and The Value Line Investment Survey published by Arnold Bernhard and Co., Inc. (Value Line)." See H. Goodman, A. Phillips, J. Burton, and M. Vasarhelyi, Illustrations and Analysis of Disclosures of Inflation Accounting Information, New York: AICPA, 1981, p. 2.

NOTES TO APPENDIX

1. R. J. Petersen, "Analysis of General Price Level Restatement," The Accounting Review, (July 1975).

2. S. Basu, Inflation Accounting: Capital Market Efficiency and Security Prices. Hamilton, Ontario: Society of Management Accountants, 1977.

3. A. Baran, J. Lakonishok, and A. Ofer, "The Information Content of General Price Level Adjusted Earnings: Some Empirical Evidence," The Accounting Review, (January 1980).

4. R. C. Morris, "Evidence of the Impact of Inflation Accounting on Share Prices," Accounting and Business Research, (Spring, 1975).

12

SUMMARY AND CONCLUSION

SUMMARY AND CONCLUSION

We have endeavored in this book to examine the financial-reporting problems that arise in periods of changing prices and to provide a comprehensive analysis of the methods and techniques for dealing with the effects of changing prices—general and specific—on financial reports. In so doing, we have attempted to illuminate the various alternative accounting models that may be used and to discuss the pros and cons of each model. This concluding chapter sums up the topics we have covered in this book.

In examining the financial-reporting problems arising from changing prices, we have restricted our focus to the environment in which investors and creditors are assumed to be the primary users of financial reports. It is assumed that investors and creditors require financial information to assess the prospective risks and returns associated with investment and lending decisions. To be relevant, financial reports should assist investors and creditors in making meaningful comparisons of the risks and returns of alternative investment opportunities. From a broader societal perspective, financial reporting should assist in allocating funds to those opportunities in which such funds can be most effectively and efficiently used. It is expected that financial reporting should create confidence among investors and thereby promote the successful operation of capital markets, which are essential to a free-enterprise economy.

There is little dispute concerning the reliability and verifiability of the financial information contained in the conventional historical-cost financial statements. However, there is a general consensus that the conventional statements are deficient in conveying meaningful eco-

259

nomic data that could help investors and creditors in their investment and lending decisions. As discussed in Chapter 1, the deficiency of the information contained in the conventional financial statements is related to unsound principles upon which the conventional model is based. Although the deficiencies of the system tend to be more pronounced during inflationary periods, it is important to recognize that the conventional model is deficient even in the absence of inflation or deflation. Reliance on the historical-cost principle generates balance sheets that do not reflect current values of resources used by a firm. The matching of historical costs with realized revenues tends to produce "inflated" profits when specific prices are increasing. Additionally, reliance on a stable monetary-unit assumption creates serious measurement problems in light of the fluctuating value of the monetary unit. In view of these deficiencies, several alternative accounting models have been proposed.

PROPOSED ALTERNATIVE ACCOUNTING MODELS

In general, the proposed accounting models can be classified as follows: (1) those that favor the modification of the conventional historical-cost accounting model, by restating historical-cost data to reflect changes in the general price-level; (2) those that call for a departure from the historical-cost model in favor of some form of current value; and (3) those that combine current values with the application of a common scale of measurement.

The historical-cost/constant-dollar model, which is also referred to as the general price-level-adjusted historical-cost model, recognizes the problems inherent in using the dollar as a unit of measurement. Thus, in order to avoid the problem of using an unstable unit of measurement in financial reporting, this model involves the restatement of the conventional historical-cost statements in terms of constant dollars. However, to the extent that this model is the historical-cost model apart from change in the unit of measurement, it does not remedy the primary weakness of the conventional model—the failure to reflect current economic conditions. Despite its shortcomings, however, the historical-cost/constant-dollar model has been seriously considered as a solution to the financial-reporting problems arising during periods of changing prices in the United States and abroad. At the present time, support for the historical-cost/constant-dollar model is limited. Even though FAS 33 has required the disclosure of historical-cost/constant-dollar data, it is widely believed that such data are of questionable relevance. [1]

At present, there appears to be considerable support for the adoption of some form of a current-value model and for the application of a constant unit of measurement in order to overcome the problems that arise from using the dollar as a measurement unit. Current-value models are intended to overcome the valuation problem caused by adherence to the historical-cost principle. However, proponents of current-value accounting do not agree on what measure best reflects current value. A disparity in views among proponents of current value models has led to the emergence of two major alternative current-value models: (1) current cost, reflecting current purchase prices and (2) current exit value, reflecting the current selling prices or the cash equivalent values. A third school of thought advocates a more flexible current-value accounting framework to reflect either current costs or current exit prices, whichever are more relevant in a given situation.

The Current-Cost Model

The essential characteristic of current-cost accounting (CCA) is the use of current entry prices as the basis for balance-sheet valuation and income measurement. As discussed in Chapter 7, there is a variety of entry prices that can be considered for application purposes. The choice between the current replacement cost of existing assets or the current replacement cost of equivalent service potential has to be made judiciously, keeping in mind that the objective is to present data that are relevant to the primary users of financial statements. Some degree of flexibility is, therefore, necessary in applying the current-cost model.

In valuing liabilities, some would argue in favor of reflecting liabilities at their current-market values. This would be particularly suitable where the market value of bonds outstanding is significantly different from the reported book value, reflecting a difference in the coupon interest rate on the bond and the current market interest rate on similar debt instruments. By contrast, there are those who argue that it is unnecessary to reflect the current values of outstanding debt simply because the financial position of the firm is unchanged as a result of changes in the current values of its debt, assuming the firm is a going concern. The valuation of assets at their current cost, and liabilities at their book values, should not be viewed as an inconsistency of the CCA model. It should be observed that the model deals only with the valuation of the assets of the entity.

Income measurement under the CCA model depends on whether financial capital maintenance or physical capital maintenance is adopted. Under financial capital maintenance, holding gains on assets would be considered a component of income for the period. Income measurement under financial capital maintenance has been criticized for its probable impairment of the firm's operating capacity during a period of increasing prices since the firm's original financial capital would be insufficient to support the same level of operating capacity. For this reason, the measurement of income under physical capital maintenance has been advocated.

Under physical capital maintenance, the distribution of the income reported should enable the firm to maintain its production capacity intact. Under physical capital maintenance, holding gains are treated as direct adjustments to stockholders' equity and are excluded in measuring the income of the period. The physical capital-maintenance concept has been criticized for its unrealistic assumption that the firm is committed to staying in a particular line of business.

In general, the CCA model should constitute a significant improvement in the relevance of financial statements compared to the conventional historical-cost model. The inclusion of holding gains (realized and unrealized) in income is, however, particularly vulnerable to criticism to the extent that this past data may conceivably be irrelevant in decision making.

It should be pointed out that the measurement-unit problem should not arise in preparing the CCA balance sheet, assuming that all balance-sheet items are stated in terms of the balance-sheet dollar. However, in preparing comparative balance sheets, it is necessary to use a common unit of measurement—i.e., common dollars. In regard to the CCA income statement, unless the rate of inflation in a given year is negligible, all income-statement items should be restated in terms of constant dollars.

The Current Exit-Price Model

According to the current exit-price model, assets are valued at their current cash equivalents or their net realizable values under conditions of orderly liquidation. Liabilities are valued either at the amounts that would be needed to settle the obligations at the balance sheet date or at the contractual amounts. Income under this model is measured by comparing the money equivalent of the net assets at the end and beginning of the period, assuming no additional investments or withdrawals are made.

In this model, various special assets that lack current resale values are reported at zero amount even if it is obvious that such assets have values in use. Since income under this model is measured by comparing current cash equivalents of the net assets at the beginning and end of the period, this approach represents a violation of the realization principle. In conventional accounting, the firm is assumed to continue its normal operations in the absence of evidence to the contrary. No such assumption is necessary using this model. One major advantage of this model is that there is no allocation problem involved in measuring income. Unlike the conventional model, the exit-price model shows the current cash equivalents of assets and liabilities in dollars on the balance sheet date. However, for purposes of inter-period comparison and for income measurement, it is necessary to use constant dollars in relation to the exit-price model.

Proponents of this model assume that the primary objective of financial reporting is to provide information that would enable inter-ested parties to evaluate the firm's ability to adapt to changing eco-nomic conditions. On the other hand, the primary objective of finan-cial reporting according to Statement of Financial Accounting Concepts No. 1 (SFAC 1) is to furnish information useful in assessing the amounts, timing, and the related uncertainties of prospective cash flows.[2] SFAC 1 assumes that investors are more interested in assess-ing the firm's prospects as a going concern rather than in assessing the firm's current cash equivalent. Thus, from the point of view of potential investors, who are primarily concerned with the prospective cash flows, the valuation of the firm's assets at their resale value and the measurement of income by comparing beginning and end-of-period net current cash equivalents of the firm's resources may not be relevant.

UNRESOLVED ISSUES

A study of the alternative accounting models suggests a number of areas that should be resolved before agreement can be reached regarding a comprehensive financial-reporting model.

As discussed earlier, the main objective of financial reporting as envisaged by proponents of the current exit-value price model, specifically Chambers, is not the same as the objective perceived by the FASB and other accounting standard-setting bodies in Canada, the United Kingdom, and Australia. Unless agreement is first reached with respect to the main objective of financial reporting, it is difficult to agree on the design of the best accounting model. Whether a given model is satisfactory or not can only be evaluated in relation to the desired objectives.

There are many unresolved issues in accounting and financial reporting. One of these issues is the measurement of income. Should income be measured using financial capital maintenance or physical capital maintenance? Is there a need for a more flexible approach that one may consider on a case-by-case analysis?

If agreement were reached on the income-measurement process then the treatment of realized and unrealized holding gains on assets could probably be resolved. Whether there is a need for a gearing (financing) adjustment to recognize a portion of realized holding gains (or a portion of total holding gains) is a question that needs to be addressed for those firms that finance their plant facilities partly with long-term debt.

Accounting for monetary items is another area that requires further research and study. The alternative accounting models that we have discussed in this book do not seem to provide satisfactory guidance for the proper computation of purchasing-power gains and losses on holding monetary liabilities during periods of changing prices. Additionally, there is no consensus on accounting for purchasing-power gains and losses on holding monetary items.

GLOBAL VIEW

United States. Among the highly industrialized countries, the United States has been the first to issue a financial-reporting standard dealing with the effects of changing prices. Statement of Financial Accounting Standards No. 33 (FAS 33) was issued in 1979 on an experimental basis, requiring large corporations to supplement their primary conventional statements with historical-cost/constant-dollar and current cost disclosures. (An analysis of FAS 33 is provided in Chapter 3.)

Although various provisions of FAS 33 have been severely criticized by parties concerned with the scope and quality of financial reports, it is important to realize the circumstances under which FAS 33 was issued, in order to appreciate its positive aspects. The FASB, as a standard-setting body in the United States, considers the views of its constituents before issuing its pronouncements. With regard to the reporting of the impact of changing prices on financial statements, the FASB was confronted with two opposing views. On the one hand, there was strong support from preparers and auditors for providing supplementary general price-level-adjusted, historical-cost data on the grounds that such data were relatively objective, verifiable, and inexpensive to generate. On the other hand, the general view expressed by users favored current-cost disclosures on the grounds that such data are more relevant albeit subjective. In view of the lack of consensus among its constituents, the FASB found it necessary to require both historical-cost/constant-dollar and current-cost supplementary data on an experimental basis.

The FASB is in the process of reviewing FAS 33. In January 1983, a conference was held at which preliminary findings were reported to the board.[3] The FASB is currently sponsoring several research projects to assist in its five-year comprehensive review of FAS 33. It is expected that various provisions of FAS 33 will be discontinued, and others will be modified or expanded.

United Kingdom. In 1980, Britain's Statement of Standard Accounting Practice No. 16 (SSAP 16) was enacted, requiring listed companies to disclose current-cost data. There are no requirements for constant-dollar data in SSAP 16. (An analysis of this statement appears in Chapter 10.)

It is probably fair to say that SSAP 16 will be amended significantly in the near future. In view of their experience with SSAP 16, many of its initial supporters "have lost their enthusiasm . . . , although there are some who remain convinced of its merits."[4] In fact, as recently reported, the members of the Institute of Chartered Accountants in England and Wales voted by a narrow margin to retain SSAP 16 for its three-year trial period.[5]

SSAP 16 is currently being carefully reviewed. Comments from many users, preparers, and auditors have been received. A revised standard is anticipated within two years. Three key points under discussion are as follows:[6]

1. Where a company is materially affected by changing prices, . . . a company's main accounts should reflect the effect of changing prices either in the arithmetic of the profit and loss account and balance sheet or in the notes to the accounts. It is implicit in this that there should be only one set of accounts.
2. The standard should prescribe more than one method of accounting for the effects of changing prices so that companies can employ a method which is appropriate to their particular circumstances and activities.
3. The standard should apply to all accounts intended to give a true and fair view, subject to a cost-benefit test, to be applied by ASC in preparing its proposals for the standard, which recognizes the differing requirements of shareholders and other users for information.

At this juncture, it is uncertain whether these points will be included as such in the revised standard.

Canada. At the end of 1982, the Canadian Institute of Chartered Accountants (CICA) issued its standard on reporting the effects of changing prices. The CICA reporting standard requires large publicly held Canadian enterprises to disclose supplementary information on the effects of changing prices in annual reports for years beginning on or after January 1, 1982. Like FAS 33, the Canadian standard was also issued on an experimental basis and will be reassessed by the CICA within five years. Although the Canadian standard is in many ways similar to FAS 33, CICA has avoided the FASB's dual disclosure of both constant-dollar and current-cost data, and has adopted essentially a current-cost approach. The CICA standard also calls for comparative information on a constant-dollar basis, reflecting changes in the general purchasing power of the dollar.

A significant difference between the U.S. and Canadian standards is the CICA's introduction of a financing adjustment as a means of reflecting the income attributable to common shareholders. (See Chapter 10 for an analysis of this standard). It is too early at this stage to tell what changes might be made in this standard in view of its recent enactment.

Australia. While Australia has long been a leader in inflation-accounting research, its CCA proposals have not yet been issued as a required standard. At this time, there is apparently a general consensus among financial-reporting constituents in Australia against mandatory disclosure of information concerning the impact of changing prices on the financial position and operating performance of the firm.

Instead, Australia is expecting to issue a set of CCA supplementary reporting recommendations, which firms may or may not follow—at their option.[7] The Proposed Standard on Current Cost Accounting issued in 1982 will presumably be released as the CCA nonmandatory standard. This statement calls for income measurement and balance sheet valuation on a current-cost basis. (See Chapter 10 for an analysis of the Proposed Standard.)

GENERAL OBSERVATIONS

Interest in inflation accounting has been waning, especially in recent months now that inflation seems to be under control at least in the short-run particularly in the United States. As Price Waterhouse observes:[8]

> This apparent lack of interest probably stems from any
> number of sources—unfamiliarity, failure to appreciate
> the significant distortions caused by inflation, the down-
> grading effect of the "supplementary" label, simply too
> many numbers to comprehend. Whatever the reason,
> clear evidence of user disinterest would force FASB to
> withdraw its FAS 33 requirements because of failure to
> pass the necessary cost-benefit test.

Nevertheless, we expect inflation accounting to flourish, especially if inflation proves to be as significant a problem in the future as it has been in the recent past. History shows that interest in inflation accounting is a function of the degree of inflation prevailing in any given time period. (See Chapter 2.) However, even if annual inflation in the future is not significant, cumulative inflation in the long run should be significant due to compounding. Accordingly, failure to recognize inflation in the financial reports would ignore a key economic factor affecting the firm. Furthermore, inflation-accounting models, which were once considered heretical, appear to be gaining acceptance in recent years among the various constituents of financial reporting. It should also be noted that as long as there are changes in the movement of individual prices, even in the absence of general inflation or deflation, departures from historical cost are inevitable in order to portray current economic conditions. Consequently, even if inflation appears to be slowing down, there is still a need to reflect the impact of specific price changes in financial reports. In this regard, we hope that the FASB and other standard-setting bodies around the world will continue their efforts to improve the accounting for the impact of changing prices.

If enthusiastic support is lacking for the inflation-accounting pronouncements considered in this book, so too is rigorous opposition in all of these countries, with the possible exception of Australia. Preparers, users, and auditors are not overly exuberant about mandatory inflation-accounting standards but seem to be willing to accept them and make recommendations for improving them.

Far from letter perfect, these pronouncements, which are all similar in terms of objectives and reporting requirements, represent a step in the right direction. As the comptroller of General Electric has observed:[9]

> I believe it is far less important how we display the impact
> of changing prices and inflation, than that we display it. I
> would hope that the standard setters would resist the temp-
> tation for complexity and conceptual tidiness and opt instead
> for a walk-before-run approach.

Finally, FAS 33 data, in particular, have not been used as prevalently as had been anticipated. But FAS 33 has, after all, been an experimental standard. As the current chief accountant of the SEC has asserted:[10]

> Experience to date with use of the data hasn't been a re-
> sounding success, but the lack of usefulness must be care-
> fully examined lest it be concluded too easily that changing
> prices data isn't needed. The data demanded by Statement
> No. 33 is complex and doesn't reach a "bottom line." Its
> relatively unused status may demonstrate a need for better
> education about what it is or a desire for more comparable

and complete data (net income, for instance). Perhaps one thing to be learned from the Statement No. 33 experiment is that users want data they can readily comprehend.

The need for educating users on the concepts and techniques of accounting for the impact of changing prices is not just limited to the United States—but also abroad. We trust that this book has contributed toward that end.

NOTES

1. See, as an example, "Special Report—FASB Conference on Use of Inflation-Adjusted Data," The Journal of Accountancy, (March 1983); 10, 12, 14.

2. Statement of Financial Accounting Concepts No. 1: "Objectives of Financial Reporting by Business Enterprises," (Stamford, Conn.: FASB, 1978).

3. See "Special Report—FASB Conference on Use of Inflation-Adjusted Data," The Journal of Accountancy, (March 1983).

4. Accounting Standards Committee, "Interim Report of the CCA Monitoring Working Party," The Accountants Magazine, (May 1983): 187.

5. "News Briefs," The Journal of Accountancy, (September 1982): 22.

6. "SSAP 16 May Remain in Force for Another Two Years," The Accountants Magazine, (May 1983): 169.

7. See "Not with a Bang But a Whimper," The Chartered Accountant in Australia, (May 1983): 56; and "Current Cost Accounting," The Chartered Accountant in Australia, (May 1983): 7.

8. Price Waterhouse and Company, Accounting Events and Trends, May 1983, p. 2.

9. T. O. Thorsen, "FASB Conference on Financial Reporting and Changing Prices," (Stamford, Conn.: FASB, May 31, 1979).

10. A. C. Sampson, "A Regulator's View of the FASB: The First 10 Years and After," The Journal of Accountancy, (August 1983): 50.

BIBLIOGRAPHY

Abdel-Khalik, A. R., and T. F. Keller, eds. Financial Information Requirements for Security Analysis. Durham, N.C.: Duke University Press, 1976.

Accounting Principles Board. "Status of Accounting Research Bulletins," APB Opinion No. 6. New York: AICPA, 1965.

Accounting Principles Board. "Financial Statements Restated for General Price Levels," APB Statement No. 3. New York: AICPA, 1969.

Accounting Principles Board. "Basic Concepts and Accounting Policies Underlying Financial Statements of Business Enterprise," APB Statement No. 4. New York: AICPA, 1970.

Accounting Research Committee. Proposed Accounting Recommendation, Re-exposure Draft, Reporting the Effects of Changing Prices. Ontario: Canadian Institute of Chartered Accountants, December 1981.

Accounting Research Committee. Section 4510, CICA Handbook: Reporting the Effects of Changing Prices, Toronto: Canadian Institute of Chartered Accountants, 1982.

Accounting Standards Committee. Inflation Accounting, An Interim Recommendation. London: ASC, 1977.

Accounting Standards Committee, Institute of Chartered Accountants of England and Wales. Statement of Standard Accounting Practice No. 16, "Current Cost Accounting." London: ASC, 1980.

Accounting Standards Committee. "Interim Report of the CCA Monitoring Working Party." The Accountants Magazine, May 1983.

Accounting Standards Committee. Proposed Statement of Standard Accounting Practice, Ed 18: Current Cost Accounting. London: ASC, November 1976.

Accounting Standards Committee. Proposed Statement of Standard Accounting Practice, Ed. 24: Current Cost Accounting. London: ASC, 1979.

Accounting Standards Steering Committee. Provisional Statement of Standard Accounting Practice No. 7 (SSAP 7) Accounting for Changes in the Purchasing Power of Money. London: ASSC, May 1974.

Ackoff, R. Scientific Method: Optimizing Research Decisions. New York: Wiley, 1962.

Agrawal, S. P. "Use of Recoverable Amounts in the Valuations Required Under FASB #33." Presented at Southeastern Regional Meeting. American Accounting Association. Virginia Beach, VA., April 1983.

Agrawal, S. P., and R. C. Hallbauer. "Inflation: Implications for Management Accounting." Cost and Management, November-December 1976.

Alexander, M. O. "FAS 33 and the Future—Research and Decisions." Presentation at American Accounting Association Annual Meeting. Chicago, August 1981.

Alexander, S. S. "Income Measurement in a Dynamic Economy," revised by D. Solomons, Studies in Accounting, eds. W. T. Baxter and S. Davidson. London: The Institute of Chartered Accountants in England and Wales, 1977.

American Accounting Association, Accounting and Reporting Standards for Corporate Financial Statements and Preceding Statements and Supplements, Iowa City, Iowa: AAA, College of Business Administration, University of Iowa, 1957.

American Accounting Association. "The Realization Concept." The Accounting Review, April 1965.

American Accounting Association, Committee on Concepts and Standards for External Financial Reports. Statement on Accounting Theory and Theory Acceptance. American Accounting Association, 1977.

American Accounting Association, Committee on Concepts and Standards—Inventory Measurement. "A Discussion of Various

Approaches to Inventory Measurement." The Accounting Review, July 1964.

American Accounting Association. Report of the Subcommittee of the Committee on Financial Accounting Standards: "Response to 'Financial Reporting and Changing Prices: Foreign Currency Translation, An Amendment of FASB Statement No. 33.'" American Accounting Association, October 1982.

American Accounting Association. A Statement of Basic Accounting Theory. Evanston, Ill.: AAA, 1966.

American Institute of Certified Public Accountants. Accounting Trends and Techniques. New York: AICPA, 1982.

American Institute of Certified Public Accountants, APB Statement No. 4, "Basic Concepts and Accounting Principles Underlying Financial Statement of Business Enterprises," New York: AICPA, 1970.

American Institute of Certified Public Accountants. Objectives of Financial Statements. New York: AICPA, 1973.

Andrews, F. "Replacement Cost Accounting Plan Adopted by SEC." The Wall Street Journal, March 25, 1976.

Arthur Andersen and Company. Inflation Accounting—A Simplified Approach. Chicago: Arthur Anderson and Company, 1979.

Arthur Young. Disclosing Replacement Cost Data. New York: Arthur Young and Company, 1977.

Arthur Young. Financial Reporting and Changing Prices: An Analysis of the FASB's Proposed Statement. New York: Arthur Young and Company, 1979.

Arthur Young. Financial Reporting and Changing Prices: Survey of Preparers Views and Practices. New York: Arthur Young and Company, 1981.

Australian Accounting Research Foundation. Current Cost Accounting Working Guide. Prepared on behalf of the Australian Society of Accountants and Institute of Chartered Accountants in Australia. Melbourne, Australia, 1978.

Australian Accounting Research Foundation. Exposure Draft. "Current Cost Accounting—Omnibus Exposure Draft." Melbourne, Australia: Australian Accounting Research Foundation, March 1980.

Australian Accounting Research Foundation. "Revised Exposure Draft: The Recognition of Gains and Losses on Holding Monetary Items in the Context of Current Cost Accounting." Insert to The Australian Accountant and The Chartered Accountant in Australia, August 1979.

Australian Society of Accountants and the Institute of Chartered Accountants in Australia, Proposed Statement of Accounting Standards: Current Cost Accounting; and Guide and Notes in Statement of Accounting Standards Current Cost Accounting, February 1982.

Axelson, Kenneth S. "Facing the Hard Truths about Inflation." Management Accounting, June 1980.

Backer, M., ed. Modern Accounting Theory. Englewood Cliffs, N.J.: Prentice-Hall, 1966.

Backer, M., and R. Simpson. Current Value Accounting. New York: Financial Executives Research Foundation, 1973.

Bailey, E. J. "The SEC and Replacement Cost: An Urgent Need to Find a Better Answer." Management Accounting, December 1977.

Ball, R., and P. Brown. "An Empirical Evaluation of Accounting Income Numbers." Journal of Accounting Research, Autumn 1968.

Baran, A., J. Lakonishok, and A. Ofer. "The Information Content of General Price Level Adjusted Earnings: Some Empirical Evidence." The Accounting Review, January 1980.

Barbatelli, E. "Implementing ASR 190." Management Accounting, December 1977.

Bastable, C. W. "Depreciation in An Inflationary Environment." The Journal of Accountancy, August 1976.

Bastable, C. W. "Is SEC Replacement Cost Data Worth the Effort?" The Journal of Accountancy, October 1977.

Baxter, W. T. Accounting Values and Inflation. London: McGraw-Hill, 1975. (Sponsored by the Research Committee on the Institute of Chartered Accountants in England and Wales.)

Baxter, W. T. "Inflation Accounting—Raising the British Standard." CA Magazine, February 1977.

Baxter, W. T., and S. Davidson, eds. Studies in Accounting. London: The Institute of Chartered Accountants in England and Wales, 1977.

Beaver, W. H. "Current Trends in Corporate Disclosure." Journal of Accountancy, January 1978.

Beaver, W. H. Financial Reporting: An Accounting Revolution. Englewood Cliffs, N.J.: Prentice-Hall, 1981.

Beaver, W. H. "The Implications of Security Price Research for Disclosure Policy and the Analyst Community." Financial Information Requirements for Security Analysis, ed. A. R. Abdel-khalik and T. F. Keller, Durham, N.C.: Duke University Press, 1976.

Beaver, W. H. "Interpreting Disclosures of the Effects of Changing Prices." Financial Analysts Journal, September-October, 1981.

Beaver, W. H. "What Should Be the FASB's Objectives?" The Journal of Accountancy, August 1973.

Beaver, W. H., A. A. Christie, and P. A. Griffin. "The Information Content of SEC Accounting Series Release No. 190." Journal of Accounting and Economics, Vol. 2, 1980.

Beaver, W. H., J. Kennelly, and W. Voss. "Predictive Ability as a Criterion for the Evaluation of Accounting Data." The Accounting Review, October 1968.

Beaver, W. H., and W. Landsman. "The Incremental Informational Content of FAS 33 Disclosures." Presented at the 1982 American Accounting Association meeting. San Diego, Calif.

Belkaoui, A. Accounting Theory. New York: Harcourt Brace Jovanovich, 1981.

Bell, P. W. American and Australian Approaches to Current Value

Accounting: How Fundamental Are the Differences? Australian Accounting Research Foundation, 1982.

Bell, P. W. "Measurement of Business Income, Part 2—Price Changes and Income Measurement," ed. M. Backer. Modern Accounting Theory, Englewood Cliffs, N.J.: Prentice-Hall, 1966.

Beresford, D. R., and J. R. Klein. "Inflation Accounting in the U.S. and U.K.—A Comparison." The Journal of Accountancy, August 1979.

Berliner, R., and D. L. Gerboth. "FASB Statement No. 33: The Great Experiment." The Journal of Accountancy, May 1980.

Bernstein, L. A. "General Price Level Financial Statements—A Review of APB Statement No. 3." New York Certified Public Accountant, January 1970.

Bierman, H. "Discounted Cash Flows, Price-Level Adjustments and Expectations: A Reply." The Accounting Review, October 1972.

Bird, P. C. "What Is Capital Gearing?" Accounting and Business Research, Spring 1973.

Bloom, R. "Reflections on the Problem of Uncertainty in Accounting." Accounting History, Vol. 4, No. 2, 1980.

Bloom, R., and A. Debessay. "A Critique of FAS No. 33." Management Accounting, May 1981.

Bloom, R., and P. T. Elgers, eds. Accounting Theory and Policy: A Reader. New York: Harcourt Brace Jovanovich, 1981.

Bloom, R., P. T. Elgers, J. R. Haltiner, and W. H. Hawthorne. "Inflation Gains and Losses on Monetary Items: An Empirical Test." Journal of Business Finance and Accounting, Winter 1980.

Blum, J. D., L. Brooks, and D. Buckmaster. "Variability in Price Level Changes: Inventory Expenses or Revenue Adjustments." Cost and Management, July-August 1975.

Boer, G. "Replacement Cost: A Historical Look." The Accounting Review, January 1966.

Bonbright, J. C. The Valuation of Property, Vol. I. New York: McGraw-Hill, 1937.

Bradford, W. D. "Price-Level Restated Accounting and The Management of Inflation Gains and Losses: A Reply." The Accounting Review, July 1975.

"Brief Guide to Sandilands." Management Accounting, October 1975.

Bronowski, J. A Sense of the Future. Cambridge, Mass.: MIT Press, 1977.

Brooks, L. D., and D. Buckmaster. "Price-Change Accounting Models and Disaggregated Monetary Gains and Losses." In Inflation and Current Value Accounting, ed. J. C. McKeown. Urbana, Ill.: College of Commerce and Business Administration, University of Illinois, 1979.

Brown, P. "Accounting for Changing Prices: A Comment." Chartered Accountant in Australia, December 1971.

Buckmaster, D., and L. D. Brooks. "Accounting for Interest and Long-Term Debt in an Inflationary Period." Management Accounting, May 1982.

Buckmaster, D. "Inflation Gains and Losses from Holding Monetary Assets and Liabilities, 1918-1936: A Study of the Development of Accounting Thought in the U.S." International Journal of Accounting Education and Research, Spring 1982.

Buckmaster, D., and L. D. Brooks. "Effects of Price-Level Changes on Operating Income." CPA Journal, May 1974.

Buckmaster, D., R. M. Copeland, and P. E. Dascher. "Relative Predictive Ability of Three Accounting Income Models. Accounting and Business Research, Summer 1977.

Burton, J. C. "Financial Reporting in an Age of Inflation." The Journal of Accountancy, February 1975.

Canadian Institute of Chartered Accountants. Exposure Draft, Proposed Accounting Recommendations: Current Cost Accounting. Toronto: Canadian Institute of Chartered Accountants, December 1979.

Canadian Institute of Chartered Accountants. Proposed Accounting Recommendations: Current Cost Accounting. Toronto: Canadian Institute of Chartered Accountants, December 1979.

Canadian Institute of Chartered Accountants, Accounting Research Committee. Proposed Accounting Recommendation, Re-exposure Draft, "Reporting the Effects of Changing Prices." Toronto: Canadian Institute of Chartered Accountants, December 1981.

Canadian Institute of Chartered Accountants, CICA Handbook, Section 4510, Reporting the Effects of Changing Prices, December 1982.

Canning, J. B. The Economics of Accountancy: A Critical Analysis of Accounting Theory. New York: Ronald Press, 1929.

Causey, D. Y. "Sweeney's Price Level Accounting—Revisited." South African Chartered Accountant, January 1975.

Caws, P. The Philosophy of Science. Princeton, N.J.: Van Nostrand, 1965.

"The CCA Experience: Progress and Prospects—Three Views." Chartered Accountant in Australia, July 1978.

Chambers, R. J. Accounting, Evaluation and Economic Behavior. Englewood Cliffs, N.J.: Prentice-Hall, 1966.

Chambers, R. J. Accounting, Finance and Management. Sydney, Australia: Arthur Andersen and Company, 1969.

Chambers, R. J. Accounting for Inflation: Exposure Draft. Sydney, Australia: University of Sydney, 1975. Reprinted in Accounting Theory and Policy: A Reader, eds. R. Bloom and P. T. Elgers. New York: Harcourt Brace Jovanovich, 1981.

Chambers, R. J. "Accounting for Inflation." 1977 Invitational Lecture of Manawater (N. Z.) Accounting Students Society. Palmerston North, New Zealand: Massey University, 1977.

Chambers, R. J. Accounting for Inflation: Methods and Problems. Department of Accounting of the University of Sydney, Australia, 1975.

Chambers, R. J. "Continuously Contemporary Accounting." In Readings in Inflation Accounting, eds. P. T. Wanless and D. A. R. Forrester. New York: John Wiley and Sons, 1979.

Chambers, R. J. "Continuously Contemporary Accounting: Misunderstandings and Misrepresentations." Abacus, December 1976.

Chambers, R. J. "Current Value Accounting—COCOA or REPCO?" Singapore Accountant, 1977.

Chambers, R. J. "Fair Financial Reporting—In Law and Practice." In the Emanuel Saxe Distinguished Lectures in Accounting 1976–1977. New York: Bernard M. Baruch College, 1977.

Chambers, R. J. "Multiple Column Accounting—oui Bono?" Chartered Accountant in Australia, March 1972.

Chambers, R. J. "NOD, COG and PuPu: See How Inflation Teases!" The Journal of Accountancy, September 1975.

Chambers, R. J. "Nonmoney Purchasing Power Unit?" The Journal of Accountancy, December 1975.

Chambers, R. J. "Price Level Problem and Some Intellectual Grooves." Journal of Accounting Research, Autumn 1965.

Chambers, R. J. Securities and Obscurities, A Case for Reform of the Law of Company Accounts. Melbourne, Australia: Gower Press, 1973.

Chambers, R. J. "Study of a Study of a Price Level Study: Response to Professor Moonitz." Abacus, August 1967.

Chatfield, M. Contemporary Studies in the Evolution of Accounting Thought. Belmont, Calif.: Dickenson, 1968.

Chippindale, W., and P. L. Defliese, eds. Current Value Accounting: A Practical Guide for Business. New York: AMACOM, 1977.

Churchman, C. W. Theory of Experimental Inference. New York: Macmillan, 1948.

Clarke, F. L. "Accounting for Inflation—A Bibliography." Chartered Accountant in Australia, March 1976.

Clarke, F. L. "CCA: Progress or Regress?" Current Cost Accounting: Identifying the Issues, eds. G. W. Dean and M. C. Wells. Second ed., Lancaster, England: International Center for Research in Accounting, University of Lancaster, and Sydney, Australia: Department of Accounting, University of Sydney, 1979.

Clarke, F. L. "Closer Look at Sweeney's Stabilised Accounting Proposals." Accounting and Business Research, Autumn 1976.

Clarke, F. L. "Inflation Accounting and the Accidents of History." Abacus, December 1980.

Clarke, F. L. "Replacement Costs and Inflation Accounting: A Demurrer." Financial Analysts Journal, January-February 1981.

Cochran, W. C., and E. M. Cox. Experimental Design. New York: Wiley, 1957.

Cohen, M. R., and E. Nagel. An Introduction to Logic and Scientific Method. New York: Harcourt, Brace and World, 1934.

Committee of Inquiry into Inflation and Taxation (Mathews Committee) Report. "Method of Accounting for Changes in the Purchasing Power of Money." Canberra, Australia: Australian Government Printing Service, 1975.

Committee on Accounting Procedures. Accounting Research Bulletin No. 43, Restatement and Revision of Accounting Research Bulletins. AICPA, June 1953. Chapter 9A, par. 17, reproduced in Financial Accounting Standards Board, Financial Accounting Standards. Stamford, Conn.: FASB, 1981.

Committee on Concepts and Standards—Long Lived Assets. "Accounting for Land, Buildings, and Equipment." The Accounting Review, July 1964.

Committee on Concepts and Standards Underlying Corporate Financial Statements. Accounting and Reporting Standards for Corporate Financial Statements—1957 Revision. Sarasota, Fla.: AAA, 1957.

Committee on Concepts and Standards Underlying Corporate Financial Statements. Supplementary Statement No. 2, Price Level Changes and Financial Statements. Sarasota, Fla.: AAA, 1951.

Committee on Concepts and Standards Underlying Corporate Financial Statements. Supplementary Statement No. 6, Inventory Pricing and Changes in Price Levels. Sarasota, Fla.: AAA, 1953.

Craswell, A. A Manual on Continuously Contemporary Accounting. Hamilton, New Zealand: University of Waikato, 1977.

Craswell, A. "CCA Adds Up to Nothing." Current Cost Accounting: Identifying the Issues, 2nd ed., eds. G. W. Dean and M. C. Wells. University of Lancaster, England, and University of Sydney, Australia, 1977.

"Current Cost Accounting." The Chartered Accountant in Australia, May 1983.

Davidson, S., and R. L. Weil. "Comments on Are You Ready for Inflation Accounting?" The Journal of Accountancy, September 1975.

Davidson, S., and R. L. Weil. "Impact of Inflation Accounting on 1974 Earnings." Financial Analysts Journal, September-October 1974.

Davidson, S., and R. L. Weil. "Inflation Accounting: The SEC Proposal for Replacement Cost Disclosures." Financial Analysts Journal, March-April 1976.

Davidson, S., and R. L. Weil. "Inflation Accounting: What Will General Price-Level Adjusted Income Statements Show?" Financial Analysts Journal, January-February 1975.

Dean, G. W., and M. C. Wells, eds. Current Cost Accounting: Identifying the Issues, 2nd ed. Lancaster, England: International Center for Research in Accounting, University of Lancaster, and Sydney, Australia: Department of Accounting, University of Sydney, 1979.

Debessay, A. An Empirical Investigation of the Impact of Replacement Cost Disclosures on Capital Market Equilibrium: A Step Towards the Resolution of the Inflation Accounting Controversy. Unpublished dissertation. Syracuse, N.Y.: Syracuse University, May 1979.

Defliese, P. L. "Inflation Accounting: Pursuing the Elusive." The Journal of Accountancy, May 1979.

Deloitte, Haskins and Sells. The Week in Review, October 23, 1981.

Deloitte, Haskins and Sells. The Week in Review, September 5, 1980.

Devine, C. T. "Research Methodology and Accounting Theory Formation." The Accounting Review, July 1960.

Dewey, J. Logic: The Theory of Inquiry. New York: Henry Holt, 1938.

Dopuch, N., and S. Sunder. "FASB's Statement of Objectives and Elements of Financial Accounting: A Review." The Accounting Review, January 1980.

Drake, D. F., and N. Dopuch. "On the Case for Dichotomizing Income." Journal of Accounting Research, Autumn 1965.

Edwards, E. O., and P. W. Bell. The Theory and Measurement of Business Income. Berkeley, Calif.: University of California Press, 1961.

Edwards, J. D., and J. B. Barrack. "Objectives of Financial Statements and Inflation Accounting: A Comparison of Recent British and American Proposals." The International Journal of Accounting, Spring 1976.

Emanuel Saxe Distinguished Lectures in Accounting. New York: Bernard M. Baruch College, 1977.

Ernst and Ernst. "SEC Replacement Cost Requirements and Implementation Guidance." Financial Reporting Developments, Ernst and Ernst, 1977.

Establishing Financial Accounting Standards. Report of the Study on Establishment of Accounting Principles. New York: AICPA, March 1972.

Executive Committee of the American Accounting Association. Accounting Principles Underlying Corporate Financial Statements, June 1941. Reproduced in American Accounting Association, Accounting and Reporting Standards for Corporate Financial Statements and Preceding Statements and Supplements. Iowa City, Iowa: AAA, College of Business Administration, University of Iowa, undated.

Fabricant, S. "Inflation and Current Accounting Practice: An Economist's View." The Journal of Accountancy, December 1971.

Fama, E. F. "Efficient Capital Markets: A Review of Theory and Empirical Work." Journal of Finance, May 1970.

FASB Highlights, cited in Deloitte, Haskins and Sells, The Week in Review, October 23, 1981.

FASB List of Research Projects [for FAS 33], 1981.

"FASB Proposed Rules of Procedure." The Journal of Accountancy, November 1972.

"FASB Statement No. 33 is Focus of 12 Research Efforts." The Journal of Accountancy, August 1982.

Fielding, J. "The Gearing Adjustment—What Is the Best Method?" Accountancy, May 1979.

Financial Accounting Standards Board. Conceptual Framework for Financial Accounting and Reporting: Elements of Financial Statements and Their Measurement. Stamford, Conn.: FASB, 1976.

Financial Accounting Standards Board. Constant Dollar Accounting. Stamford, Conn., 1979. (Exposure Draft, March 2, 1979. Supplement to Proposed Statement of Financial Accounting Standards. Financial Reporting in Units of General Purchasing Power.)

Financial Accounting Standards Board. Discussion Memorandum: Reporting the Effects of General Price-Level Changes in Financial Statements. Stamford, Conn.: FASB, February 1974.

Financial Accounting Standards Board. FASB Discussion Memorandum: Conceptual Framework for Financial Accounting and Reporting: Elements of Financial Statements and Their Measurement. Stamford, Conn.: FASB, December 2, 1976.

Financial Accounting Standards Board. Financial Reporting in Units of General Purchasing Power. Stamford, Conn.: December 1974.

Financial Accounting Standards Board. Statement of Financial Accounting Concepts No. 1, "Objectives of Financial Reporting by Business Enterprises." Stamford, Conn., November 1978.

Financial Accounting Standards Board. Statement of Financial Accounting Concepts No. 2, "Qualitative Characteristics of Accounting Information." Stamford, Conn., May 1980.

Financial Accounting Standards Board. Statement of Financial Accounting Standards No. 33. "Financial Reporting and Changing Prices." Stamford, Conn.: FASB, 1979.

Fisher, I. The Money Illusion. New York: Macmillan, 1925.

Fisher, I. The Nature of Capital and Income. New York: Macmillan, 1906.

Fisher, I. The Purchasing Power of Money. New York: Macmillan, 1911.

Fisher, I. The Rate of Interest. New York: Macmillan, 1907.

Fisher I. The Theory of Interest. New York: Macmillan, 1930.

Flesher, D., and J. Soroosh. "Controllers Say FAS 33 Is Not Very Useful." Management Accounting, January 1983.

Freeman, R. N. "Alternative Measures of Profit Margin: An Empirical Study of the Potential Information Content of Current Cost Accounting." Presented at the 1982 American Accounting Association Meeting. San Diego, Calif.

Friedman, L. A. "An Exit-Price Income Statement." The Accounting Review, January 1978.

Friedman, L. A. "What is Current Value?" CPA Journal, November 1978.

Friedman, M. Essays in Positive Economics. Chicago: University of Chicago Press, 1953.

Gandele, G. O. "Concepts of Capital Maintenance." Journal of Accounting, Auditing and Finance, Spring 1981.

Garner, D. E. "Survey of Financial Statement Users: The Need for Price-Level and Replacement Value Data." The Journal of Accountancy, September 1972.

Gaumnitz, B. R. "Income Determination and Closed-End Investment Companies." Unpublished doctoral dissertation, Madison, Wis.: University of Wisconsin, 1982.

Gerboth, D. L. "Research, Intuition, and Politics in Accounting Inquiry," The Accounting Review, July 1973.

Gheyara, K., and J. Boatsman. "Market Reaction to the 1976 Replacement Cost Disclosures." Journal of Accounting and Economics, June 1980.

Goodman, H., A. Phillips, J. Burton, and M. Vasarhelyi. Illustrations and Analysis of Disclosures of Inflation Accounting Information. New York: AICPA, 1981.

Grinyer, J. R., and T. W. Symon. "Maintenance of Capital Intact: An Unnecessary Abstraction?" Accounting and Business Research, Autumn 1980.

Gynther, R. S. "Accounting for Changing Prices: Some Recent Thinking, Recommendations and Practice." Chartered Accountant in Australia, December 1971.

Gynther, R. S. "Accounting for Inflation: Developments in Australia and Overseas." Unpublished paper presented at the New South Wales Congress of the Australian Society of Accountants, February 10, 1982.

Gynther, R. S. "Accounting for Monetary Items Under CCA: A Comment." Accounting and Business Research, Spring 1983.

Gynther, R. S. "Accounting for Price Changes—Theory and Practice." Australian Society of Accountants, Society Bulletin. Melbourne, Australia: Accountants Publishing, 1968.

Gynther, R. S. Accounting for Price Level Changes: Theory and Procedures. London: Pergammon Press, 1966.

Gynther, R. S. "Capital Maintenance, Price Changes, and Profit Determination." The Accounting Review, October 1970.

Gynther, R. S. "CCA: Its Expected Effects." Part I. The Australian Accountant, April 1978.

Gynther, R. S. "CCA—Some Answers to Some Unasnwered Questions." Australian Accountant, June 1977.

Gynther, R. S. Correspondence with the authors. March 8, 1982.

Gynther, R. S. "Why Use General Purchasing Power?" Accounting and Business Research, Spring 1974.

Hakansson, N. H. "On the Relevance of Price-Level Accounting." Journal of Accounting Research, Spring 1969.

Hakansson, N. H. "Purchasing Power Fund: A New Kind of Financial

Intermediary." Financial Analysts Journal, November–December 1976.

Hatfield, H. R. "An Historical Defense of Bookkeeping." In Contemporary Studies in the Evolution of Accounting Thought, ed. M. Chatfield. Belmont, Calif.: Dickenson, 1968.

Hawkins, D. F. "The Development of Modern Financial Reporting Practices Among American Manufacturing Corporations." The Business History Review, Autumn 1963.

Henderson, M. S., and C. G. Peirson. CCA and Purchasing Power Gains and Losses on Monetary Items. Australian Accounting Research Foundation, August 1977.

Henderson, M. S., and C. G. Peirson. "Purchasing Power Gains and Losses on Monetary Items and Current Cost Accounting." Accounting Education, May 1978.

Hendriksen, E. S. Accounting Theory, 4th ed. Homewood, Ill.: Richard D. Irwin, 1982.

Hicks, J. R. Value and Capital, 2nd ed. Oxford, England: Clarendon Press, 1946.

Hong, H. "Inflation and the Market Value of the Firm: Theory and Tests." Journal of Finance, September 1977.

Horngren, C. "How Should We Interpret the Realization Concept?" The Accounting Review, April 1965.

Horngren, C. "The Marketing of Accounting Standards." The Journal of Accountancy, October 1973.

Ijiri, Y. "In Defense of Historical Cost Accounting." In Asset Valuation and Income Determination, ed. R. R. Sterling. Lawrence, Kans.: Scholars Book, 1971.

Ijiri, Y. "Price-Level Restatement and Its Dual Interpretation." The Accounting Review, April 1976.

Irish, R. A. "The Evolution of Corporate Accounting." In Contemporary Studies in the Evolution of Accounting Thought, ed. M. Chatfield. Belmont, Calif.: Dickenson, 1968.

Inflation Accounting: Report of the Inflation Accounting Committee.
    London: Her Majesty's Stationery Office, 1975.

The Institute of Chartered Accountants in Australia and Australian
    Society of Accountants. "Explanatory Statement: The Basis of
    Current Cost Accounting." Insert to The Australian Accountant,
    November 1976.

The Institute of Chartered Accountants in Australia and Australian
    Society of Accountants. "Statement of Provisional Accounting
    Standards: Current Cost Accounting." Insert to The Australian
    Accountant, August 1978.

Institute of Chartered Accountants in England and Wales. Statement
    of Standard Accounting Practice No. 16: Current Cost Account-
    ing. London: Institute of Chartered Accountants in England and
    Wales, 1980.

International Encyclopedia of Unified Science, 2nd enlarged ed.
    Chicago: University of Chicago Press, 1970.

Invitation to Comment on Financial Reporting and Changing Prices,
    FASB, 1981.

Kaplan, R. S. "Purchasing Power Gains on Debt: The Effect of
    Expected and Unexpected Inflation." The Accounting Review,
    April 1977.

Keister, O. R. "The Mechanics of Mesopotamian Record-Keeping."
    In Contemporary Studies in the Evolution of Accounting Thought,
    ed. M. Chatfield. Belmont, Calif.: Dickenson, 1968.

Kenley, W. J. "Current Value Accounting and Price-Level Restate-
    ments." Chartered Accountant in Australia, June 1972.

Kessel, R. A. "Inflation-Caused Wealth Redistribution—A Test of a
    Hypothesis." American Economic Review, March 1956.

Kieso, D. E., and J. J. Weygandt. Intermediate Accounting, 3d. ed.
    New York: John Wiley & Sons, 1980.

Kuhn, T. S. "The Structure of Scientific Revolutions." International
    Encyclopedia of Unified Science, 2nd enlarged ed. Chicago:
    University of Chicago Press, 1970.

Largay, J., and J. L. Livingstone. "Current Value Accounting Neglects Liabilities." Financial Analysts Journal, March–April 1978.

Largay, J., and J. L. Livingstone. Accounting for Changing Prices: Replacement Cost and General Price Level Adjustments. Santa Barbara, Calif.: Wiley/Hamilton, 1976.

Lay, D. W. "CCA—Canada's Proposed Solution to Inflation Accounting." CA Magazine, February 1980.

Lee, T. A. Income and Value Measurement: Theory and Practice. Baltimore, Md.: University Park Press, 1975.

Lemke, K. "The Achilles Heel of Sandilands." The CA Magazine, September 1976.

Lindsay, R., ed. The Nation's Capital Needs: Three Studies. New York: Committee for Economic Development, 1979.

Lintner, J. "Security Prices, Risk and Maximum Gains from Diversification," Journal of Finance, December 1965.

Littleton, A. C. Accounting Evolution to 1900. New York: Russel and Russel, 1933; reprinted 1966.

MacNeal, K. Truth in Accounting. Philadelphia, Pa.: University of Pennsyvalnia Press, 1939; new ed., Houston, Tex.: Scholars Book, 1970.

Magee, R. P. "Accounting Measurement and Employment Contracts: Current Value Reporting." Bell Journal of Economics, Spring 1978.

Marriott, R. G. "CCA: A Comparison of the Australian and U.K. Proposals." The Australian Accountant, October 1979.

Mattessich, R. "An Evolutionary Survey and Comparisons of Current Cost and General Purchasing Power Hypothesis and Their Applications." Unpublished paper, 1980.

Mattessich, R. "On the Evolution of Inflation Accounting—With a Comparison of Seven Major Models." Working paper. University of British Columbia: Vancouver, Canada, 1981.

Mattessich, R. "Still Shooting with Bow and Arrow?—To the CICA Re-exposure Draft on 'Reporting the Effects of Changing Prices.'" Cost and Management, November-December, 1982.

May, G. O. Financial Accounting: A Distillation of Experience. New York: Macmillan, 1943.

May, G. O. "The Influence of Accounting on Economic Development." The Journal of Accountancy, January 1936.

May, R. G., G. G. Mueller, and T. H. Williams. A New Introduction to Financial Accounting, 2nd ed. Englewood Cliffs.: N.J.: Prentice-Hall, 1980.

McCosh, A. M. "Implications of Sandilands for Non-U.K. Accountants." The Journal of Accountancy, March 1976.

McKeown, J. C., ed. Inflation and Current Value Accounting. College of Commerce and Business Administration, University of Illinois, 1979.

Merino, B., ed. Business Income and Price Levels. New York: Arno Press, 1980.

Meyers, J. H. "The Critical Event and Recognition of Net Profit." The Accounting Review, October 1959.

Middleditch, L., Jr. "Should Accounts Reflect the Changing Value of the Dollar?" The Journal of Accountancy, February 1918.

Miller, E. L. Inflation Accounting. New York: Van Nostrand Reinhold, 1980.

Modigliani, F., and R. Cohn. "Inflation, Rational Valuation and the Market." Financial Analysts Journal, March-April 1979.

Modigliani, F., and M. Miller. "The Cost of Capital, Corporate Finance and the Theory of Investment." American Economic Review, June 1958.

Moonitz, M. Accounting Research Study No. 1. "The Basic Postulates of Accounting." New York: AICPA, 1961.

Moonitz, M. "Chambers on the Price Level Study." Abacus, August 1967.

Moonitz, M. Changing Prices and Financial Reporting. International Centre for Research in Accounting, University of Lancaster, 1973.

Moonitz, M. Correspondence with the authors. February 16, 1982.

Moonitz, M. "Inflation and the Lag in Accounting Practice: Critique." Accounting in Perspective. Cincinnati, Ohio, 1971.

Morgan, R. A. "TB—TC" The Accounting Forum, December 1981.

Morpeth, D. S. "The CCA Experience." Chartered Accountant in Australia, July 1978.

Morpeth, D. S. "Practical Problems of Inflation Accounting." Accountant, April 8, 1976.

Morris, R. C. "Evidence of the Impact of Inflation Accounting on Share Prices." Accounting and Business Research, Spring 1975.

Mossin, J. "Equilibrium in a Capital Asset Market." Econometria, October 1966.

Most, K. Instructor's Manual to Accompany Accounting Theory, 2nd ed. Columbus, Ohio: Grid, 1982.

Mullen, L. E. "Are You Ready for Inflation Accounting?" The Journal of Accountancy, June 1975.

Nagel, E. The Structure of Science. New York: Harcourt, Brace and World, 1961.

"News Briefs." The Journal of Accountancy, September 1982.

Norby, W. C. Rejoinder to F. L. Clarke, "Accounting for Financial Analysis." Financial Analysts Journal, January–February 1981.

"Not With a Bang But a Whimper." The Chartered Accountant in Australia, May 1983.

Noreen, E., and J. Sepe. "Market Reaction to Accounting Policy Deliberations: The Inflation Accounting Case." The Accounting Review, April 1981.

O'Connor, M. C., and G. Chandra. "SEC (ASR 190) Required Replacement Cost Data Disclosures." Collected Papers of the Annual Meeting of the American Accounting Association. Sarasota, Fla., August 1978.

Ovadia, A., and J. Ronen. "On the Value of Current-Cost Information." Journal of Accounting, Auditing and Finance, Winter 1983.

Paton, W. A. Accounting Theory, 1922 original ed.; reprinted, Houston, Tex: Scholars Book, 1973.

Paton, W. A. "Depreciation, Appreciation and Productive Capacity." The Journal of Accountancy, July 1920.

Paton, W. A. "The Significance and Treatment of Appreciation in the Accounts." Michigan Academy of Science. Twentieth Annual Report, ed. G. H. Coons (Ann Arbor, Mich., 1918). Reprinted in S. A. Zeff, ed., Asset Appreciation, Business Income and Price-Level Accounting: 1918-1935, New York: Arno Press, 1976.

Paton, W. A., and W. A. Paton, Jr. Asset Accounting. New York: Macmillan, 1952.

Paton, W. A., and R. A. Stevenson. Principles of Accounting. Ann Arbor, Mich., 1918.

Peasnell, K. V. "The CCA Depreciation Problem." Abacus, December 1977.

Petersen, R. J. "Analysis of General Price Level Restatement." The Accounting Review, July 1975.

Petersen, R. J. "Interindustry Estimation of General Price-Level Impact on Financial Information." The Accounting Review, January 1973.

Peterson, R. J., and T. K. Keller. "Asset Valuation, Income Determination and Changing Prices." The Accounting Review, October 1972.

Platt, W. H. "Analysis of Aspects of the Treatment of Monetary Gains and Losses in the Hyde Guidelines and ED24." Journal of Business Finance and Accounting, Winter 1979.

Popoff, B. "Chambers, Inflation, and CoCoA Addiction." Accountants' Journal, June 1976.

Prakash, P., and S. Sunder. "The Case Against Separation of Current Operating Profit and Holding Gains." The Accounting Review, January 1979.

Price Waterhouse and Company. Accounting Events and Trends, May 1983.

Price Waterhouse and Company. Common-Sense Accounting in an Era of Persistent Inflation. Position Paper, New York, 1977.

Rappaport, A. "Inflation Accounting and Corporate Dividends." Financial Executive, February 1981.

Report of Study Group on Business Income. Changing Concepts of Business Income. Houston, Tex.: Scholars Book, 1975.

Report of the (Trueblood) Study Group on the Objectives of Financial Statements. Objectives of Financial Statements. New York: AICPA, 1973.

Report of the Subcommittee of the Committee on Financial Accounting Standards. "Response to 'Financial Reporting and Changing Prices: Foreign Currency Translation, An Amendment of FASB Statement No. 33.'" Sarasota, Fla.: American Accounting Association, October 1982.

Revsine, L. "Accounting Data, Inflation and Resource Allocations." The Accounting Forum, December 1978.

Revsine, L. "Inflation Accounting for Debt." Financial Analysts Journal, May-June 1981.

Revsine, L. "Let's Stop Eating Our Seed Corn." Harvard Business Review, January-February 1981.

Revsine, L. "On the Correspondence Between Replacement Cost Income and Economics Income." The Accounting Review, July 1970.

Revsine, L. Replacement Cost Accounting, Englewood Cliffs, N.J.: Prentice-Hall, 1973.

Revsine, L. "The Theory and Measurement of Business Income: A Review Article." The Accounting Review, April 1981.

Revsine, L., and J. B. Thies. "Price Level Adjusted Replacement Cost Data." The Journal of Accountancy, May 1977.

Revsine, L., and J. J. Weygandt. "Accounting for Inflation: The Controversy." The Journal of Accountancy, October 1974.

Ro, B. T. "The Adjustment of Security Returns to the Disclosure of Replacement Cost Accounting Information." Journal of Accounting and Economics, Vol. 2, 1980.

Ro, B. T. "The Disclosure of Replacement Cost Accounting Data and Its Effect on Transaction Volumes." The Accounting Review, January 1981.

Ronen, J., and G. H. Sorter. "Providing Relevant Financial Statement Information in a Period of Changing Prices." The Nation's Capital Needs: Three Studies, ed. R. Lindsay. Committee for Economic Development, New York, 1979.

Ronen, J., and G. H. Sorter. "Relevant Accounting." Journal of Business, April 1972.

Rosen, L. S. "Replacement-Value Accounting." The Accounting Review, January 1967.

Rosenfield, P. "Confusion Between General Price-Level Restatement and Current-Value Accounting." The Journal of Accountancy, October 1972.

Rosenfield, P. "General Price-Level Accounting and Foreign Operations." The Journal of Accountancy, September 1971.

Rosenfield, P. "GPP Accounting-Relevance and Interpretability." The Journal of Accountancy, August 1975.

Rosenfield, P. "Inflation and the Lag in Accounting Practice: Critique," eds. R. R. Sterling and W. F. Bentz. Accounting in Perspective. Cincinnati, Ohio, 1971.

Rosenfield, P. "Is There Such a Thing as a General Purchasing Power Unit?" The Journal of Accountancy, December 1975.

Ross, H. "Inflation Accounting: A Case of Misplaced Zeal." Accountancy, June 1972.

Saftner, D. V. Stock Market Reaction to Replacement Cost Disclosures Required by the Securities and Exchange Commission. Unpublished manuscript, December 1979.

Sampson, A. C. "A Regulator's View of the FASB: The First 10 Years and After." The Journal of Accountancy, August 1983.

Samuelson, R. "Should Replacement-Cost Changes Be Included in Income?" The Accounting Review, April 1980.

Sandilands' Committee. Inflation Accounting: Report of the Inflation Accounting Committee. London: Her Majesty's Stationery Office, 1975.

Schiff, M. "Inflation Accounting: U.S. and U.K." CPA Journal, March 1976.

Schmidt, F. "The Basis of Depreciation Charges." Harvard Business Review, April 1930.

Schmidt, F. "The Impact of Replacement Value." The Accounting Review, September 1930.

Schmidt, F. "Is Appreciation Profit?" The Accounting Review, December 1931.

Scott, G. M. Research Study on Current-Value Accounting Measurements and Utility. New York: Touche Ross Foundation, 1978.

Securities and Exchange Commission. Accounting Series Release No. 150. Washington, D.C.: U.S. Government Printing Office, 1973.

Securities and Exchange Commission. Accounting Series Release No. 190: "Notice of Adoption of Amendments to Regulation S-X Requiring Disclosure of Certain Replacement Cost Data." SEC Docket, Vol. 9, No. 5, April 6, 1976. Washington, D.C.: U.S. Government Printing Office.

Seed, A. H. The Impact of Inflation on Internal Planning and Control. New York: National Association of Accountants, 1981.

Seed, A. H. Inflation: Its Impact on Financial Reporting and Decision Making. New York: Financial Executives Research Foundation, 1978.

Sepe, J. "The Impact of the FASB's 1974 GPL Proposal on the Security Price Structure." The Accounting Review, July 1982.

Sharpe, W. "Capital Asset Prices: A Theory of Market Equilibrium Under Conditions of Risk," Journal of Finance, September 1967.

Sharpe, W. Portfolio Theory and Capital Markets. New York: Mc-Graw-Hill, 1970.

Shaw, J. C. "The Hyde Gearing Adjustment." Accountants Magazine, March 1978.

Sherwood, K. "Are You in Gear for 'Hyde' and Seek?" Accountancy, May 1978.

Skousen, K. F. An Introduction to the SEC, 2nd ed. Cincinnati, Ohio: Southwestern, 1980.

Smith, A. An Enquiry into the Nature and Causes of Wealth of Nations. London: George Routledge, 1890.

Solomons, D. "The Politicization of Accounting." The Journal of Accountancy, November 1978.

Sorter, G. H. "An 'Events' Approach to Basic Accounting Theory." The Accounting Review, January 1969.

"Special Report—FASB Conference on Use of Inflation-Adjusted Data." The Journal of Accountancy, March 1983.

Sprouse, R. T. "Inflation: Symptom or Disease?" Financial Analysts Journal, January-February 1979.

Sprouse, R. T. "Understanding Inflation Accounting." CPA Journal, January 1977.

Sprouse, R. T., and M. Moonitz. A Tentative Set of Broad Accounting Principles: Accounting Research Study No. 3. New York: AICPA, 1962.

"SSAP 16 May Remain in Force for Another Two Years." The Accountants Magazine, May 1983.

Stamp, E. "Income and Value Determination and Changing Price Levels: An Essay Towards a Theory." Accountants' Journal, August 1972.

Standish, P. E. M. "Can Auditing Survive Sandilands?" Accountancy, November 1976.

Staubus, G. J. "Effects of Price-Level Restatements on Earnings." The Accounting Review, July 1976.

Sterling, R. R., ed. Asset Valuation and Income Determination. Lawrence, Kans.: Scholars Book, 1971.

Sterling, R. R. "Costs (Historical versus Current) Versus Exit Values." Abacus, December 1981.

Sterling, R. R. "Relevant Financial Reporting in an Age of Price Changes." The Journal of Accountancy, February 1975.

Sterling, R. R. Theory of the Measurement of Enterprise Income. Lawrence, Kans.: University Press of Kansas, 1979.

Sterling, R. R., and W. F. Bentz, eds. Accounting in Perspective. Houston, Tex.: Scholars Book, 1979.

Stickney, C. P., and D. O. Green. "No Price-Level Adjusted Statements, Please (pleas)." CPA Journal, January 1974.

Sunder, S. "Note on Estimating the Economic Impact of the LIFO Method of Inventory Valuation." The Accounting Review, April 1976.

Sunder, S. "Why Is the FASB Making Too Many Accounting Rules?" The Wall Street Journal, April 27, 1981.

Sweeney, H. W. "Capital." The Accounting Review, September 1933.

Sweeney, H. W. "Effects of Inflation on German Accounting." The Journal of Accountancy, March 1927.

Sweeney, H. W. "Reporting the Financial Effects of Price-Level Changes: Accounting Research Study No. 6: A Critique." The Accounting Review, October 1964.

Sweeney, H. W. Stabilized Accounting. New York: Harper and Brothers, 1936. Also reprinted in 1964 by Holt, Rinehart and Winston, with a foreword by S. A. Zeff, W. A. Paton, and Sweeney's own twenty-three page memoir, "Forty Years After: Or Stabilized Accounting Revisited."

Thorsen, T. O. "FASB Conference on Financial Reporting and Changing Prices." Stamford, Conn.: Financial Accounting Standards Board, May 31, 1979.

Tierney, C. V. "General Purchasing Power Myths." The Journal of Accountancy, September 1977.

Touche Ross and Company. "Economic Reality in Financial Reporting." New York, 1976.

Tweedie, D. T. "Current Cost Accounting: U.K. Controversies and Overseas Solutions." eds. P. T. Wanless and D. A. R. Forrester. In Readings in Inflation Accounting. Chichester, Great Britain: Wiley, 1979.

Vancil, R. F. "Funds Flow Analysis During Inflation." Financial Analysts Journal, March-April 1976.

Vancil, R. F., and R. L. Weil. "Current Replacement Cost Accounting, Depreciable Assets and Distributable Income." Financial Analysts Journal, July-August 1976.

Vancil, R. F., and R. L. Weil. Replacement Cost Accounting: Readings on Concepts, Uses and Methods. Glen Ridge, N.J.: Thomas Horton and Daughters, 1976.

Wanless, P. T., and D. A. R. Forrester, eds. Readings in Inflation Accounting. Chichester, Great Britain: Wiley, 1979.

Watts, R., and J. Zimmerman. "Towards a Positive Theory of the Determination of Accounting Standards." The Accounting Review, January 1978.

Whittington, G. "The Role of Research in Setting Accounting Standards: The Case of Inflation Accounting." In Accounting Standards Setting: An International Perspective, eds. M. Bromwich and A. Hopwood. London: Pitman, 1983.

Wright, F. K. "Accounting for Inflation." Australian Accountant, July 1963.

Zeff, S. A. "Constant Dollar Accounting: Which Approach Tells the Story?" The Journal of Accountancy, October 1979.

Zeff, S. A. "Episodes in the Progression of Price-Level Accounting in the United States." In Contemporary Studies in the Evolution of Accounting Thought, ed. M. Chatfield. Belmont, Calif.: Dickenson, 1968.

Zeff, S. A. "The Rise of Economic Consequences." The Journal of Accountancy, December 1978.

Zeff, S. A. "Truth in Accounting: The Ordeal of Kenneth MacNeal." The Accounting Review, July 1982.

Zeff, S. A., ed. Asset Appreciation, Business Income and Price-Level Accounting: 1918-1935. New York: Arno Press, 1976.

ANNUAL REPORTS

Anderson Clayton and Company, 1981
Colt Industries, 1980
Consolidated Edison of New York, Inc., 1980
Genuine Auto Parts Company, 1980
Gulf Oil, 1981
Heileman Baking Company, 1981
Hilton Hotels Corporation, 1981
J. P. Morgan, 1981
Kennecott Corporation, 1980
Knight-Ridder Newspapers, 1980
Marathon Oil Company, 1980
McDonald's, 1980
Norlin Corporation, 1980
Pan American World Airways, Inc., 1980
PepsiCo, 1980
R. R. Donnelley and Sons, 1981
Squibb Corporation, 1981
Textron, 1980
United States Gypsum, 1981
Weyerhaeuser Company, 1980

INDEX

ABOUT THE AUTHORS

ROBERT BLOOM is currently professor of accounting at the University of Wisconsin-Whitewater. He has previously taught at Rutgers University, College of William and Mary, and Illinois Institute of Technology.

Dr. Bloom has published many articles in the areas of accounting and finance. He is the coeditor of two other books on accounting.

Dr. Bloom holds a B.A. from Queens College in New York, an M.B.A. from Columbia University, and a Ph.D. from New York University.

ARAYA DEBESSAY is currently associate professor of accounting at the University of Delaware, where he has taught since 1978.

Dr. Debessay has published a number of articles in the area of accounting in the professional literature. He is the coeditor of a book on behavioral accounting.

Dr. Debessay received a B. Com. from Haile Selassie University in Ethiopia and an M.S., M.B.A., and Ph.D. from Syracuse University. He holds a Certificate in Management Accounting.